The Hunt for a
Reds October

The Hunt for a Reds October

Cincinnati in 1990

CHARLES F. FABER *and*
ZACHARIAH WEBB

McFarland & Company, Inc., Publishers
Jefferson, North Carolina

ALSO OF INTEREST AND FROM MCFARLAND

*Baseball Prodigies: Best Major League Seasons
by Players Under 21,* Charles F. Faber (2014)

*The American Presidents Ranked by Performance,
1789–2012,* 2d ed., Charles F. Faber *and* Richard B. Faber (2012)

*Major League Careers Cut Short: Leading Players
Gone by 30,* Charles F. Faber *and* Richard B. Faber (2011)

*Baseball Ratings: The All-Time Best Players at Each Position, 1876 to
the Present,* 3d ed., Charles F. Faber *and* Richard B. Faber (2008)

The American Presidents Ranked by Performance, Charles F. Faber
and Richard B. Faber (2000; softcover 2006)

Spitballers: The Last Legal Hurlers of the Wet One,
Charles F. Faber *and* Richard B. Faber (2006)

Baseball Pioneers: Ratings of Nineteenth Century Players,
Charles F. Faber *and* Richard B. Faber (1997)

ISBN 978-0-7864-7951-1 (softcover : acid free paper) ∞
ISBN 978-1-4766-2095-4 (ebook)

LIBRARY OF CONGRESS CATALOGUING DATA ARE AVAILABLE

British Library cataloguing data are available

Front cover: Team photograph of the 1990 World Series
champion Cincinnati Reds with owner Marge Schott's
St. Bernard, Schottzie (National Baseball Hall
of Fame Library, Cooperstown, New York)

Printed in the United States of America

*McFarland & Company, Inc., Publishers
Box 611, Jefferson, North Carolina 28640
www.mcfarlandpub.com*

To my family, who made me what I am. For many years they have supported me in all my endeavors. This dedication is small acknowledgment of their love, help, and encouragement, but they know it is heartfelt.

—Charles F. Faber

To my grandfather and co-author Charles Faber, for instilling within me at an early age a love for baseball and an appreciation for academic study. To my father and mother, Jay and Deborah Webb, and my sister, Kyffin Bland, for all the wiffleball, youth baseball, and Reds games we enjoyed together as a family. To my 1990 *MC Steel/Silver Grove Fleeting* Knothole team, especially Chaz Weber, Eric Rath, Nick Mohr, and Nick Thomas, for all the joy we shared on the field and off as our Reds won their championship. Finally, to my nephew Wakiza, who I hope gets as much joy out of baseball as I have!

—Zachariah Webb

Acknowledgments

This book is a collaborative effort, as most books are. The two authors received help from numerous sources. Jay Webb and Danny Faber read the early drafts and provided helpful and constructive criticism. As always, Deborah Webb was there when we needed her. Mindy Faber and Paul Scheuerlein made valuable contributions. We appreciate the help of John Horne, photo archivist at the National Baseball Hall of Fame. The online research program of the Society for American Baseball Research was invaluable. Other sources, cited in the text, were indispensable.

Table of Contents

Abbreviations

A—Assists

AA—American Association

AB—At Bats

AL—American League

ALCS—American League Championship Series

BA—Batting Average

CG—Complete Games

DH—Designated Hitter

DL—Disabled List

DP—Double Plays

E—Errors

ERA—Earned Run Average

G—Games

GB—Games Behind

GS—Games Started

HR—Home Runs

L—Losses

MLB—Major League Baseball

MLBPA—Major League Baseball Players Association

MVP—Most Valuable Player

NCBBL—National Colored Base Ball League

NL—National League

NLCS—National League Championship Series

NLDS—National League Division Series

OBP—On-Base Percentage

OPS—On-Base Percentage Plus Slugging Average

Pct—Percentage

PO—Put Outs

R—Runs

RBI—Runs Batted In

SB—Stolen Bases

SHO—Shutouts

SLG—Slugging Average

SO—Strikeouts

TC—Total Chances

W—Wins

WBC—World Baseball Classic

WHIP—Walks Plus Hits per Nine Innings Pitched

WR—Weighted Rating

Preface

This is the story of the world champion Cincinnati Reds of 1990 and the environment in which they played. The great Cincinnati teams of the 1970s were known as the Big Red Machine, but a baseball club is not a machine. It is a collection of human beings—players, owners, managers, coaches, executives, and support personnel—working together as a team. We discuss the contributions of these individuals to the success of he club. The 1990 Cincinnati Reds did not exist in a vacuum. They belonged to a city, a community that had a history, a culture, and an ethos. The team did not spring into existence on Opening Day 1990. It had a long history, a tradition that affected the team and the fans who embraced it. We provide some orientation to the setting, the history, and the traditions of the Cincinnati Reds.

In Chapter 1 we explore some of the geographic, demographic, and economic characteristics that have influenced the course of baseball in Cincinnati, making it into a baseball town, par excellence. The Cincinnati Reds are considered a small-market club. Only three metropolitan areas with populations less than that of Cincinnati field major-league clubs, and none of these areas has supported baseball as long or as fervently as Cincinnati.

During professional baseball's formative years in the latter part of the nineteenth century, Cincinnati was almost always represented in one major league or another, whether it was the National League, American Association, Union Association, or Players' League. Geography played a role. Cincinnati was an ideal location for the growth of baseball. In 1880 the center of population of the United States was only eight miles away from Cincinnati, giving the baseball town a large fan base. There were no major league clubs in the South. Only St. Louis could compete with the Reds in the entire area south of the Ohio River clear to the Gulf of Mexico. Relatively prosperous, Cincinnati residents could afford the cost of attend-

1

ing baseball games. Brewers were important to the development of baseball in Cincinnati. Several of the early club owners were involved in the brewing industry. The owners allowed local clubs to play baseball on Sundays and sell beer in the ballpark, leading to the club's temporary expulsion from the National League and the establishment of the American Association, known as the Beer and Whiskey League.

In 1869 the Cincinnati Red Stockings became the first openly all-professional baseball team in the world. The modern-day Reds and their fans owe a debt of gratitude to Aaron Burt Champion, Harry Wright, and other pioneers. In Chapter 2, then, we look back at Cincinnati's long history in professional baseball. In a book about the 1990 Reds, why do we mention the 1869 Red Stockings and other teams from a bygone era? Perhaps the words of Luke Salisbury provide some insight. Salisbury wrote, "Unlike other sports, baseball's past is always relevant; its distant past mirrors the present, and the present revives the past."[1] Salisbury suggested that baseball is like a novel: "It is an ongoing, hundred-year-old work of art, peopled with thousands of characters, full of improbable events, anecdotes, folklore, and numbers."[2]

Our book doesn't have thousands of characters, but it has its share of improbable events, anecdotes, folklore, and numbers. Some mention is made of Cincinnatians who contributed to the development of baseball, for example Garry Herrmann, who chaired the National Commission and has been called "The Father of the World Series." We pay our respects to the Cincinnati teams that won the World Series in 1919, 1940, 1975, and 1976, but we reserve most of our space for the champions of 1990.

The story of the Reds in 1990, of course, occupies most of this book. The championship team of 1990 was not assembled in that calendar year alone. Its roots go back some time. Certain events of 1989 must be narrated in order to provide an understanding of 1990. The downfall of Pete Rose, the employment of Bob Quinn and Lou Piniella, the acquisition of key players Hal Morris and Mariano Duncan, and especially the trade for Randy Myers were important parts of the tale of the 1990 Reds, although they had occurred during the previous year. Without those events the Reds of 1990 would not have been the team they were.

As the new year dawned there was uncertainty over whether there would be a 1990 season. The current Basic Agreement had expired. Negotiations between owners and players were going nowhere. On February 15, 1990, the owners refused to open spring training camps, locking the players out. We provide some analysis of the issues and the settlement that was reached more than a month later. We discuss briefly the impact of abbreviated spring training on the Reds and their new manager. We tell what happened to the traditional Opening Day. But mostly we recount the progress of the team through the season.

In 1990 the underdog Reds won the National League West, defeated the favored Pittsburgh Pirates in the League Championship Series and swept the powerful Oakland Athletics in the World Series. The bulk of the book is devoted to portraying that season and the personnel who made the Reds' improbable success possible. Under the ownership of the controversial Marge Schott and managed on the field by the mercurial Lou Piniella, the Reds led their division from Opening Day through the end of the season, one of the few National League clubs ever to accomplish that feat. Stars such as Barry Larkin, Eric Davis, and a trio of relievers known as the Nasty Boys deserve a lot of credit for the success, but lesser-known players, including Billy Hatcher, Glenn Braggs and others, made significant contributions. We give these players their due, and we discuss the role of the underappreciated general manager, Bob Quinn.

The Reds were not expected to advance past the NLCS, with the Pittsburgh Pirates standing in their way. The Pirates were led by the National League's Most Valuable Player, Barry Bonds, hard-hitting Bobby Bonilla, and Cy Young Award winner Doug Drabek. We recount how the Reds prevailed, mainly on the strength of some timely hitting, great fielding, and the outstanding relief pitching by the Nasty Boys.

Cincinnati was given little chance against the defending world champion Oakland Athletics, who were sparked by the greatest leadoff man in baseball history, Rickey Henderson, and powered by the Bash Brothers, Jose Canseco and Mark McGwire. We explain how the Reds were able to sweep this potent aggregation and bring the title to that baseball town known as the Queen City.

In the Appendix we provide biographical and statistical data on club personnel, tell how the 1990 team was dispersed, discuss the radio and television broadcasters.

In this complex modern world, with its joys and sorrows, hopes and fears, and serious problems in desperate need of solutions, inquiring minds might ask, "Why write a book about a baseball club?" We answer, "Because baseball is important." As Jacques Barzun famously wrote, "Whoever wants to know the heart and mind of America had better learn baseball."[3]

Readers of this book may agree with Gerald Early, who wrote, "I think there are only three things that America will be known for 2,000 years from now when they study this civilization: the Constitution, jazz music, and baseball. They're the three most beautifully designed things this culture has ever produced."[4]

Will the Cincinnati Reds be remembered 2,000 years from now? We don't know. We have tried only to write a book that 21st century readers will find informative and enjoyable.

Introduction: A Short History of Baseball in Cincinnati, 1869–1989

What's past is prologue.—William Shakespeare

The 1869 Red Stockings are frequently said to be the first professional club in the history of baseball. Baseball historian John Thorn maintains that is not quite true.[1]

Several other clubs were openly paying some of their players as early as 1868. Perhaps it is more accurate to say that the Red Stockings were the first club to pay *all* of their players. In 1865 a Cincinnati lawyer, Aaron Burt Champion, became one of the organizers of the Union Cricket Club in Cincinnati. Shortly thereafter, the Cincinnati Base Ball Club was organized in his offices. Albert T. Goshorn, a Cincinnati businessman and civic leader, was elected president of the club, but soon turned the presidency over to Champion. Although Goshorn remained active in helping fund the club, his name is seldom mentioned in modern accounts of the old Red Stockings. The baseball club played its games on grounds adjacent to the cricket field. Harry Wright, who had starred in both sports in the East, had moved to Cincinnati after the Civil War to pursue his career as a cricketer. After watching a game on the baseball field, Wright decided to convert to baseball. Following a conversation with Champion, Wright led a mass exodus of cricketers to the baseball club. This enhanced club played its first game as a team on September 26, 1866. Admission to games ranged from ten to 25 cents for men; women were admitted free of charge. The Cincinnati club quickly became the strongest team in the Midwest. In 1867 they won 17 of 18 contests.

Within two years Champion and Wright had assembled the famous Red Stockings, a dominant team that toured the country, sweeping the opposition, and enhancing the popularity of baseball. The team put together by Champion and Wright consisted of some of the most talented amateur players in the country, many of whom had probably maintained their amateur status by accepting jobs with supporters of the clubs—jobs that often paid well and duties that allowed them ample time for practicing and playing baseball (or cricket). Several of them had been recruited in 1868 or earlier, before the club became avowedly professional. First baseman Charlie Gould was the only native Cincinnatian on the club. An 18-year-old outfielder, Cal McVey, came from Indianapolis to join the club. McVey had been born on a farm near Montrose, Iowa, the first professional baseball player born west of the Mississippi River. He moved to Indiana with his parents when he was in his early teens and became a star on Indianapolis nines. All of the other Red Stockings were recruited from the East. One of them—Doug Allison—was the first catcher to take his position immediately behind the batter's box. While playing for Cincinnati in 1870, he became the first player to use a fielder's glove. Among the recruits was Harry Wright's brother, George. (Both Wright brothers are in the Hall of Fame.) Other clubs adopted the practice of paying all of their players, and professional baseball was on its way.

Before the 1868 season began, Wright hired seamstress Bertha Betram to create new uniforms. She made white flannel jerseys, soft-collared and flared at the neck, with a bright red Gothic C stitched on the front. She added white knickers with a clasp below the knee. The knickers were an innovation. Previously players had worn long trousers, but it was believed that they could run faster in knickers than in longer, restricting trousers. For the final touch Betram added long, bright red stockings. The hose inspired a nickname for the team—the Red Stockings. In 1868 they won 36 games while losing seven. Many of the games were so lopsided that the public lost interest, and gate receipts declined. Competitors such as Champion and Wright wanted to expand operations by creating a traveling team that would tour the East, taking on all comers. In order to do this successfully, the club would have to become openly professional and pay all of its players, the first club to do so.

Champion remained president of the club, responsible for paying the salaries. As captain of the team, Harry Wright took on tasks that today would be considered responsibilities of the general manager, field manager, traveling secretary and scout. On April 17, 1869, the Red Stockings took the field for their first game as the first all-professional club. In April and May they played severely overmatched Midwestern amateur teams. On May 31 they embarked on a tour of the East to test their strength against

After defeating all the Midwestern teams they faced in April and May 1869, the Red Stockings embarked on a tour of the East to face the powerful teams in that section of the country. They returned to the Queen City undefeated and were treated to a parade and presented with a giant 27-foot wooden bat, weighing 1,600 pounds. The bat is now stored in the Cincinnati Reds Hall of Fame and Museum. Because of its huge size, it is brought into the exhibit area only on special occasions (Library of Congress).

the powerful teams in that section of the country. Upon completing the tour undefeated, the Red Stockings returned to the Queen City and were treated to a parade. They were presented with a giant 27-foot wooden bat, weighing 1,600 pounds. (The bat is now stored at the Cincinnati Reds Hall of Fame and Museum. Because of its huge size it is brought into the exhibit area only on special occasions.) An ecstatic Champion declared that he would rather be president of the Cincinnati Base Ball Club than president of the United States.

Having defeated the best teams in the Midwest and the East, they had one area left to conquer—the West Coast. The team left Cincinnati on September 14. After stopping in St. Louis to win two games, 70–9, and 31–9, the team boarded a stage coach for the trip to Omaha. At Omaha they boarded a train, becoming the first baseball team to travel on the new transcontinental railroad. In San Francisco the Red Stockings trounced three California teams by a combined score of 289–22. On the return trip they stopped in Omaha and defeated the local team by a 64–

The Cincinnati Red Stockings were the first openly all-professional baseball club in the world. Standing from left to right are Cal McVey, Charlie Gould, Harry Wright, George Wright and Fred Waterman. Seated are Andy Leonard, Doug Allison, Asa Brainard, and Charlie Sweasy (4doxies.com).

run margin in front of Vice President Schuyler Colfax. In November they defeated their most respected rivals, the New York Mutuals, thus completing a perfect season of 57 wins and no losses.

The winning streak continued well into the 1870 season, probably reaching nearly 90 in a row against other professional clubs.[2] After winning all the early games on a long road trip, the Red Stockings arrived in New York in June to face the Atlantics of Brooklyn. The game was anticipated with great excitement. Greg Rhodes quoted a *New York World* article: "All Brooklyn seemed awake to the event of the day. Stores were deserted, boys who could not obtain permission to leave school played hooky, and hundreds who could or would not produce the necessary fifty-cent stamp for admission looked on through cracks in the fence, or even climbed boldly to the top, while others were perched in the topmost limbs of the trees, or on the roofs of surrounding houses."[3]

The game lived up to its advance billing. The lead went back and forth until nine innings had been played with the score tied, 5–5. The game continued into extra innings. In the 11th inning the Red Stockings took a two-run lead, but the Atlantics rallied. With one man on base, Joe Start drove a ball over Cal McVey's head in right field. The ball rolled into the crowd, and an exuberant fan jumped on McVey's back, preventing him from throwing the ball back to the infield until a runner had scored and Start was safely at third base. Brooklyn scored two more runs to win the game, 8–7. Cincinnati's fabulous winning streak was over. Champion telegraphed home: "The finest game ever played. Our boys did nobly, but fortune was against us. Eleven innings played. Though beaten, not disgraced."[4]

In 1871 dissension struck the club. Two major cliques emerged, divided over opinions about drinking and discipline. Some opposed what they considered rowdy behavior; the others had a different opinion, particularly about off-field conduct. During the controversy, Champion resigned as club president. The stockholders voted to return to amateur status. Harry Wright moved to Boston and joined the Boston Red Stockings of the new National Association, taking his brother George and Cal McVey with him. Baseball's first avowedly all-professional club was no more, but the concepts advanced by Champion and Wright lived on. Authors Greg Rhodes and John Erardi wrote: "To Aaron Champion and Harry Wright go the credit for casting the mold for the professional sports team.... They established that the all-salaried club, the scouting and training of junior-level players, regular training procedures, systematically conducted practices, and carefully devised strategies and teamwork could produce results far superior to any system that had been tried."[5]

The National League Reds, 1876–1880

When the National League replaced the unstable National Association in 1876, Cincinnati was ready for major league baseball. Cincinnati businessmen George and Josiah Keck had constructed a new ballpark in 1875 and paid the $100 fee for a franchise in the new loop. Known as Avenue Grounds, the park had a grass infield, while the outfield was hard clay. Left field was deeper than right field, and center field had a semicircular fence with an entrance for carriages.[6] The club had no official nickname, but cranks (as fans were known as in those days) called the club the Red Stockings, frequently shortened to the Reds. The new league aspired to restore respectability to baseball by preventing drunkenness and gambling in the ballparks. Liquor sales were prohibited in the parks. The pool box, where gamblers congregated, was removed from the ball grounds.

The Keck brothers charged the standard admission rate of 50 cents.

In efforts to increase attendance the club tried some innovative marketing practices. After the fifth inning, a special price of ten cents was set. The first Ladies Day in the major leagues was held in 1876, when all women, escorted or unescorted, were admitted to the park free. On other days women were frequently charged a reduced rate of 25 cents. However, no marketing gimmicks could make up for the poor performance of the team. The club occasionally had an outstanding player, but none of the stars

stayed long enough in Cincinnati to generate fan loyalty.

The club's most spectacular player was Mike "King" Kelly, who played his first two major league seasons for the Red Stockings, only to be released after the 1879 campaign, reportedly in order to cut the club's payroll. Deacon White was the only future Hall of Famer to play as many as three years (1878–1880) for the club. In an effort to increase revenue, the owners took to renting the ball park to local clubs, allowing them to play on Sundays and sell beer on the grounds. For these transgressions, the other owners voted to expel Cincinnati from the league. During its first incarnation as a National League club, Cincinnati won 125 games while losing 217, for a .365 percentage.

Michael "King" Kelly was one of the most colorful, flamboyant, and popular players of the 19th century. He started his major league career in Cincinnati, but was released after the 1879 season and went on to stardom in Boston and Chicago. He retuned to the Queen City in 1891 as player-manager of the Cincinnati Porkers in the American Association The club, sometimes known as "Kelly's Killers," did not survive the season. Kelly is a member of the National Baseball Hall of Fame, not for what he did in Cincinnati, but for his exploits elsewhere (Library of Congress).

The American Association Reds, 1882–1889

Resentment of the actions of the National League owners was centered in Cincinnati, but not confined to the Queen City. Businessmen in other cities were angry about the National League's monopolistic power to curtail expansion and prevent entrepreneurs from having the opportunity to tap into the riches that might flow from a new franchise. Agitation for formation of a new league arose in several quarters. One of the earliest outspoken advocates of a new league was Oliver Perry Caylor, sports editor of the *Cincinnati Enquirer.*

Caylor enlisted the help of Justin Thorner, who was connected to a local brewery and was an ex-president of the now bankrupt Cincinnati club, in securing support from local businessmen in creating a new club. The greatest boost from outside the Queen City came from a St. Louis saloonkeeper named Chris von der Ahe. He believed workingmen ought to be able to see a game for a quarter, rather than the 50 cents charged by the National League. He thought they should be allowed to enjoy a beer during the game and on Sundays, too. Von der Ahe and representatives from several other cities met in Cincinnati on November 2, 1881, and established the American Association, which was dubbed the Beer and Whiskey League, because it allowed the sale of alcoholic beverages in the ballparks.

JOHN McPHEE, 2d B. Cincinnati

COPYRIGHTED BY GOODWIN & CO. 1888

OLD JUDGE
CIGARETTES.
GOODWIN & CO., New York.

A 21-year-old rookie, Bid McPhee led the Reds to a pennant in the first season of the American Association. Regarded as the best fielding second basemen of his era, McPhee was the last major leaguer to field without using a glove. He played eight seasons for the AA Reds and ten years for the National League Reds, leading his league in fielding eight times. He has been inducted into the National Baseball Hall of Fame (Library of Congress).

Thorner was installed as president of the Reds. Pop Snyder, a veteran catcher, became player-manager. Snyder and all the other starters, with one exception, had played in the National League before being enticed to join the Reds. The one exception was a 22-year-old rookie, Bid McPhee. Arguably the best fielding second baseman of his era, McPhee was the last player to field without a glove, just two decades after a fellow Cincinnati player (Doug Allison) introduced the fielder's glove. McPhee was elected to the Hall of Fame in 2000. The Reds were a strong team, led by McPhee, third baseman Hick Carpenter, and pitcher Will White. This aggregation won the American Association pennant in the circuit's first year. Although they never won another championship in the American Association, the Reds were in contention most years and compiled a record of 549 wins and 396 losses, for a .581 percentage.

In 1889 the City of Cincinnati began enforcing a law against Sunday baseball. Reds owners tried moving Sunday games first to Ludlow, Kentucky, then to Hamilton, Ohio, but they ran afoul of authorities in both places. Sunday baseball was no longer feasible in Cincinnati. Meanwhile, the National League was seeking to expand by stealing clubs away from the American Association.

The Reds accepted an invitation to join the senior circuit. A dispute between the Cincinnati ownership and Chris von der Ahe of the St. Louis Browns over the selection of a new American Association president may have also influenced the decision. At any rate, the Reds jumped to the National League on November 14, 1889, taking most of their players with them.

Cincinnati Baseball: Cuban and African American Players

The Cincinnati Reds of the American Association were among the first major league clubs to give an all-black team the chance to prove that it could compete on an even basis with a big league club.[7] The Cuban Giants, the first salaried black baseball team, defeated the Reds on July, 21, 1886, the first victory by an all-black team over a major league club.

The first professional baseball league for black players, called the National Colored Baseball League (NCBBL) was founded in 1887.[8] The Cincinnati Browns were charter members. On May 6, 1887, the league made its debut in Pittsburgh with a street parade and a brass band concert. However, within a short time the new loop began to struggle. Every club in the circuit suffered financial losses, and the league collapsed after only a few weeks.[9] For some time the Browns continued to play as an independent club.[10] Few records of the Browns or the NCBBL survive.

For several years after the failure of the NCBBL, opportunities for black professional ball players were limited to barnstorming or playing in the minor leagues. Several blacks, including Bud Fowler, Fleetwood Walker and his brother Welday, had played in the majors earlier, but blacks were effectively excluded from the majors by 1887. Some minor leagues fielded racially integrated (and even some all-black teams) in the 1890s. But blacks were soon barred from Organized Baseball for the next half-century.

J. L. Wilkinson was largely responsible for restoring black baseball to a place of prominence in America's national pastime. Wilkinson created an integrated barnstorming club, the All-Nations, made up of players of 11 different nationalities or ethnicities. He moved the team to Kansas City and formed the Kansas City Monarchs. Together with Rube Foster, he organized the Negro National League in 1920. Although white, Wilkinson was accepted by his black colleagues and became the league secretary. He helped the league become the nation's most prominent venue for African-American ball players.[11] Other Negro Leagues tried to emulate the success of the Negro National League—the Negro American League, the Eastern Colored League, and the Negro Southern League, for example. Some survived only a short time; none left complete records of their players and their games, but they all made an impact on the game of baseball.[12]

Over the years Cincinnati was represented by a half-dozen clubs in Negro leagues, starting with the Cincinnati Browns of the ill-fated National Colored Base Ball League. Members of the Negro American League included the Cincinnati Cubans in 1921; the Cincinnati Tigers in 1937; the Cincinnati Buckeyes in 1942; the Cincinnati Clowns in 1943; and the Indianapolis-Cincinnati Clowns in 1944 and 1945.[13]

On April 17, 1954, Chuck Harmon became the first African American to play for the Reds, seven years after Jackie Robinson had broken the color barrier. He was not the first black, however. That honor went to Nino Escalera, a Puerto Rican. Harmon and Escalera made their debuts in the same inning of the April 17 game, both as pinch-hitters, with Escalera leading off the seventh inning with a single and Harmon following him to the plate. Neither man had much of a major league career. Much more impactful was Bob Thurman, a veteran of the Negro National League, who joined the Reds in 1955. Cincinnati had been slow to integrate its baseball teams, but Thurman's pleasant personality and leadership skills made him popular with teammates and fans alike. Within a few years

African Americans such as Frank Robinson and Vada Pinson were numbered among the biggest fan favorites ever to ply their trade in the Queen City.

Rafael Almeida and Armando Marsans, who made their major league debuts on the same day, July 4, 1911, were the first Cuban-born players to perform for the Reds and among the earliest to play for any major league club. By far the most famous Cuban to play for the Reds before the color line was broken was Dolf Luque. He had gone from Cuban baseball to the Boston Braves before being sold to Cincinnati in 1918. For many years the right-handed hurler was the best pitcher on the Reds staff and one of the best in the National League. In a long career he won 194 games, 154 of

ALMEIDA-CINN.-NAT.

Rafael Almeida (left) and Armando Marsons (right), both of whom made their major league debuts on July 4, 1911, were the first Cuban-born players to perform for the Reds, and among the earliest to play for any major league club. Early Cuban teams were composed of both black and white players. Light-skinned Cubans could move back and forth between Cuban baseball, Negro Leagues Baseball, and Organized (white) Baseball (Library of Congress).
Armando Marsans shared with Rafael Almeida the distinction of being the first Cuban-born player to perform for the Cincinnati Reds. Both men were signed by the Reds while playing for integrated teams in Cuba and assigned to a farm team in New Britain before being promoted to the major leagues. They were inducted into the Cuban Baseball Hall of Fame in 1939 (Library of Congress).

them for Cincinnati. Adding the 106 games he won in Cuban leagues gives Luque a total of exactly 300 wins as a professional pitcher.

Luque was the first Latin American player to star in the major leagues. Now, of course, the majors abound with Latinos, many of whom are among the game's biggest stars. The Most Valuable Player of Cincinnati's 1990 World Series triumph was Jose Rijo, a native of the Dominican Republic. The Reds' Most Valuable Player during the regular season was Barry Larkin, an African American born in Cincinnati. The 1990 World Champions' roster included five Latinos, seven African Americans, and a black Jamaican.

The Union Association "Outlaw Reds," 1884

The Union Association was the creation of a millionaire St. Louis sports enthusiast, Henry V. Lucas. An entrepreneur, he envisioned adding a baseball club to his business enterprises. His sincere, heart-felt opposition to the reserve clause was perhaps his main motivation for starting the new league. He said, "It

Dolf Luque was the most famous Cuban to play for the Reds before baseball integrated. He started his major league career with the Boston Braves before being traded to Cincinnati in 1918. For many years he was the best pitcher on the Reds and one of the best in the National League. He won 194 games in the majors and 106 in Cuba for a total of 300 professional wins. Following his retirement as a player, Luque coached in the major leagues and managed clubs in Cuba (Library of Congress).

isn't so many years ago that a great American president—Abraham Lincoln—freed negro slaves. Now we have leagues which practice a reserve clause which holds athletic young men in perpetual bondage."[14] He built a lavish baseball facility in St. Louis and set about convincing businessmen in other cities to sponsor clubs in the new circuit. His pleas fell upon fertile ground in the Queen City. A former owner of Cincinnati clubs in both the National League and American Association, Justus Thorner, paid the franchise fee, signed a lease with the owners of the Bank Street Grounds (evicting the AA Reds), and set about signing players.

The St. Louis Maroons of Henry Lucas were by far the best team in the Union Association. In mid-season Thorner and his colleagues made an attempt to catch the Maroons by raiding the Cleveland Blues of the National League. By offering each man a bonus of $1,000 for jumping leagues, they obtained catcher Fatty Briody, shortstop Jack Glasscock, and pitcher Jim McCormick. Briody's bonus was exactly twice as large as the $500 salary he was drawing at Cleveland.[15] The three newcomers transformed the Outlaw Reds into a formidable outfit. Briody hit .337; Glasscock hit an amazing .419 as well as continuing to be the best fielding shortstop in baseball; McCormick won 21 games while losing only three during the remainder of the season. Cincinnati finished the season 69–36 (.657). However, it was not enough to catch the powerful St. Louis club.

Union Association clubs drew well in St. Louis, Cincinnati, and a few other places, but could not compete with National League or American Association rivals in most cities. A few clubs folded, others changed locations, and Lucas loaned money to some in an attempt to keep them afloat. But there were not enough cranks to support three major leagues in 1884. The Union Association expired at the end of its one and only season. Overcoming the reserve clause was a noble idea, but its time did not come until nearly a century later.

The American Association
Porkers, 1891 (Kelly's Killers)

The winter of 1890–1891 was a confusing time for Cincinnati baseball cranks. The Reds had left the American Association and rejoined the National League for the 1890 season. However, the club did not fare well in its return to the senior circuit. By the end of the year, the Reds were teetering on the edge of bankruptcy. The club was purchased by Frank Brunell and Albert Johnson, who planned to move the Reds to the Players' League. However, the Players' League folded. The new owners accepted an invitation to join the American Association. The National League decided to put a new club in the Queen City, moving the Indianapolis Hoosiers to the banks of the Ohio. Brunell and Johnson then sold the Reds back to the National League. John T. Brush, president of the Hoosiers, became the new owner of the Reds. The club had committed to three different leagues during the off-season. The American Association did not give up and awarded a new Cincinnati franchise to Chris von der Ahe, who also owned the St. Louis Browns. (Multiple ownership of clubs in the same league was not a new experience for von der Ahe.)

So when the 1891 season got under way, there were two professional clubs in Cincinnati. They were in two different leagues but competing for the same fan base. The American Association club was called the Porkers because of the city's eminence in the meat-packing industry. The club was led by player-manager Mike "King" Kelly, one of the most prominent stars of the 19th century. For this reason the Porkers were sometimes called "Kelly's Killers." Despite the popularity of King Kelly, his club did not draw well in 1891. The ball park, called Pendleton Park, was located in the sparsely populated East End of the city, right on the banks of the Ohio River. Fans could get to the park by boarding a steamboat downtown at the foot of Walnut Street; the Pennsylvania Railroad passed right by the main entrance to the park. Streetcars also ran to the park, but they were slow and overcrowded. Despite these multiple means of access, the club had difficulty attracting fans to the East End; the competition of the National League club was too much to overcome. The attendance for the season totaled only 63,000. On August 27, the AA suspended the 43–57 (.430) club, canceling the remaining games on the Cincinnati schedule.

National League Reds, 1890–Present

1890–1919

John T. Brush was a clothier, the owner of a department store in Indianapolis. He purchased the Indianapolis Hoosiers in 1887 as a means of advertising his store. The Indianapolis club folded in 1889. A year later Brush invested in the New York Giants and helped keep that club solvent. When Brush assumed ownership of the Reds, he retained his interest in the Giants. Actually, promoting the fortunes of the New York club seemed to be his top priority. Brush also owned the Baltimore Orioles of the American Association, and he used this position to strengthen the Giants. In 1902 he enticed John McGraw to leave Baltimore to manage the Giants and released future Hall of Famers Roger Bresnahan and Joe McGinnity from Orioles contracts so they could join the Giants. His greatest deal came at the expense of Cincinnati. He traded young pitcher Christy Mathewson to New York for washed-up hurler Amos Rusie. The one-time "Hoosier Thunderbolt" never won a game for Cincinnati, while Mathewson posted 372 wins for the Giants, the most victories attained for one National League club by any pitcher.

What is now called the first modern World Series was played in 1903 between National League champion Pittsburgh and the Boston club of the upstart American League. The fact that the American League was in a position to challenge the National League for baseball supremacy was largely due to the efforts of a former Cincinnati sports editor. Ban Johnson had succeeded the Oliver Perry Caylor as sports editor of the *Cincinnati Commercial Gazette.* Johnson was appointed president of the Western League in 1893. Under his aggressive leadership, the league expanded into Eastern metropolises and soon rivaled the NL in attendance. Johnson changed the name of the circuit to the American League in 1900, jettisoned its salary cap, and raided the National League for some of its biggest stars. In 1901 he announced that the American League was now a major league. He made his audacious proclamation come true.

Upon their return to the National League in 1890, the Reds enjoyed little success, never contending for a championship and finishing as high as third only three times in their first quarter-century in their present reincarnation. In 1902 Brush sold the Reds for $150,000 to a group of Cincinnati politicians headed by George "Boss" Cox, Mayor Julius Fleishmann and his brother Max, and the boss's protégé, Garry Herrmann. The Fleishmann brothers were sons of a Jewish immigrant from Central Europe who founded the Fleishmann Yeast Company, as an adjunct to the distillery industry. Like many of Cincinnati's early baseball figures, Herrmann was the son of German immigrants. He was named president of the club and rapidly rose to be one of the most influential baseball figures of the first two decades of the 20th century, second only to Ban Johnson. On January 10, 1903, the fierce battle between the American and National Leagues was ended by the "Cincinnati Peace Treaty," now known as the National Agreement. Herrmann's contribution to the settlement was costly to the Reds (he gave up their claim to future Hall of Famer Sam Crawford). But it brought enduring stability to major league baseball. The agreement stipulated that henceforth baseball was to be governed by a three-person National Commission, consisting to the two league presidents and a club president acceptable to both. Herrmann was selected as the club representative and served as chairman of the commission. For nearly the next 20 years, baseball was ruled by Garry Herrmann, Ban Johnson, and a succession of National League presidents. It was not until the Black Sox scandal and the appointment of Kenesaw Mountain Landis as baseball's first commissioner that Herrmann's power ended.

NATIONAL BASEBALL COMM JAN 09
HARRY PULLIAM - AUG. HERRMANN   BAN JOHNSON   J. E. BRUCE, Sec'y

From 1903 until 1920 Organized Baseball was ruled by a three-person commission, consisting of the presidents of the National and American Leagues and a club president acceptable to both. August "Garry" Herrmann, president of the Reds, served as chairman of the commission for nearly 20 years. From left to right in this 1909 photograph are National League president Harry Pulliam, Herrmann, American League president Ban Johnson, and commission secretary J. E. Bruce (Library of Congress).

From 1884 through 1901, the Reds played in a succession of ball fields, all of which were in the same general locality of the 20th century Redland (Crosley) Field. On Opening Day 1884, the stands collapsed, leading to a rumor that a fan had been killed. Actually, there were no fatalities, although many fans were injured.[16] Constructed of wood, the stands in the early ball parks were susceptible to fire. One large fire at Cincinnati's National League Park occurred in 1900. In the fall of 1901, after the end of the season, the entire ball park burned down. It was replaced by the Palace of the Fans, the second park in the nation to use steel and concrete for the major portion of its foundation and superstructure.[17] With pillars and columns inspired by the 1893 Columbian Exposition in Chicago, the Palace was quite an elegant structure. However, it did not have sufficient seating capacity to accommodate the growing number of fans in Cincinnati, the baseball town.

In 1912 the Palace of the Fans was replaced by Redland Field, capable of seating 25,000 customers. With a lifespan of 58 years, this park was by far the longest lasting of all stadia in the Queen City. When Powel Crosley, Jr., purchased the Reds in 1934, the name was changed to Crosley Field, but it was still the same ball park. Redland Field was located at the intersection of Findley Street and Western Avenue. That area had been the home of the Reds since 1884. The various National League parks and the Palace of the Fans were all located at Findley and Western, although with differing configurations. The most notable feature of the park was the 15-degree outfield slope. The incline was a way to make up the difference between field level and street level. A terrace had not been necessary in the older parks built on the site, but the playing field was expanded when

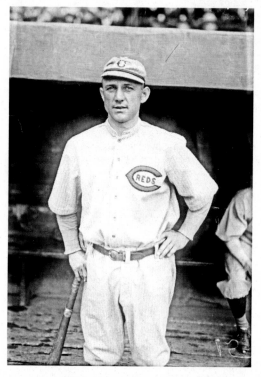

One of the leaders of the 1919 World Champions was third baseman Heinie Groh, who led the league in on-base percentage and ranked in the top five in batting average, slugging percentage, bases on balls, runs scored, and runs batted in. An excellent fielder, he led the loop's third sackers in putouts and double plays (Library of Congress).

Redland Field was built in 1912. The new construction placed the outfield well below street level. A very high wall could have been built in order to provide a level playing field. Instead designers of the park decided to use a sloping terrace to make up the difference in grade. Although the terrace was most prominent in left field, it extended clear across the outfield. All outfielders had to go uphill to chase a long fly ball. The slope warned fielders they were approaching the wall, so no dirt or gravel warning track was necessary.

The Reds were not pennant contenders in the last part of the 19th century nor the early part of the 20th. Their brightest star, Wahoo Sam Crawford, jumped to the American League in 1903. In 1905 outfielder Cy Seymour won the club's first batting title. Another outfielder, Bob Bescher, led the league in stolen bases four consecutive years from 1909–1912, but these individual exploits did not translate into club success. From 1890–1918 the Reds never finished above third place, usually languishing in the second division, sometimes in the basement. Led by third baseman Heinie Groh, outfielder Edd Roush, and a fine pitching staff, the Reds turned things around briefly. From 1917 through 1920 Cincinnati had a winning record four years in a row for the first time since 1902–1905.

1919

Under first-year manager Pat Moran, the Cincinnati Reds won their first National League pennant in 1919 and faced the Chicago White Sox in the World Series that October. Modern accounts of the Series tend to imply that the Sox were overwhelming favorites to take the championship. Not so. A review of contemporary newspaper articles revealed that most observers thought the clubs were evenly matched. Chicago newspapers tended to favor the White Sox; Cincinnati papers were more likely to see the Reds as probable winners.[18]

The Sporting News asked leading baseball writers of the day to predict the outcome of the Series. The writers whose opinions were printed in the paper were divided seven to seven in their predictions. James Gould of the *St. Louis Evening Star* wrote that "perhaps there never has been a World's Series the winner of which is harder to pick in advance."[19]

Early betting odds favored the White Sox, largely because the American League had won the last four World Series titles. By game time the odds had shifted; gamblers betting on the Reds were forced to accept even-money wagers. The view that the Reds could not have won had the Sox not thrown the Series is unwarranted. Both teams were formidable outfits.

The Reds were led by future Hall of Fame outfielder Edd Roush. Jake Daubert at first base was one of the top players of his time. Third baseman Heinie Groh was far and away the best National League third sacker of his era. Even second baseman Morrie Rath, who did not have a great career, was the most productive National League player at his position in 1919.[20] Rath and shortstop Larry Kopf made a surprisingly good keystone combination.[21] Moran had two experienced catchers, Ivy Wingo and Bill Rariden. In the outfield Roush was flanked by Greasy Neale in right and either Rube Bressler or Pat Duncan in left. It was in pitching, however, that the Reds really stood out. Moran's strength in the World Series, as in the pennant race, was that he had a lot of starters, any one of whom could win on any given day. Cincinnati pitchers posted a 2.23 earned run average.

The Reds' defense allowed the opposition to score only 401 runs, compared to the 534 given up by the White Sox. Dutch Ruether led the NL in winning percentage and ranked third in ERA. With a record of 21–7, Slim Sallee was second in percentage and tied for second in wins. Hod Eller was second in strikeouts and fourth in winning percentage. Ray Fisher ranked among the league's best in fewest base runners allowed.

The Reds won 96 games in the shortened season, a .686 pace that would have given them 106 victories in a normal 154-game season (or 111 wins in today's 162-game season). The 1919 Cincinnati Reds were no pushovers.

Their opponents, the Chicago White Sox, were a strong team, but not invincible. During the regular season the Sox had won 88 games, eight fewer than the Reds. Furthermore, the Sox were a team filled with dissension. Sportswriter Tom Meany quoted Eddie Collins as saying, "They seethed with discord and bitterness. Time after time they were close to open fighting with fists among themselves."[22] Collins, a future Hall of Fame second baseman, was leader of one faction of the team, which included catcher Ray Schalk and pitchers Red Faber and Dickie Kerr. Opposing them were some disgruntled players who resented what they considered favored treatment given to the Collins faction. Collins was not on speaking terms with first baseman Chick Gandil, an angry malcontent. Center fielder Happy Felsch, whose demeanor belied his nickname, was a sixth-grade dropout, a son of dirt-poor immigrants, who was often ridiculed by his better-educated teammates. Pitcher Eddie Cicotte was known as a surly troublemaker and an anti-management agitator.[23]

In short, the White Sox were not a group of happy campers. Furthermore, they played the 1919 World Series without the services of their best pitcher, Red Faber. A future Hall of Famer, Faber had won three games in the 1917 World Series, a feat that has never been surpassed. But he was unavailable for the 1919 Series. He had been plagued all year, first by an ankle injury, followed by a sore arm, and finally by a late-season bout of the influenza that was sweeping the country that year.

It took eight games for the Reds to wrap up the Series, five games to three. Not all of the White Sox players were in on the fix, and some who were wanted to win some games. But the Reds prevailed, and the world championship came to that baseball town known as the Queen City. It would be 20 years before the Reds played in another World Series.

Through no fault of their own, the 1919 Reds have not received the respect they deserve. The Black Sox stole that from them. Eight Chicago players were later accused of accepting bribes from gamblers to throw the Series. Although acquitted of fraud by a trial jury, Cicotte, Felsch, Gandil, Fred McMullin, Swede Risberg, and Lefty Williams probably were involved in throwing games. Joe Jackson's involvement is questionable. Buck Weaver did not participate in the fix, but he knew about it and did not report it. Commissioner Landis banned all eight from baseball for life. *The Sporting News* wrote that the "Reds won fair and square and well deserve honors."[24] The Series was not on the up-and-up, but that should not take away from the accomplishments of the Reds. The 1919 Cincinnati Reds achieved the highest winning percentage (.682) of any team in the history of the franchise and the highest of any National League club in the 32-season stretch from 1910–1941.

The events surrounding the bribery of the Chicago White Sox players in 1919 are among the most widely reported in the history of baseball. Yet an attempt to bribe a Cincinnati Reds pitcher in the same Series has received little attention. According to Roush's granddaughter, Susan Dellinger, her grandfather's suspicions were aroused by a tip from a Cincinnati newsstand operator, Jimmy Widmeyer, who was known as the "millionaire newsboy" because he had reportedly made and lost a fortune by investing on suggestions given to him by stockbroker customers. Roush mulled it over and decided if it was true, it had to be the pitchers who were guilty.

In the clubhouse meeting before Game 8, Roush informed manager Pat Moran of what he had heard. Moran took Roush and captain Jake Daubert into an adjacent shower room. The three decided to confront Hod Eller, the projected starting pitcher. Moran

In 1915, in his first year as a major league manager, Pat Moran led the Philadelphia Phillies to the National League championship. After four years in the City of Brotherly Love, Moran took his talents to Cincinnati, again leading his club to a pennant in his initial season. The former catcher added a World Series title to his 1919 accomplishments (Library of Congress).

said, "Hod, I want the truth. Did any gamblers approach you and offer you money to throw today's game?"

Eller replied, "Yep, some fella followed me up to my hotel room.... He walked right up to me and held up five 1,000 dollar bills. These are yours if you throw the game tomorrow. And there'll be five more just like them after the game."

"What did you tell him?" asked Moran.

"Why I told him to get outta my sight right quick or I would punch him square on the nose! I don't have any use for those kinda guys."

Moran believed his pitcher. Eller started Game 8, and the record shows that he pitched the game that won Cincinnati's first World Series. As Dellinger put it, "Moran's most interesting and brilliant moundsman threw an elegant array of raw fastballs combined with his famous talcum powder and paraffin shine balls to win the day."[25]

1920–1940

Roush became the first player primarily identified with the National League Reds to be elected to the National Baseball Hall of Fame. He was followed into those hallowed precincts by Eppa Rixey, the club's best pitcher of the 1920s. Rixey's efforts were not enough to bring another pennant to Redland. The Reds finished second three times in the twenties (1922, 1923, and 1926), before falling upon hard times. Not once from 1927–1937

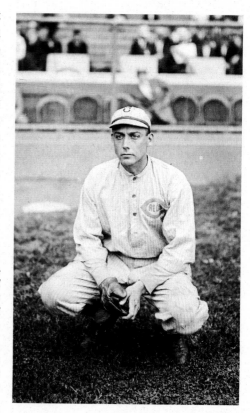

For many years Edd Roush was one of the top outfielders in the National League. In 18 big league seasons he compiled a .323 career batting average and won two batting titles, including one in the Reds' championship year of 1919, when he was probably the Reds' most valuable player. He has been inducted into the National Baseball Hall of Fame (Library of Congress).

did they finish in the first division, occupying the cellar five times during that span of mediocrity.

Herrmann resigned from the National Commission on January 8, 1920. Soon thereafter the Commission was abolished, and Kenesaw Mountain Landis became sole commissioner of the game. Herrmann continued as president of the Reds until 1927, when he resigned because of ill health. He was succeeded as club president by C. J. McDiarmid, a Cincinnati attorney. Ownership of the Reds was dispersed among many stockholders. Sidney Weil, a Jewish businessman whose ancestors had immigrated from Germany, started in his father's livery business, switched from horses to automobiles in 1919, and became owner of the largest Ford dealership in Cincinnati. Within ten years it had become the largest dealership under one roof in the United States.[26] He had invested in the stock market and accumulated what he described as "a small fortune."[27] He decided to acquire ownership of the Cincinnati Reds. In April 1929, he achieved his dream by becoming majority owner. Six months later the stock market crashed, taking most of Weil's fortune down the tubes. Although he struggled mightily, he was unable to recover his losses. He declared bankruptcy in 1933. When he was unable to repay a bank loan of $100,000, the franchise was sold to Powel Crosley, Jr., one of the bank's directors. Weil's greatest achievement as president of the Reds was the acquisition of Paul Derringer in a trade for Leo Durocher. (Four lesser players were also involved in the 1933 deal.) Derringer was a major contributor to the Reds pennants in 1939 and 1940.

Under owner Crosley and general manager Larry MacPhail, the Reds introduced several innovations into the game. On June 8, 1934, the Reds became the first major league club to travel by plane, when they flew to Chicago. The event drew very little coverage in the press at the time, probably because it was considered a novelty rather than the start of a trend.

Press coverage was extravagant a year later, however, when MacPhail and Crosley unveiled another innovation, one that was eventually copied by every major league club. On May 24, 1935, the Reds hosted the Philadelphia Phillies in the first night game ever played in the majors. Playing under the lights was not new to baseball. Baseball had been played under artificial illumination for nearly half a century, but never in the major leagues. J. L. Wilkinson, who surpassed even MacPhail as an innovator, had added a lighting system to his portable ball park for use in exhibition games at night. After he founded the Kansas City Monarchs, night games were sometimes played in the Negro American League. The Monarchs frequently played exhibition games against the House of David, which traveled throughout the country with portable lights mounted on their equipment truck. The first night game in Organized Baseball was played May 2, 1930, in Des Moines, Iowa, when the home team hosted Wichita in a Western League contest. *The Sporting News*, however, saw no future for baseball under the lights: "It would seem that night baseball is definitely on its way out. The mourners will probably be few. It was a noble experiment, but like so many others, it didn't live up to the expectations of its supporters."[28]

It took all of MacPhail's considerable powers of persuasion to get permission from the conservative powers who ran baseball to try his project. Fortunately, Crosley, the club owner, came aboard. Crosley contracted with Cincinnati Gas & Electric Company to design the lighting layout, the Ken Rad Company of Owensboro, Kentucky, to provide the Mazda lights, and General Electric to coordinate the project. President Franklin D. Roosevelt, sitting at his desk in the White House, pressed a gold telegraph key, which signaled MacPhail to throw a switch lighting all 632 Mazda lamps on the eight light towers.[29] Night baseball had arrived in the major leagues.

Excitement about the innovation obscured interest in the outcome of the game. For the record, Paul Derringer pitched a masterpiece and the Reds beat the Phillies, 2–1. Reaction of the players was enthusiastic. Billy Sullivan, the Cincinnati first baseman, said, "No pun intended, but there was electricity in the air, on the field, in the stands, and in the dugout. Ballplayers did not get blasé. They got fired up, too."

Reporters for the *Cincinnati Enquirer* shared Sullivan's enthusiasm. Jack Ryder wrote, "The theory that the players cannot see the ball well under the lights was shot to pieces by the staging of some of the finest defensive plays seen here this season."[30] His colleague James T. Golden waxed lyrical: "The field showed up in a more uniform light, green and tan, than it does in daytime.... What clouds there were were so thin that the ball, when it flew high, shone through them like a bald head in a steam room. And when there was no mist, the sphere stood out against the sky like a pearl against dark velvet."[31]

Not all of MacPhail's fellow owners were optimistic about the future of baseball after dark. Clark Griffith, owner of the Washington Nationals (frequently called the Senators), did not conceal his disdain for Cincinnati and its fans when he opined, "There is no chance of night baseball ever being popular in the bigger cities. People there are educated to see the best there is and will stand for only the best. High-class baseball cannot be played at night under artificial light."[32] One might agree or disagree with the Old Fox about his opinion of Cincinnati and the Reds fans, but it is beyond dispute that he misperceived the future of night baseball. By 1990 every major league club had installed lights, and night games were more frequent than day games.

After years of mediocrity, the fortunes of the Cincinnati Reds rose rapidly in the late 1930s. From eighth and last place in the National League in 1937, the Reds climbed to fourth in 1938, and won the pennant in both 1939 and 1940. The highlight of the 1938 season was provided by Johnny Vander Meer, who pitched two consecutive no-hit, no-run games, a feat never before accomplished in the major leagues and not likely to be duplicated in the future. The Reds' revival coincided with the arrival of future Hall of Famer Bill McKechnie as manager in 1938. Of course, McKechnie was not solely responsible for the Reds' improvement. On June 13, 1938, Cincinnati obtained pitcher Bucky Walters in a trade to join Paul Derringer in what would soon become the league's best pitching staff. First

Bill McKechnie was the first National League manager ever to win the World Series with two different clubs, having led the Pittsburgh Pirates in their triumph over the Washington Nationals in 1925, before guiding the Reds to victory in 1940. In a quarter of a century as a major league skipper McKechnie accumulated 1,896 wins, second only to John McGraw among National League managers. In this photograph, McKechnie (left) and Bucky Harris, Washington's manager (right) watch as President Calvin Coolidge (center) prepares to throw out a ball to start the 1925 World Series (Library of Congress).

baseman Frank McCormick and center fielder Harry Craft played their first full seasons in 1938. In 1939 the Reds acquired veteran third baseman Bill Werber in a trade, and rookie Junior Thompson emerged as a pitching star. By 1939 the Reds were a very good club. Cincinnati lost the 1939 World Series to the New York Yankees, but took the 1940 World Championship by defeating the Detroit Tigers. Future Hall of Fame catcher Ernie Lombardi had won both the National League batting title and the Most Valuable Player Award in 1938. Bucky Walters won the Triple Crown for pitchers and the MVP Award in 1939. Between the two of them, Walters and Derringer won 52 games in 1939, the most wins by NL teammates since 1916.

In 1940 Cincinnati won 100 games, only the third National League club with that many victories in more than a quarter of a century. The defensive-minded Reds set a new NL record with a .981 fielding percentage, and Harry Craft set a record for outfielders with a .997 mark. Walters led the league in wins, ERA, complete games, and innings pitched. Derringer was second to his teammate in wins and complete games and led the loop in fewest bases on balls per nine innings pitched. McCormick was named the league's Most Valuable Player, the third consecutive year that the MVP Award had gone to a Red. McKechnie became the first National League manager ever to win the World Series with two different clubs, having led the Pittsburgh Pirates to their triumph over the Washington Nationals in 1925.

1939 World Series

Good as the 1939 Reds were, they were no match for their World Series opponents. The 1939 New York Yankees are considered one of the strongest teams of all time. The Yankees won 106 games en route to their fourth consecutive American League pennant, the first AL club to accomplish that feat. They finished 17 games ahead of the runner-up Boston Red Sox. The Bronx Bombers were led by future Hall of Fame manager Joe McCarthy and had five future "immortals" in their lineup—catcher Bill Dickey, second baseman Joe Gordon, center fielder Joe DiMaggio, and pitchers Red Ruffing and Lefty Gomez.

After losing the first three games of the Series, the Reds sent Game 4 into extra innings. With the Yankees batting in the top of the tenth, Frankie Crosetti drew a base on balls. Red Rolfe sacrificed him to second. Charlie Keller was safe on an error by shortstop Billy Myers. DiMaggio singled, and right fielder Ival Goodman didn't handle it cleanly. Seeing this, Keller rounded the bases and headed for home, crashing full-tilt into Lombardi just as Goodman's throw arrived. The catcher lay prone on the ground as DiMaggio came charging around the bases and scored before Lombardi could recover from the stunning impact of the collision with Keller. The press made a big deal about Lombardi's "snooze" at the plate. The big catcher took a lot of unjustified criticism. Actually, the hit he took in the groin area incapacitated him momentarily; he recovered as quickly as he could. His so-called snooze did not cost the Reds the World Series. Crosetti had already scored what turned out to be the winning run before this incident took place.

Losing the 1939 World Series to the powerful Yankees was no disgrace, but the Reds resolved to make amends for the loss in their next chance.

1940 World Series

After four straight pennants, the Yankees failed to repeat in 1940, and the Detroit Tigers represented the American League in the World Series that October. The Tigers were a worthy opponent. Future Hall of Famer Hank Greenberg, the American League's Most Valuable Player, led the league in home runs, runs batted in, doubles, total bases, slugging percentage, and OPS. Another future Hall of Famer, Charlie Gehringer, was solid at second base. The excellent pitching staff was led by veterans Bobo Newsom, Tommy Bridges, and Schoolboy Rowe. The evenly matched World Series that resulted was deemed "one of the best in years."[33]

The two clubs took turns winning, alternating victories through the first six games. In Game 7, pitching on only two days' rest, Derringer held Detroit to only one run as the Reds won, 2–1, and captured the Series four games to three. Walters and Derringer each accounted for two of the Reds' wins.

Ecstatic fans poured through the downtown streets of the Queen City and gathered at Fountain Square to celebrate the victory. Rowdy fans upset a streetcar and caused some other minor damage, bringing the baseball town the unwelcome distinction of perhaps being the first city to engage in a destructive celebration after winning a championship.

Cincinnati had its first World Championship since 1919 and its first-ever untarnished crown. The 1939 loss was put behind them. There were no charges that the 1940 title was an undeserved gift. The 1940 Cincinnati Reds were proud champions.

Fountain Square in the heart of downtown Cincinnati is the favorite gathering place for Queen City residents and visitors. Following the World Series of 1940, fans crowded into the square to celebrate the victory. Rowdy fans upset a streetcar and cause some other minor damage, bringing the baseball town the distinction of becoming perhaps the first city to celebrate a championship by engaging in destructive behavior (Library of Congress).

1941–1961

Following their championship years of 1939–1940, the Reds again relapsed, finishing in the first division only seven out of the next 20 years. During the era of McCarthyism, the club changed its nickname to Redlegs from 1953 through 1958, fearing that fans would think the term Reds showed affinity for communism. Fortunately, the scourge of McCarthyism abated, and some semblance of sanity returned to the nation. The Reds became the Reds again, although in the minds of most fans they had never stopped being the Reds.

Another chapter in the up-and-down saga of the Cincinnati Reds started in the mid–1950s as they began acquiring future stars. At the age of 20, Frank Robinson was Rookie of the Year in 1956. Two years later, in 1958, 19-year-old Vada Pinson, from the same Oakland high school as Robinson, and pitcher Jim O'Toole debuted, and hurler Bob Purkey was obtained from Pittsburgh. The Reds' two best hitters and two of their leading pitchers were now in place. The final touch was added in 1961 when pitcher Joey Jay was obtained from Milwaukee. Behind the hitting of Robinson and Pinson and the hurling of the three pitchers, Cincinnati became the surprise team of 1961.

On March 28, 1961, Powel Crosley, Jr., died of a heart attack. During his 27 years as owner of the club, the Reds had introduced night baseball to the major leagues, won two pennants, and set the stage for another. During his regime, future stars Frank Robinson, Tony Perez, and Pete Rose were acquired by the Reds. A year after Crosley's death, Bill DeWitt purchased the club from the Crosley Foundation. As owner and general manager, DeWitt was destined to make some good moves and one huge mistake (trading away Frank Robinson in 1965). He sold the club after an unhappy season in 1966.

In some ways the season of 1961 was a strange one. From April 20 through the first game of a doubleheader on April 30, the Reds lost eight straight games, falling to last place in the National League. In the second game of that doubleheader, the Reds started a nine-game winning streak, climbing from eighth to second place in a matter of ten days. Cincinnati took the league lead on May 30 and battled the Los Angeles Dodgers for first place throughout the summer, taking the lead for good on August 16. Spurred on by the performance of Robinson and the league's best pitching staff, the Reds won the pennant. Robinson led the league in slugging percentage and OPS. He finished in the league's top five in runs scored, doubles, home runs, total bases, runs batted in, and stolen bases. Pinson led the loop in hits and was second in stolen bases. Jay tied for the league lead with 21 wins and four shutouts and was third in both winning percentage and complete games. O'Toole was third in wins, second in both winning percentage and earned run average, and fourth in strikeouts. Purkey was among the league leaders in fewest bases on balls per innings pitched and lowest batting average by opponents. The starting pitchers were abetted by two outstanding relievers, Jim Brosnan and Bill Henry, who saved 16 games each, only one fewer than the league leaders.

1961 World Series

For the second time in 23 years, the Reds faced the New York Yankees in a World Series. The 1939 encounter had resulted in a four-game sweep by the Bronx Bombers, rated as one of the best teams in history. The 1961 aggregation was almost as powerful, with three future Hall of Famers—Yogi Berra, Whitey Ford, and Mickey Mantle. Led by the M&M boys, Mantle and Roger Maris, the Yankees set a new major-league club record with 240 home runs. Maris beat out Mantle in a race to break Babe Ruth's record for most home runs by an individual during a season, with Maris clubbing number 61 on the final day. Maris won the AL MVP Award for the second year in a row, with Mantle close behind. The Yankees won 109 games, only one fewer victories than their fabulous 1927 team had garnered. Ford, Ralph Terry, and Luis Arroyo ranked one-two-three in pitcher's winning percentage. It is quite easy to see why the Yankees were overwhelming favorites in the Series.

Cincinnati lost three out of the first four games. The Yankees closed out the Series by winning a slugfest in Game 5, 13–5. Two of the Yankees' future Hall of Famers, Yogi Berra and Mickey Mantle, were held out of the game by minor injuries. They were replaced by Johnny Blanchard and Hector Lopez, both of whom hit home runs in the lopsided contest. Frank Robinson and Wally Post clouted round-trippers for the Reds, but that was not enough. The Reds had now twice lost the World Series to the Yankees. Nobody could know it at the time, but revenge was coming 15 years in the future.

1962–1970

Throughout the 1960s the Reds remained a strong ball club. In 1962 they won 98 games, the most victories they had attained since their championship season of 1940, but it was still not enough to cop the pennant.

The San Francisco Giants won 103 games in 1962, and the Los Angeles Dodgers won 102, but with no wild cards at the time both the Dodgers and the Reds were left out of post-season play. In 1964 the Reds came very close to winning the pennant, but fell short in a three-team race as the Cardinals clinched the pennant on the last day of the season. Baseball's amateur free agent draft was instituted in 1965. DeWitt made a superb choice by selecting Johnny Bench in the second round, after taking Bernie Carbo as his first pick. Cincinnati had a winning season in every year of the decade except 1966, but was unable to snare another flag in the sixties.

After the 1965 season, DeWitt made a trade that is considered by most Reds fans as the worst in the history of the club. He sent the club's greatest star, Robinson, to Baltimore in exchange for Milt Pappas, Jack Baldschun, and Dick Simpson. When Cincinnati fans complained bitterly about the deal, DeWitt responded by saying that Robinson is a "fading talent, increasingly hobbled by injuries."[34] Told that Robinson was only 30 and probably had many productive years ahead of him, DeWitt unwisely said, "He's an old 30." Robinson immediately set out to prove his former owner was wrong about him. He did so with a vengeance. In 1966 he won the Triple Crown by leading the league in batting average, home runs, and runs batted it; led the Orioles to the pennant and a four-game sweep over the Dodgers in the World Series; was named MVP of the Series; and was voted the American League MVP, the first player ever to win the award in both leagues. Meanwhile, the Reds got little production from the players traded to them. Arthur Daley, respected sportswriter for the *New York Times*, wrote that the trade was the "most colossal blunder in history by dealing off the explosive outfielder to the Orioles for inferior players who contributed virtually nothing in the exchange."[35]

Although DeWitt had made some moves that strengthened the Reds, the one huge blunder soured him in the minds of Cincinnati fans. In December 1966 he sold the Reds to a local ownership group that included the *Cincinnati Enquirer* and the Cincinnati Gas and Electric Company. A major factor in DeWitt's decision to sell the team was the negotiations to build a new stadium downtown that would require the Reds to sign a 40-year lease. DeWitt felt that he could not make such a long-term commitment to Cincinnati.[36] The new owners employed Bob Howsam as general manager.

Even without Robinson, the 1970s were the best decade in the long and storied history of the Cincinnati Reds. Several changes were made by the club in 1970. The most important was Howsam's employment of the unheralded Sparky Anderson as the new manager. A Cincinnati newspaper greeted the announcement of the hiring with the headline, "Sparky Who?"[37] Three rookies made important contributions to the team's success: Bernie Carbo in left field, Dave Concepcion at shortstop, and pitcher Wayne Simpson. The hard-throwing Simpson had a record of 14–3 before he suffered a season-ending arm injury with 30 games left in the season. Unfortunately, Simpson never regained the form that he had shown before the injury. The Reds also changed ball parks during the season, moving from Crosley Field to Riverfront Stadium on June 30. The Reds hosted the 1970 All-Star Game in their new park, a game that is remembered mainly for the hard slide by Pete Rose into Ray Fosse at home plate. The club got off to a fast start and led the National League West for all but one day of the season (April 11). They won the West with a club-record 102 victories in 1970, for a 14½-game margin over the Dodgers. Johnny Bench led the league in home runs and runs batted in, with Tony Perez close behind in both categories. Bench was named the National League MVP. At 22 he was the youngest ever to win that honor. Wayne Granger saved 35 games, at the time a record for a National League reliever, and he was named Fireman of the Year.

Regarded as one of the greatest catchers of all time, Hall of Famer Johnny Bench was the National League Rookie of the Year in 1968 and the loop's Most Valuable Player in 1970 and 1972. He was a 14-time All Star and the winner of ten Gold Gloves. In 1990 Bench telecast games on the Reds' TV Network (National Baseball Hall of Fame Library).

In the NLCS the Reds swept the Pittsburgh Pirates, winners of the East, in three straight games. The powerful Pirates, even with Roberto Clemente and Willie Stargell, were able to score only three runs in the three games against Cincinnati pitching. Although the Reds won all three games, it was a close, hard-fought series, with the Pittsburgh hurlers nearly matching their Cincinnati counterparts. The scores were 3–0, 3–1, and 3–2. The last game was a thriller. The Pirates scored a run in the top of the first inning, but the Reds overtook them in the bottom of the frame on successive home runs by Perez and Bench. Pittsburgh tied the game in the fifth. The game was still tied with two out in the home half of the eighth, when pinch-hitter Ty Cline drew a walk, went to second on a single by Pete Rose, and scored on a single by Bobby Tolan, barely beating Stargell's throw to the plate. When Granger allowed Clemente to reach base with two outs in the ninth inning, Anderson brought in a 19-year-old rookie, Don Gullett, to preserve the victory and give the Reds their first National League title of the 1970s. It was Gullett's second consecutive save in the NLCS.

1970 World Series

Cincinnati manager Sparky Anderson was excited to reach the World Series in his first year as a big-league skipper. "It just thrilled me to be in the 1970 Series and every day was like another day in my favorite dream.... I consider myself an average guy, but even an average guy likes to touch royalty once in a while and the World Series is the very royalty of baseball."[38]

Cincinnati again faced a powerful American League opponent in the World Series. Baltimore had won 108 games while posting its second straight AL title. The Orioles won the East by a 15-game margin over the New York Yankees and swept the Minnesota Twins in the ALCS. The Birds had the league's best pitching staff, featuring Mike Cuellar, Dave McNally, and Jim Palmer, each of whom was a 20-game winner. Paced by MVP Boog Powell and ex-Red Frank Robinson, the Orioles led the loop in scoring.

In four of the five games, the Reds scored first, but the Birds were too powerful and took the Series four games to one. Lee May of the Reds set a World Series record by driving in eight runs in a five-game Series, but it was not enough to win the championship. Baltimore third baseman Brooks Robinson was named Most Valuable Player of the Series. He hit .429, broke the record for total bases in a World Series, and put on a sensational show of fielding. *Total Baseball* credited the third sacker with "other-worldly defense that gave Reds hitters nightmares through the Series."[39]

1971–1972

Although favored to repeat, the Reds slipped badly in 1971, falling all the way to a tie for fourth place in the NL West. Bobby Tolan missed the entire season due to an injury. Jim Merritt, a 20-game winner in 1970, won only one game in 1971, and his career was effectively over. After the end of the season, the Reds traded slugging first baseman and clubhouse leader Lee May, popular second baseman Tommy Helms, and reserve outfielder Jimmy Stewart to Houston for Ed Armbrister, Jack Billingham, Cesar Geronimo, Denis Menke, and Joe Morgan. The trade was met with skepticism and even hostility by Reds fans, who remembered the disastrous trading away of Frank Robinson a few years earlier.

General manager Bob Howsam explained that in order to play successfully in Riverfront Stadium, the club needed to get more speed into the lineup. Sparky Anderson welcomed the additional speed. With Rose leading off and Morgan batting second, Cincinnati had one of the best top-of-the-lineup combinations in baseball, setting the stage for power hitters Bench and Perez. As it turned out, Geronimo and Morgan became vital pieces of the Big Red Machine, and the other three, especially Billingham, made contributions in the not-too-distant future. The deal clinched Howsam's reputation as the chief architect of the Big Red Machine. Five of the so-called Great Eight—Morgan, Concepcion, Foster, Griffey, and Geronimo—were secured during his tenure.

In 1972 the Reds got off to a slow start, picked up the pace in May and June, and took over the division lead for good on June 25, winning the West by a comfortable 10½-game cushion over Houston. Bench led the league with 40 home runs and 125 RBI and won the NL MVP Award. Rose led the circuit in hits, and Morgan was tops in runs scored. Gary Nolan led the loop's pitchers in winning percentage, and Clay Carroll set a new saves record with 37.

Cincinnati faced the defending world champion Pittsburgh Pirates in the NLCS. After the clubs split the first four games, the decisive Game 5 was a memorable contest. Pittsburgh took a 2–0 lead in the second inning. The Reds got their first run on a RBI double by Rose in the fourth, but the Pirates had upped their lead by also scoring a run in the fourth. The Reds cut the lead to 3–2 on a fifth-inning home run by Geronimo. Neither team could score again until the bottom of the ninth. With Pittsburgh needing only three more outs to advance to the World Series for the second year in a row, Bench hit a game-tying homer. Perez hit a single and was replaced by pinch-runner George Foster. Menke hit safely to put runners on first and second. Pittsburgh brought in Bob Moose in relief. Foster advanced to third on a fly out and stayed there as the next batter popped up. With two out and the potential winning run on third base, Hal McRae came up to pinch-hit. Moose let loose a wild pitch and Foster scampered home with the pennant-winning run.

1972 World Series

The three-year reign of the Baltimore Orioles as American League champions came to an end as the Oakland Athletics started their own three years atop the junior circuit. The A's copped their first flag in more than 40 years and their first after the move to the West Coast, largely due to the pitching of Ken Holtzman, Catfish Hunter, Blue Moon Odom, Vida Blue, and relievers Darold Knowles and Rollie Fingers.

The World Series showcased a sharp contrast between the conservatism of the Reds and the unconventional appearance of the A's in their day-glo uniforms. The trivial matter of hair styles is illustrative. Charlie Finley, owner of the Oakland club, paid $300 each to his players to grow beards and present an array of mustaches, long hair, and heavy sideburns. Fingers stood out with a handlebar mustache that exceeded anything seen in a ballplayer for 100 years, if ever. On the other hand, the Reds had a strict rule barring long hair and mustaches. The Series was called "The Hairs vs. the Squares."[40]

The two clubs battled evenly through the first six games, each winning three. The hard-fought 1972 World Series came down to a decisive seventh game. Fittingly, it was a nail biter. Oakland took a 1–0 lead on an unearned run in the first inning. Cincinnati tied it in the fifth on a sacrifice fly by pinch-hitter Hal McRae. In the sixth the A's regained the lead, 3–1, on RBI doubles by Gene Tenace and Sal Bando. The Reds scored one run in the eighth, but Fingers shut them down in the ninth. Oakland won the game and the World Series, 3–2, the first of three consecutive world championships for Finley's unorthodox crew.

1973–1976

The defending National League champion Cincinnati Reds got off to a poor start in 1973. Early on, Menke, Geronimo, and Tolan were all mired in deep slumps. At the end of June the Reds were in fourth place at 39–37, 11 games behind the league-leading Los Angeles Dodgers. The team got blazing hot in July, going 24–7 in the month. Led by Rose, who won the NL batting title and MVP honors, and powered by Morgan, Bench, and Perez, the Reds continued winning during the remainder of the season, compiling a major-league best 99 wins. They were heavily favored to defeat the New York Mets in the NLCS. However, the Mets lived up to their slogan, "Ya Gotta Believe," and took a hotly contested series, three games to two. Despite having the best record in baseball, the Reds were denied a chance to perform in the 1973 fall classic.

Cincinnati fielded an excellent team again in 1974, winning 98 games, which would usually be enough to capture the pennant. But the Dodgers were four wins better, and the flag went to Los Angeles. One of the headline-grabbing events of the season came at Riverfront Stadium on Opening Day, when Hank Aaron tied Babe Ruth's all-time home run record. The Reds hit more than a few home runs themselves, leading the league with 126 round-trippers. Rose led the league in runs and doubles, Morgan was tops in on-base percentage, and Bench led in total bases. George Foster and Dan Driessen were added to the starting lineup, and Clay Kirby joined an already excellent pitching staff, but it was not enough to catch the Dodgers. Kirby was acquired in a trade for Tolan, who had fallen into disfavor with the Reds' front office for his refusal to abide by the club's no facial hair policy. Once the club had suspended him, but he appealed to the Players Association and filed a grievance, which he won because there were no league rules against beards or mustaches.[41]

The Big Red Machine is regarded as a great hitting team. Less well recognized is that they were one of the greatest defensive clubs in the history of the sport. Particularly down the middle—catcher, shortstop, second base, and center field—where defensive play is most important, they were incomparable. From 1974–1977 Bench, Concepcion, Morgan, and Geronimo each won four consecutive Gold Gloves. Bench won ten in his career.

Near the end of the 1974 season, Cincinnati strengthened its good, but overworked, bullpen by promoting Rawley Eastwick and Will McEnaney from their Indianapolis farm club. There was also a perceived weakness at third base. Although Driessen was an excellent hitter, he was not a third baseman by trade. He could not play third base the way the Reds wanted it played. Third base is called the "hot corner" because, as Joe Posnanski wrote, "Baseballs rush at you like angry wasps."[42] Driessen couldn't handle the hot smashes. General manager Bob Howsam wanted to trade Perez for a star third baseman like George Brett or Graig Nettles, and move Driessen to first base. He couldn't get the superstar he wanted, so he settled for slick-fielding, weak-hitting John Vukovich. "With our lineup, you won't need his hitting," Howsam told manager Sparky Anderson. "We'll still score plenty of runs. Just put him at third base and let him make all the plays. Every hit he gets will be a bonus."[43]

If there was a weakness at third base, the outfield on the other hand had a surfeit of capable players. Geronimo and Rose had been joined by George Foster and Ken Griffey. All were capable of big league stardom, but four players were too many to play every day in three positions. Sparky Anderson played favorites. It was no secret; he admitted it. During 1975 spring training, he said there were four superstars—Rose, Morgan, Bench, and Perez. Those four could make their own rules. "The rest of you are turds," he said.[44] (Darrel Chaney had "Turd" T-shirts made for his fellow outcasts.)[45]

Vukovich was lowest on Anderson's totem pole. Anderson never accepted him, treating him with contempt, and complaining loudly and often that the Reds could never win with that "turd" at third base. Eventually, the manager went to Pete Rose and asked him if he would consider taking over at the hot corner. Rose agreed, and never reluctant to blow his own horn, was effusive in his praise for himself for making the move. "Who else would just agree to play third base in the middle of the season? Just like that. Who else? You name me one star player who would do that. I was an All-Star in left field.... Now you tell me, who would agree to switch positions to help the club? Do you know any great player that would have done that?"[46]

Rose deserved the credit he gave himself for accepting the switch. It freed up his three erstwhile outfield mates for full-time play and enabled Driessen to assume a role as the club's best pinch-hitter and back-up to Perez at first base. He could even play the

Known as "Charlie Hustle" for playing with reckless abandon, Pete Rose was one of the greatest players in the history of baseball. The game's all-time hits leader, he won three batting titles, two Gold Gloves, and one Most Valuable Player Award. As manager of the Reds (1984–1989), he led the team to five consecutive second-place finishes before being permanently suspended from baseball for betting on games (National Baseball Hall of Fame Library).

outfield when needed. The Big Red Machine was now assembled and ready to dominate baseball. And dominate they did! The club was an even .500 at 12–12 before Rose moved to third base on May 3. For the rest of the season they played at a .696 clip, winding up the season with 108 wins, the most by any National League team since 1909. The move to third did not hurt Rose's offensive numbers. He led the league in hits and runs scored and was second to Morgan in on-base percentage. Morgan not only led in OBP, but he was also tops in on-base plus slugging and finished in the top five in batting average, runs scored, and stolen bases, leading to a well-deserved MVP Award. Bench, Perez, and Foster each ranked among the league's five best in at least one hitting category each. Bench, Morgan, Concepcion, and Geronimo all won Gold Gloves. Although the quiet, Bible-reading Foster did not receive the award, he was certainly worthy of one. Gullett led NL pitchers in winning percentage, Eastwick led in saves, and Nolan allowed the fewest walks per innings pitched.

As a club the 1975 Cincinnati Reds led the National League in runs scored, difference between runs scored and runs allowed, stolen bases, fielding average, and saves by the pitching staff. In the NLCS they faced a strong Pittsburgh club, which had won its fourth NL East title in five years. The Pirates turned out to be no match for the Big Red Machine. The Reds swept the NLCS and advanced to the World Series.

1975 World Series

The Reds expected to face the Oakland A's in the World Series, but a surprise team represented the junior circuit. The Boston Red Sox had won the AL East and then upset the three-time defending world champions in the ALCS. Few people gave them a chance in the World Series. Pitcher Rick Wise came up with the idea to have the Red Sox players wear T-shirts with a giant letter **U** and then underneath the word **"Underdog"** written in script.[47] In *The Sporting News*, Furman Bisher wrote: "The Reds come with muscle. They hit the ball a long way and a lot. They play like figures off tintypes of another age, when caps looked like saucepans with bills and fans got to the park by streetcar. You would surely say that if the matchup were between the Reds and Boston, the Reds would win."[48]

Wise was correct. The underdog Red Sox were underrated. Stars like outfielders Carl Yastrzemski and Dwight Evans, catcher Carlton Fisk, and pitcher Luis Tiant had been joined by sensational rookies Fred Lynn and Jim Rice. Those who had predicted a rout for the Reds soon had to eat their words. The Red Sox were no pushovers.

The World Series that the Reds were expected to win in a breeze turned out to be one of the most exciting, hotly contested classics ever played, filled with passion, tension, drama, and glory such as sport has seldom seen. Joe Posnanski wrote that it was the greatest World Series that ever was.[49] Baseball (and America) needed this kind of respite from the travails of economic misery, the Vietnam War, and Watergate. The game was being criticized as being too slow, too old-fashioned, and not as exciting as the nation's more violent pastime, football. Baseball needed some exciting games to bring the fans back. That is exactly what the Reds and Red Sox provided in 1975.[50]

Bill James wrote that "The 1975 World Series showed millions of Americans how good baseball had become and annihilated forever the feeling that the game had become passé."[51]

Not everyone agreed on the greatness of the 1975 World Series. It would not be baseball, or America, or human nature if everyone agreed on anything. The official historian of Major League Baseball and his colleagues wrote an article about the year 1975, featuring the signing of Catfish Hunter by the New York Yankees, the hiring of Frank Robinson as manager by the Cleveland Indians, and the end of the Oakland Athletics dynasty as the three major stories of the year. The World Series got one paragraph at the end of the piece, with no comment about it being exciting or important in any way.[52]

After five games, the Reds led the Series three games to two. Three days of rain in Boston delayed Game 6 until October 21. The rain did not dampen the enthusiasm of the fans. Resumption of the Series was eagerly anticipated. The rain finally stopped and a capacity crowd poured into Fenway Park, some paying exorbitant prices to scalpers and others buying standing-room-only tickets or perching atop nearby structures. Millions more tuned in on television, more than had ever watched a baseball game. When the game was finally played, it was "one of the greatest games in baseball history."[53]

The teams battled on even terms. First one would gain the lead, then the momentum would shift. At the end of nine innings, the score was tied, 6–6. The game moved into extra innings. Neither team could score in the tenth or the 11th.

Cincinnati got two runners on base in the top of the 12th, but couldn't score. Fisk led off the home half of the 12th. Pat Darcy's first pitch was high for ball one. His second pitch was low and inside. Fisk reached down and hit a towering drive down the left field line. Would it be foul or fair? Fisk hopped sideways down the first-base line, watching the flight of the ball, waving his arms, urging, begging, willing the ball to stay fair. Joseph Wallace quoted Roger Angell describing Fisk as "waving wildly, weaving and writhing and gyrating along the first-base line, as he wished that ball fair, *forced* it fair with his entire body."[54] Ecstatic fans rushed out of the stands and engulfed the field, trying to reach their hero, who was already being mobbed by his teammates.

"How can a manager of a losing team call it the greatest game ever played?" asked Sparky Anderson. "Well, winning or losing a man can't lie to himself."[55] Peter Gammons wrote in the *Boston Globe*, "At 12:34 a.m. in the 12th inning, Fisk's historic home run brought a 7–6 end to a game that will be the pride of historians in the year 2525, a game won and lost what seemed like a dozen times, and a game that brings back summertime one more day."[56] We can't speak for the historians of 2525, but we know memories of this game will endure for many years. In 2011 Major League Baseball's MLB network rebroadcast the game, calling it the greatest game of the past 50 years.[57] Rose told Bob Costas, host of the MLB program, "I was having fun. I mean win, lose, or draw. Man, I was happy to play in that game. Let me tell you something, man, I played 3,500 games and that's the most exciting game I ever played in."[58]

Some people may think Fisk's dramatic homer won the 1975 World Series for Boston. Not so. There was still Game 7 to be played, although Bill Lee didn't think it was necessary. "These teams are so close that they should call the game off, declare us co-champions of the world, and stage a picnic at old Fenway," the Spaceman said.[59]

The game was not called off. Game 7 was played, and there are those of us who believe it should get as much ink as Game 6. After all, it was the game that decided the winner of the World Series and was as close as the previous game. A one-run game with the winners coming from three runs behind to win the championship sounds exciting enough. Perhaps writers, broadcasters, fans, and players had used up all their superlatives on Game 6 and had run dry by the time Game 7 came around. For whatever reason, the deciding game did not get the attention it deserved.

It was Lee versus Gullett in the championship game. Both hurlers started well, but Gullett lost command of his pitches in the bottom of the third. He gave up only two hits, but walked four, allowing the Red Sox to plate three runs. Billingham replaced Gullett in the fifth. The Reds got to Lee in the sixth. Perez hit a home run with Rose on base to reduce the deficit to 3–2. Roger Moret replaced Lee in the seventh after Griffey's walk and allowed the Reds to tie the game. Griffey stole second and scored on a hit by Rose. The score remained tied, 3–3, until the ninth inning.

With Jim Burton now pitching for Boston, Griffey and Rose both walked. Morgan delivered a single, driving in Griffey with the go-ahead run. McEnaney shut the Red Sox down in the bottom of the ninth. Cincinnati won, 4–3, for their first world championship since 1940.

Roger Angell explained why the 1975 World Series so touched the hearts of even the most casual fans. The Series reminded us, he wrote, of the deep satisfaction of *"caring*—caring deeply and passionately, really caring—which is a capacity or an emotion that has almost gone out of our lives.... Naivete—the joy that sends a grown man or woman to dancing and shouting in the middle of the night over the flight of a distant ball— seems a small price to pay for such a gift."[60]

1976 World Series

The Big Red Machine had won a World Series. To validate their claim as one of the greatest teams of all time, they needed to win another. Cincinnati boasted the same starting lineup that had been victorious in 1975. The squad was augmented by two outstanding rookie pitchers, Santo Alcala (11–4) and Pat Zachry (14–7). The Reds set out on the path toward their goal early in the 1976 season. During April and May they were at or near the top of the standings. After May 28 they were never out of first place. With 102 wins, they outpaced the Los Angeles Dodgers by ten games and became the first National League team to post two consecutive 100-win seasons since World War II. Morgan won his second straight MVP Award, with a terrific season in which he led the league in on-base percentage and slugging, and was in the top five in batting average, runs, home runs, and RBI. Rose led in hits, doubles, and runs. Griffey and Foster also had outstanding seasons. The Reds were the best fielding team in the league. Bench, Morgan, Concepcion, and Geronimo all won Gold Gloves, and Foster deserved one. Philadelphia won the National League East, but fell to the Reds in three straight games in the NLCS. The sweep gave the Reds their second straight NL pennant.

The once-dominant New York Yankees won their first pennant in 12 years in 1976. Most members of the Big Red Machine were not yet born when the Yankees beat the Reds in the 1939 World Series. But fans with long memories were eager for revenge. They got it.

The Reds swept the Yankees four games straight. Counting their three-game sweep over the Phillies, the Big Red Machine had now won eight straight post-season games. Cincinnati celebrated its second consecutive World Series title, something no other National League club had accomplished since 1922. Through 2014, no other NL club has won two world championships in a row since 1976.

Most observers would now proclaim the Big Red Machine as one of baseball's greatest teams. But not Billy Martin. The Yankees' skipper, never a gracious loser, won the sour grapes competition by claiming, "A good team, not great. Lucky. Bloops, pop-ups that fell in, every umpire's decision, every break."[61]

1977–1989

Could the Reds win again in 1977? Could they become the first National League club ever to win the World Series three times in a row? To do that they had to keep their stars on board, despite the lures of free agency. Arbitrator Peter Seitz had ruled that a player could escape the reserve clause by playing a season without a contract in their option year. Asked about the possibility of losing players, Anderson said, "I would like to think we will not lose any player by playing out their option. If money is put before anything else, then we are a mighty sick society."[62] They lost one immediately—Don Gullett. Anderson decried the pitcher's "disloyalty" and said he would never use his name again.[63] In the minds of some conservative baseball people, a player was to be condemned as disloyal if he tried to better himself by playing out his contract, but a club had the right to trade players away at any time, regardless of the player's wishes.

Through a combination of free agency, trades, and retirement, the Big Red Machine dissipated over time. None of the so-called Great Eight stayed with the Reds throughout the 1970s and 1980s. Tony Perez was traded away on December 16, 1976, even before Anderson complained about Gullett accepting free agency. General manager

One of the most productive members of the Big Red Machine, Cuba-born Tony Perez was a fan favorite in Cincinnati for many years. Traded away in 1976, he returned to the Queen City in 1984. Pete Rose appointed him to his coaching staff and Piniella retained him in that position (National Baseball Hall of Fame Library).

Bob Howsam, who had been given major credit for assembling the Big Red Machine, traded Perez because he thought the younger Driessen would be an acceptable replacement at first base. Howsam later admitted it was the biggest mistake he ever made.[64] He had underestimated the importance of Perez as a clubhouse leader. Howsam was bitterly opposed to free agency and refused to sign any free agents for the Reds. His disappointment with the direction baseball was taking led to his resignation in April 1978. He was succeeded by Dick Wagner, his longtime assistant. At the end of the season, Wagner fired Anderson, Cincinnati's most successful manager. Sparky led the Detroit Tigers to a world championship in 1984, the first manager ever to win the World Series in both leagues.

Rose became a free agent in 1978; Morgan followed suit in 1979. Geronimo and Griffey left via the trade route in 1981, and Foster was dealt in 1982. Bench retired as a Red in 1983. He and Concepcion were the only members of the Great Eight to spend their entire careers in the Queen City. Concepcion was granted free agency in 1986, but re-signed with the Reds, before being released in 1988. Except for Ken Griffey, he was the last member of the Great Eight to play for Cincinnati, although several of the others returned in different capacities.

Cincinnati finished second in their division in 1977 and again in 1978. In 1979 they won the NL West, but were swept by the Pirates in the NLCS. They fell to third in 1980. The Reds had the best record in the NL during the strike-shortened 1981 season, but because of the peculiarities of the split season were not eligible for the playoffs. They were not in contention from 1982 through 1984. In August 1984, the Reds reacquired Pete Rose and installed him as player-manager. On September 11, 1985, Rose broke Ty Cobb's record for most career hits. He retired as a player a year later but stayed on as manager. Under Rose and new owner Marge Schott, the Reds rebounded and finished second in their division four straight years from 1985 through 1988, but never qualified for the post-season.

The 1989 season was a huge disappointment, reaching its nadir with a lifetime ban from baseball imposed on Rose. When the 1990 season got under way the veteran Ken Griffey, who had returned to the Reds after stints in New York and Atlanta, was the only surviving member of the Big Red Machine playing in the Queen City.

From 1890 through 1989, this Cincinnati franchise had won 7,713 games, while losing 7,540, a percentage of .506. They had won eight National League pennants and four World Series championships. They had called six different ball parks home and played under 11 different principal owners.

The club record by decade:

	W	L	Pct.	
1890s	729	639	.533	Best finish was third in the National League in 1896, 1898
1900s	705	769	.478	Best finish was third in the National League in 1904
1910s	717	782	.478	World Series champions in 1919
1920s	798	735	.521	Best finish was second in the National League in 1922, 1923, 1926
1930s	664	866	.434	Won National League pennant in 1939
1940s	765	769	.499	World Series champions in 1940
1950s	741	798	.481	Best finish was third in National League in 1956
1960s	860	742	.537	Won National League pennant in 1961
1970s	953	657	.592	Won four pennants and two World Series championships
1980s	781	783	.499	Had the best record in the National League West in 1981

A Baseball Town

Cincinnati is a baseball town. By 1990 it had carried that distinction for well over a century. The Society for American Baseball Research has published a book titled *Inventing Baseball: The 100 Greatest Games of the Nineteenth Century*.[1] Of the 100 games, 75 involved professional clubs; teams from Cincinnati were principals in nine of these contests. As is well known, the Cincinnati Red Stockings of 1869 were the first openly all-professional baseball club in the world. John Thorn has written that most veteran baseball observers believe that a game between the Red Stockings and the Brooklyn Atlantics in 1870 was the greatest in the game's history until Bobby Thomson hit "the shot heard around the world" in 1951.[2] Cincinnati joined the National League in 1876 and has had a club in the major leagues every year except one since then. During most of the years from 1869 to 1990, baseball was the only professional game in the Queen City. Truly, Cincinnati was and is a baseball town.

At the high school level, Cincinnati has produced many state champions in all three revenue sports. Archbishop Moeller High School won the state football title five times between 1972 and 1990, with Princeton taking the championship twice. In basketball the boys state tournament was twice won by Cincinnati teams. Princeton High School captured the girls title twice. However, it was in hardball that the teams from the baseball town dominated. Between 1923 and 1990, nine area high schools shared 27 state championships. Elder High School led the parade with ten titles, while Western Hills won the championship five times. At least 32 future major leaguers played high school ball in Cincinnati, including such luminaries as Ken Griffey, Jr., and Barry Larkin at Moeller and Pete Rose at Western Hills. Before the days of high school baseball and organized youth leagues, perhaps nearly 200 major leaguers learned the game on Cincinnati sandlots and playgrounds.[3]

The first native of Cincinnati to be inducted into the National Baseball

Hall of Fame in Cooperstown was Miller Huggins. Called the "Mighty Mite" for his lack of height (five feet, six and one-half inches), Huggins was an outstanding second baseman. Playing first for his hometown Reds and later for the St. Louis Cardinals, he earned a place among the best second sackers of all time, tied with Lou Whitaker for 20th place in the Faber System rankings.[4] However, it was not as a player but as a manager that Huggins won admission to the Hall of Fame. In a 17-year managerial career with the Cardinals and the New York Yankees, Huggins won 1413 games and lost 1134, for a winning percentage of .555. In his tenure with the Yankees, the club won six American League pennants and three World Series championships. His 1927 Yankees won 110 games and are often considered one of the best baseball clubs of all time. Huggins was named to the Hall of Fame by the Veterans Committee in 1964.

The first native of Cincinnati to be inducted into the National Baseball Hall of Fame was the "Mighty Mite," Miller Huggins. The diminutive second baseman was an outstanding player for his hometown Reds and later for the St. Louis Cardinals, but he earned his Hall of Fame credentials as a manager. In a 17-year managerial career with the Cardinals and the New York Yankees, Huggins won 1,413 games, while losing 1,134 for a winning percentage of .565 (Library of Congress).

In 2013 Huggins was joined in the Hall of Fame by another native son of the Queen City. Barry Larkin had an outstanding career both in the field and at the plate. He was named to 12 All-Star teams and won three Gold Glove Awards and nine Silver Slugger Awards. Larkin was one of the leaders of the Reds' 1990 championship team and was the National League's Most Valuable Player in 1995. In 19 major league seasons, the Cincinnati native played in 2,180 regular-season games, every one of them for his hometown Reds. The Faber System ranked him the tenth-best shortstop in major league history.[5] Larkin was elected to the Cooperstown shrine in 2012 by the Baseball Writers' Association of America and inducted in 2013.

Three members of the 1990 Cincinnati Reds were born in

the baseball town—Larkin, Bill Doran, and Ron Oester. At least 11 other Cincinnati natives played in the major leagues in 1990. Among the more prominent were outfielders Daryl Boston, Lance Johnson, and David Justice, and pitchers Rich Dotson, Roger McDowell, and Jeff Russell. Justice was the National League Rookie of the Year in 1990.

Baseball is played on many different levels in Cincinnati. The Cincinnati Cobalts are a semipro club founded in 1985 that competes at the highest level of play. They have consistently been ranked nationally. The Cincinnati Spikes baseball program was started in 1990. The players were selected from knothole teams in suburban Blue Ash, Loveland, and Montgomery, and found success in the Southwest Ohio League. The Spikes have since divided into three different age divisions—ten and up, 13 and up, and college age. By 1990 clubs from the city's American Legion posts had won 23 state championships, including eight in a row from 1951–1958. They had captured seven national titles, including three consecutive championships in 1956–1958. Other titles were claimed in 1944, 1947, 1952, and 1988.

The best amateur baseball club in metropolitan Cincinnati is the Midland Redskins. Indeed, the Redskins may well be the most successful amateur baseball nine on the planet. The club was founded in 1958 by Joe Hayden, then chairman of the Midland Insurance Company. It plays its home games in a stadium on the campus of the insurance company in Clermont County, about 20 miles east of the Queen City. A graduate of Miami University, Hayden named his club the Redskins in honor of his alma mater. (Out of sensitivity to the concerns of American Indians, the university changed its nickname to Red Hawks in 1997, but the Midland club kept its original name.)

In 1990 the Redskins were the defending Connie Mack World Series champions. Four alumni of the club were playing for the Cincinnati Reds that season—Todd Benzinger, Bill Doran, Barry Larkin, and Ron Oester. The defending champion Redskins did not make it to the World Series that year, but the following season they started a string that had stretched to 23 consecutive appearances by 2013. Cincinnati has won the Connie Mack World Series 14 times, a number equal to the combined total of the next three cities—Dallas, Texas; Long Beach, California; and Marietta, Georgia.[6] The Redskins have sent around 250 of their former players into professional baseball, including about 40 to the major leagues.[7] One, Barry Larkin, is enshrined in the National Baseball Hall of Fame in Cooperstown; another, Ken Griffey, Jr., will soon join him there.

Author Lonnie Walker paid tribute to the baseball town. "Perhaps

Midland's success is because so many of its players are Cincinnati kids. Perhaps that is Midland's advantage—that it plays out of Cincinnati, the only city uncool enough yet rich enough in baseball tradition that its most celebrated young jocks can actually be persuaded to do what the coach says and be grateful for the privilege; the only city whose best schoolboy athletes still believe that this is an incredible way to spend a teenage summer."[8]

Little Leagues and other youth leagues flourish in Cincinnati. At a less advanced level, dozens of baseball clubs are sponsored by churches, park and recreation departments, and industries. Regardless of skill, almost any youth or adult wishing to play baseball can find a home in this baseball town.

Knothole baseball has been a Cincinnati tradition since 1932. Around 1990 the Greater Cincinnati Knothole Baseball Association was formed. There are over 100 leagues in the area, including separate leagues for different age groups from sixth grade through high school. Weather permitting, practice normally starts in mid–March. League games start the third week in April and run through the end of June, followed by tournaments in July.

The Cincinnati Reds organization and former Reds players are instrumental in the success of Reviving Baseball in Inner Cities, a youth outreach program designed to promote interest in baseball, increase self-esteem in disadvantaged youngsters, and encourage kids to stay in school and off the streets. It was formed by Major League Baseball in an attempt to increase the number of youngsters from underserved populations (primarily inner city black youth) who are prepared to play college and professional baseball, but the program also stresses life skills and educational opportunities. The Cincinnati Reds are among the sponsors of the program. Eric Davis, an outfielder for the 1990 Reds, is an outstanding booster of RBI, as is Joe Morgan, a star of the Big Red Machine. "It's not the excitement of the game or the lack of marketing wizardry that hurts baseball," said Davis. "It's economics. Inner-city African American kids play basketball and football because they view these sports as avenues to college scholarships.... If you live in the inner city, your parents can't afford to send you to college. You need a scholarship. So what are you going to play?"[9] It is appropriate that people from a baseball town support this program that makes it possible for more youngsters to play hardball.

Cincinnati is home to two major universities, Xavier and the University of Cincinnati, both of which field athletic teams. Neither has enjoyed outstanding success in baseball, having no College World Series appearances between them. However, both have sent alumni to the major leagues. A total of 23 ex-Cincinnati Bearcats or ex-Xavier Musketeers have made it to The Show. Among them are three Hall of Famers—Miller Huggins and Sandy Koufax from the Bearcats and Jim Bunning from Xavier. Perhaps best known among recent baseball players who plied their craft for a Queen City college is Cincinnati native Kevin Youkilis, who played for the Bearcats.

In football and basketball the Cincinnati institutions have made a mark. It is in basketball that the Bearcats have really stood out. The team won the NCAA championship in both 1961 and 1962. In 1990 the basketball Bearcats were members of the Metro Conference, while the football team was not affiliated with a conference. Xavier had discontinued football in 1973. The Musketeer basketball team was a member of the Midwestern City Conference in 1990, and had not yet achieved national renown, but it was on its way up. The team reached the NCAA's Sweet Sixteen for the first time in 1990 and is now recognized as a perennial national power.

Pro basketball had a brief existence in the Queen City. The Rochester Royals moved to Cincinnati in 1957. Despite having some great players, such as Bob Cousy, Oscar Robertson, and Jerry Lucas, the Royals never enjoyed much success, either on the court or at the box office. After missing the NBA playoffs for the fifth consecutive season, the Royals moved to Kansas City in 1972. (Later they were to become the Sacramento Kings.)

After three failed attempts to establish a professional pigskin club in Cincinnati in the late 1930s and early 1940s, the American Football League (AFL) finally succeeded, creating the present Bengals franchise in 1968. The club struck a deal with the city, Hamilton County, and the Cincinnati Reds for the construction of a multipurpose stadium which could host both baseball and football games. In 1970 the AFL merged with the National Football League (NFL). The Bengals have enjoyed considerable success in the NFL. In 1990 the club made its seventh playoff appearance.

Neither basketball nor football has yet overturned the perception that Cincinnati is a baseball town. Yes, Cincinnati is a baseball town and especially a Cincinnati Reds baseball town. Cincinnati is where the professional game began. Cincinnati sportswriter Paul Daugherty described the hold the game has on the fans of this baseball town: "Baseball is not a diversion here. It's not some beer-drinking, beach ball-bopping party. Other places, people go to baseball games the way they go to a movie.... They don't take the game personally. We take it personally."[10]

In his memoir, baseball star Bill Werber wrote:

The best fans I can recall from my thirteen years in the game were in Cincinnati, where I played from 1939 through 1941. Of course, we had all the ingredients for a close relationship with the community during those years: a hustling, winning ballclub; a ballpark (Crosley Field), which provided a feeling of intimacy between fans and players, and a population financially able to fill the seats. The Queen City was simply a great baseball town, with its professional roots running all the way back to the 1869 Red Stockings of Harry Wright.[11]

Baseball historian Paul DeBono wrote, "Like clam chowder in Boston, or money on Wall Street, baseball is [at] home in Cincinnati."[12]

If they were musically inclined, Cincinnatians could sing this parody of Neil Young's "Railroad Town."

"Baseball Town"[13]

When the red sun sets
On the baseball town
The bars begin to laugh
With a happy sound.
And the dreams you're having
They won't let you down
If you just follow the Reds
'Cause you know
Where they're bound.
I'll still be here, Reds
Right on your side.
There'll not be another
In my heart, Reds, but you!

Geography

Long before the term "River City" was popularized by *The Music Man*, Cincinnati could well have been called River City USA. Rivers defined its very existence. Located on the north bank of the Ohio River, halfway between its source in Pittsburgh and its confluence with the mighty Mississippi near Cairo, its exact site was determined by the junction of the Ohio with the Licking River, flowing up from Kentucky. At a time when waterways provided the chief means of transportation, both for people and goods, Cincinnati's growth was further enhanced by its location between the Great Miami and Little Miami Rivers in Ohio. Between 1825 and 1845, the Miami and Erie Canal was constructed, connecting Cincinnati to Toledo on Lake Erie about 200 miles to the north. From Toledo goods could be shipped through the Great Lakes to the Erie Canal and down the Hudson River to New York City and the Atlantic Ocean. In the other direction, products could be sent down the Ohio and Mississippi Rivers to New Orleans and the Gulf of Mexico. Thus, Cincinnati was the hub of the interstate transportation system of the day.

Cincinnatians did not embrace the appellation River City USA. Instead they preferred to be known as the Queen City because of the beautiful setting. The early settlement was in a narrow, steep-sided valley. From the river's edge a series of terraces were built, rising to the business district, and then up the hills to the residential districts, affording beautiful vistas and giving the city a picturesque landscape. In his poem "Catawba Wine," Henry Wadsworth Longfellow referred to Cincinnati as the "Queen of the West." In the mid–1800s Cincinnati had another, less romantic, nickname—Porkopolis, but that is a story for another place.

Besides its importance to transportation, the Ohio River served another very important function in the ante-bellum days. It was the dividing line between free territory and slave states. The growing city became a leading station on the Underground Railway. Although Harriet Beecher Stowe did not mention Cincinnati by name in *Uncle Tom's Cabin,* she clearly had in mind the place where she had lived from 1832 to 1850.

Geologists tell us that Cincinnati lies in the Cincinnati Arch province, situated between the Illinoian and Appalachian Basins, and is composed of limestone and shale. According to a geologist at the University of Cincinnati, sedimentary rocks were formed during the Ordovician Period and were exposed during the Illinoian Glaciation Period, which was responsible for forming both the Great Miami and Little Miami Rivers.[14]

The area has a continental climate with a wide range of temperatures from summer to winter. Winters are rather cold, with considerable cloudiness and an average snowfall of almost 24 inches. Cincinnati has an earlier spring than most of the cities further north, helping make the Opening Day tradition viable. Summers are warm and humid, with temperatures sometimes reaching into the 90s, which makes playing baseball in the dog days somewhat uncomfortable, but heat and humidity are apparently no deterrent to the popularity of the game. Average annual precipitation is just above 40 inches, and the average daily temperature ranges from about 29 degrees in January to over 75 in July. Local folklore insists that summer storms travel up the Ohio River from the southwest and hit the Queen City oftener than they do places further from the river. This belief is not supported by data, which show that Lexington, some 80 miles to the south, receives more precipitation during the summer months than does the city on the river.

In some ways Cincinnati was in an ideal location for the growth of baseball in the late 19th century. The 1880 census showed that the center of United States population was just eight miles southwest of Cincinnati in Boone County, Kentucky, giving the Queen City access to a large fan base. The only major league cities further south than Cincinnati were St. Louis and Washington. Only the St. Louis clubs could compete with the Reds for the loyalties of fans in a wide swath of the country stretching from Kentucky, south through Tennessee, Mississippi, and Alabama, all the way to the Gulf of Mexico.

Demography

According to the Bureau of the Census, the population of Cincinnati in 1990 was 364,040, ranking 45th among cities of the United States. This ranking seriously underrates the importance of the Queen City. The Census contains two other figures that more accurately reflect Cincinnati's standing. The Consolidated Statistical Metropolitan Area (CSMA), consisting of 13 counties tied to Cincinnati economically, had a population of 1,884,915, placing Cincinnati 23rd in the nation.[15] The Urbanized Area had a population of 1,212,675, ranking it 28th in the United States. These statistics reflect more accurately the population of the area that most people think of as Cincinnati. Unlike the CSMA, which is delineated by county boundaries, the Urbanized Area includes only densely populated communities outside the city boundaries, excluding the rural portions of the CSMA. Thus, neither of the Indiana counties in the CSMA is part of the Urbanized Area.

Founded in 1788, within a few years Cincinnati became the first major inland city in the country. By the early 1800s it was rivaling the larger cities on the East Coast in size. At every decennial census from 1830 to 1900, Cincinnati ranked among the ten most populous cities in the nation. With the shift from steamboats to railroads, Cincinnati's prominence decreased and it was surpassed by other inland cities, such as Chicago and St. Louis. Throughout the 1900s its ranking declined, reaching its low point in 1990. The majority of the population was white, with blacks making up the only other sizeable group. No other race contributed more than two per cent of the total. Principal ancestral origins of the whites were German, Irish, and English.

In 1990 the population of the city was 37 percent African American. Roman Catholics were a prominent component of the population. Neither of these facts was true in the city's early days. What brought about the change? A look at the city's history will shed some light.

Cincinnati's earliest settlers were mainly white Protestant migrants from the Eastern part of the United States, and largely of English and Scottish stock. Although a Catholic church—a plain, barn-like structure—was built as early as 1822, it was not until the 1850s that Catholics flourished in the city. The Irish potato famine of 1848 and political disturbances in Germany about the same time brought an influx of European immigrants to Cincinnati for the first time, changing the character of the city forever.

Many of the Irish immigrants had peasant backgrounds and came to the United States mainly because they were starving as a result of the famine in their home country. In 1842 there were only about 1,000 Irish in Cincinnati; by 1851 there were nearly 14,000, comprising 12 percent of the city's population. They found work along the riverfront, digging the Miami and Erie Canal, and working on the railroads. Many of the jobs were unskilled, dangerous, and low-paying. More desirable jobs were difficult to obtain, as "No Irish need apply" signs abounded. Discrimination against Irish immigrants was based on their Catholic religion, their frequenting saloons that served alcoholic beverages, and their perceived rowdy and boisterous behavior. More genteel Cincinnatians tended to look down on the newcomers.

Located in the Over-the-Rhine section of Cincinnati, Findlay Market is one of the oldest surviving farmers' markets in the Midwest. Since 1920 it has been known to baseball fans as the starting point for the Queen City's Opening Day Parade (Library of Congress).

Discrimination again Irish and other immigrants was not limited to Cincinnati, of course. It was nation-wide in scope. Nativist political parties sprang up in many states. The American Party, widely known as the Know-Nothings, nominated former President Millard Fillmore as a presidential candidate in the 1856 election, and he garnered 874,534 votes, actually acquiring the eight electoral votes of Maryland.

German immigrants fared better in Cincinnati than did their Irish brethren. There were many more of them, 28 percent of the city's population in 1852. Unlike the Irish, many Germans came with funds with which to buy homes. They clustered in one area of the city, known as Over-the-Rhine. Often they worked as butchers, bakers, or tailors. Many of them were well-educated and prosperous, and became successful businessmen in their new home. German immigrants established the breweries for which 19th century Cincinnati was famous. It was largely due to the influence of German (and Irish) immigrants that the Reds allowed the sale of beer on the grounds, which led to the club's expulsion from the National League and their joining the American Association, the so-called Beer and Whiskey League, in 1882. Several of the early owners of the Reds of German extraction were connected with breweries. Not all of the German immigrants were skilled, of course. In order to support their families, some of them were forced to accept dangerous and low-paying jobs on the canals, the docks, or meat-packing plants.

German immigrants built Over-the-Rhine into perhaps the most notable section of Cincinnati. It was so called because many residents walked across bridges over the Miami and Erie Canal, which separated the area from downtown Cincinnati. The district was the center of the city's brewery industry and home to Findlay Market. The market is one of the oldest surviving farmers' markets in the Midwest. For over a century it was the starting point of the parade that marked baseball's Opening Day. It was placed on the National Register of Historic Places in 1972.

German immigrants and their descendants changed the culture of Cincinnati. The Art Academy of Cincinnati was founded in Over-the-Rhine in 1869. The Cincinnati Music Hall was built in the area in 1878. The original home of the Cincinnati Symphony Orchestra was in Over-the-Rhine. The same thing is true of many other landmarks in the arts, music, and the theatre. Perhaps the most distinctive thing about Over-the-Rhine was its architecture. It contains the most outstanding collection of Italianate architecture in the United States. Most of the ornate buildings were constructed by German immigrants from 1865 through the 1880s. Over-the-Rhine was added to the National Register of Historic Places in 1983.

In the 1940s another wave of migrants entered Cincinnati. Hardworking people from the economically depressed, coal-mining regions of the Southern Appalachians poured into Cincinnati, searching for better paying jobs. Most were successful and merged into the life of the city with little difficulty. However, a significant portion lacked skills and found that Cincinnati had little demand for unskilled labor. These unfortunates moved into tenements in the deteriorating Over-the-Rhine area. Many of them were forced to go on welfare in order to survive. By 1990 Over-the-Rhine had fallen into disrepute. Most of its prosperous residents had moved into the hills overlooking the city or into the suburbs. The population had declined from 44,475 in 1900 to 9,572 in 1990. Absentee landlords had allowed the houses to fall into disrepair. Many of the buildings were vacant or occupied illegally by vagrants, prostitutes, or drug addicts. In recent years an effort has been made to preserve the historic buildings and restore the reputation of the city's former showplace.

As the largest city on the Ohio River, the dividing line between the slave-holding South and the free states of the North, Cincinnati was in the forefront of racial agitation in the pre–Civil War years. Residents of the city were among the country's leading abolitionists. The city also hosted some violent anti-abolitionists. As early as 1829, a riot occurred when anti-abolitionists attacked black residents, causing over 1,000 blacks to leave the city for Canada. In 1836 a mob attacked black neighborhoods, as well as the press run by James M. Birney, publisher of an anti-slavery weekly, *The Philanthropist.* Often fugitive slaves crossed the Ohio River at Cincinnati to escape to freedom. Many stations of the Underground Railroad were located in Cincinnati. After the Fugitive Slave Act was passed in 1850, some Cincinnatians became "slave catchers" who attempted to earn rewards by capturing runaways and returning them to their masters.

After the Civil War, Cincinnati did not attract many new black residents. Because of its commerce with slave states and the large number of Southerners among its population, Cincinnati was not viewed as friendly to blacks, despite the history of abolitionists and the Underground Railroad. In 1900 the black population was 14,340—about 4.4 percent of the total. Most of the black population lived in the flats along the riverfront, until industrial and business interests took over the area. Most of the black residents then moved into the West End. Following World War I, a Great Migration of blacks flowed from the rural South into the industrial cities of the North. A much greater migration followed World War II. Although Cincinnati gained over 100,000 black residents between 1920 and 1990, the city's increase was much less than that of some other destinations, such as Chicago, Cleveland, and Detroit. The Second Great Migration changed the residential patterns of Cincinnati. It occurred at the same time that many whites were leaving the city core for the suburbs—a phenomenon sometimes known as white flight. African Americans moved into the areas vacated by the whites. Most of the blacks remained near the lower elevations of the city, although some moved up into the heights, such as into the College Hill area. In 1990 at least 18 of the city's 52 neighborhoods had a significant black population.

By 1990 the racial composition of Cincinnati was far different from the first census 190 years previously.[16] Racial discrimination still existed in Cincinnati in 1990, of course. The scourge of the past will continue to haunt much of America for many years to come, but at least progress was beginning. Sports offered an opportunity for a small number of talented blacks to advance. Out of the many millions of young people who aspire to become professional athletes, only a tiny percentage make it. By 1990 some doors were open that had previously been closed. Seven years after Jackie Robinson broke the major leagues' so-called color barrier, Nino Escalera, a black Puerto Rican, and Chuck Harmon, an African American, made their major league debuts for Cincinnati. The Big Red Machine of 1975–1976 fielded nine Hispanics or African Americans (Ed Armbrister, Pedro Borbon, Dave Concepcion, Dan Driessen, George Foster, Cesar Geronimo, Ken Griffey, Joe Morgan, and Tony Perez). The 1990 contingent numbered at least ten, not counting manager Lou Piniella or coach Tony Perez (Glenn Braggs, Eric Davis, Mariano Duncan, Billy Hatcher, Barry Larkin, Luis Quinones, Jose Rijo, Rosario Rodriguez. Rolando Roomes, and Alex Trevino). Larkin, a future Hall of Famer, was an African American born and raised in Cincinnati.

Among the millions who have lived, loved, and labored in the Cincinnati area are many who have contributed to the American dream. Some are known only to friends and family. The working men and women of Cincinnati deserve honor and respect. Their lives are no less valuable or virtuous than those of individuals who have achieved national prominence. However, space limitations make it impossible to pay homage to more than a few Cincinnatians in these pages.

Two Cincinnatians served as President of the United States. The 19th president, Rutherford B. Hayes, was born in Delaware, Ohio, on October 4, 1822. He attended Webb Preparatory School in Middletown, Connecticut, Kenyon College, and Harvard Law School. In 1850 the young man moved to Cincinnati, married Lucy Ware Webb, started his family and entered politics in the Queen City. He served as city solicitor from 1858 to 1861.Wounded during the Civil War, he rose to the rank of brevet major general. He was nominated to run for Congress from the Cincinnati area in 1864, but refused to campaign for office, feeling it was his duty to remain in the army. Nevertheless, he won the election and took office after the war ended in 1865. Hayes served three terms in Congress and later three terms as governor of Ohio. In 1876 the Republican party, for the first time, held its national convention in Cincinnati and nominated Hayes as its presidential candidate. Following a disputed election, a special electoral commission declared that Hayes had won the presidency over Samuel J. Tilden, the Democratic candidate. Hayes lived up to his pledge to served only one term.

Unlike Hayes, the 27th president, William Howard Taft, was a lifelong Cincinnatian. Born into a prominent Cincinnati family on September 15, 1857, Taft lived his entire life in his home town, except when he was away in the service of his country. Like Hayes, Taft married (Helen Herron), started his family, and began his political career in Cincinnati. A graduate of Cincinnati's Woodward High School and Yale College, Taft attended Cincinnati Law School and worked as a court reporter for the *Cincinnati Commercial* until he was appointed assistant prosecutor for Hamilton County. He moved quickly up the ladder—assistant county solicitor and superior court judge in Cincinnati, taking time out briefly to serve President Arthur as collector of internal revenue. President Harrison appointed him United States solicitor general and then judge for the sixth judicial circuit. In 1901 he was appointed governor-general of the Philippines by President McKinley. In 1903 President Theodore Roosevelt appointed him secretary of war. As the candidate of the Republican party for President of the United States in 1908, Taft defeated William Jennings Bryan, the Democratic candidate. During Taft's administration, he and Roosevelt had a falling out, with the ex-president forming his own Progressive or "Bull Moose" party. As a result of the split in Republican ranks, Democratic candidate Woodrow Wilson won the presidency in 1912. In 1921 President Harding appointed Taft chief justice of the United States. Taft became the only ex-president ever to serve on the Supreme Court of the United States. Despite all his distinguished accomplishments in public life, Taft is best remembered by baseball fans for a few moments at Washington's National Park on April 14, 1910. President Taft became the nation's first chief executive to celebrate baseball's Opening Day by throwing out the ceremonial first pitch. It seems altogether fitting for a native of a baseball town to have that distinction.

William Howard Taft was the only native of Cincinnati to be elected President of the United States. In 1910 he started the custom of throwing out the first pitch of the baseball season, a practice that since has been followed by most of the nation's chief executives. In this photograph the President is flanked by unidentified members of his party at a 1911 game in Washington, D.C. (Library of Congress).

The Taft tradition of public service was carried on by William Howard Taft's eldest son, Robert Alphonso Taft. Born in Cincinnati on September 8, 1889, Bob Taft was educated at Yale College and Harvard Law School. After opening a law office in Cincinnati in 1922, he served in the Ohio legislature. He was elected to the United States Senate in 1938 and was re-elected in 1944 and 1950. Because of his influence as a policy-maker in his party, he was called "Mr. Republican." He unsuccessfully sought the Republican party's presidential nomination in 1940 and 1948. In 1952 he was the front-runner for the nomination, and early polls showed him a likely winner in the November general election. However, the charismatic General Dwight D. "Ike" Eisenhower entered the fray and won both the coveted nomination and the White House.

Others with Cincinnati connections to achieve national prominence in government service include: John Boehner and Nicholas Longworth, who have served as Speaker of the House; cabinet officials Neil McElroy, Charles Sawyer, and Kathleen Sebelius; Supreme Court Justice Potter

Stewart; and John McLean, who served variously as congressman, cabinet officer, and Supreme Court justice.

Albert T. Goshorn, a businessman and civic leader, was born in Cincinnati in 1833. He was the owner of a paint company and served on the city council. For two decades he organized the Cincinnati Industrial Expositions, annual exhibitions of Cincinnati arts and industries. He was so successful in his undertakings that he became world famous. He was appointed Director-General of the Centennial Exposition, a world's fair held in Philadelphia in 1876, 100 years after the Declaration of Independence was signed in that city. The fair was a resounding success, appealing not only to Americans but to Europeans as well. Queen Victoria was so impressed that she knighted Goshorn. To sports fans, however, Goshorn is best remembered for his role in the development of baseball. He was the first president of the Cincinnati Base Ball Club, established in 1866, holding that position as the club evolved from a local amateur organization into the full-fledged professional Cincinnati Red Stockings under the leadership of Aaron Burt Champion and Harry Wright.

Economy

The early economy of Cincinnati was based on its Ohio River location and the proximity to rich agricultural lands and hardwood forests. Within a few decades of its founding, the city had developed industries such as boat building, breweries, furniture manufacture, and meat packing. As always, the river played a dominant role in commerce. Barges were the chief means of transportation. Inexpensively built out of native lumber, they floated down the river, carrying passengers and their goods to their new homes and transporting products to southern and western markets. Having no means of propulsion, the early barges could not travel upstream, so they were usually dismantled when they reached their destination, with the lumber being used in the construction of houses or other buildings. By 1990, barges were towed (more correctly, pushed) by tugboats and could travel in either direction, busily carrying huge loads of coal, petroleum products, sand and gravel, and other materials up and down the river. The barges of 1990 were much larger than those that carried the early settlers to the West. They averaged nearly 200 feet in length and could carry 1,500 tons. Barges continued to offer economical transportation on the Ohio River.

In the very early days, keelboats were used for passenger service on

the Ohio River. Weekly passenger service between Cincinnati and Pittsburgh began in 1793. By 1811 keelboats were making the round-trip between Cincinnati and New Orleans in 78 days at a cost of $160 per passenger.[17] The days of the keelboats were numbered. The first steamboat to traverse western waters visited Cincinnati in 1811 on its way from Pittsburgh to New Orleans. After the development of the steamboat, Cincinnati became one of the leading river ports in the United States. Passengers occupied the upper decks, while cargo was loaded below decks. (In 1817 the *Zebulon Pike*, built in Cincinnati, became the first vessel designed exclusively for passenger service.) Steamboats made two-way traffic possible. Not only could products be transported downriver, but goods from New Orleans could be carried upstream. At the peak of the steamboat era in 1852, about 8,000 landings were recorded at Cincinnati. The coming of the railroads caused a decrease in the use of steamboats, and the industry declined rapidly during the Civil War and subsequent years. By 1990 only the *Delta Queen* called Cincinnati home. It was used mainly for excursions from the Queen City to Louisville and New Orleans.

Located near a rich farming area and with quick and easy access via waterways to the nation's markets, Cincinnati was in an ideal strategic position to emerge as one of the leading meat-packing centers in the United States. Meat packing was so important to 19th century Cincinnati that the city earned the nickname Porkopolis. Cattle and hogs were transported by horse-drawn wagons or driven on foot from farms to the city. Before the days of refrigeration, beef was not readily preserved without losing its flavor, so pork became the meat of choice. In Cincinnati hogs were slaughtered, processed, packed in barrels of brine, and transported to markets in the East, South, or West, usually by river or canal. Before Henry Ford made the assembly line famous, the modern assembly line was developed in meat-packing plants in Cincinnati, where overhead trolleys were used to transport the carcasses from worker to worker. The trolleys moved the carcasses past the laborers at a steady pace, at a speed dictated by the machine, not by the worker. The work, often performed by Irish or German immigrants, was unpleasant and dangerous. With no labor unions or government regulators to help them, the lot of the workers

Opposite: *Development of the steamboat helped Cincinnati become one of the leading river ports in the United States. Passengers occupied the upper decks, while cargo was stowed below. In the peak year of 1852, about 8,000 landings were recorded at Cincinnati. The coming of the railroads caused a decrease in the use of steamboats, and the industry declined rapidly during the Civil War and subsequent years (Library of Congress).*

was deplorable. Toiling long hours at low pay, they were at the mercy of their employers. Of course, they had no health insurance, unemployment compensation, or retirement benefits. If workers became injured on the job, bosses routinely fired them. If they could not keep up the pace set by the machines, the employers replaced them with younger, more productive employees. Upton Sinclair's expose of the meat-packing industry in Chicago could well have described conditions in Porkopolis.[18]

Despite Cincinnati's lovely location, the section where the packing plants were situated was not a pleasant place in which to live or work. The industry produced a tremendous amount of pollution. There was no Environmental Protection Agency in the 19th century. In the area's relatively high temperatures, meat spoiled quickly, resulting in horrible odor. Waste from the butchered animals was thrown into the Ohio River. After the Civil War, the continuing westward movement of the population, expansion of railroads, and development of refrigerated cars enabled Chicago to surpass Cincinnati as the nation's leading processor of meat. In the words of Carl Sandberg, Chicago came to be hog butcher for the world. The legendary American cowboy, driving herds of cattle from Texas to railheads in the Great Plains, for trans-shipment to Chicago, helped in the demise of Cincinnati as a meat-packing center. Refrigerated railroad cars enabled beef to be preserved and eventually to replace pork as America's favorite meat. Long before 1990, meat packing had virtually disappeared from the Cincinnati area.

Of course, pork was not the only valuable product of the meat-packing industry. In the 19th century, lard, obtained from the fat of butchered hogs, was a necessity in every home in America. Lard was used as a lubricant, an ointment, and in the manufacture of soap and candles. With so many synthetic products on the market today, it is difficult for a modern American to comprehend the importance that lard played in the lives of his or her ancestors.

One of Cincinnati's most prominent families, the Emerys, started on their road to eminence via the lard business. Thomas Emery came to Cincinnati in 1832 and opened a store to sell lard. Eventually, he became a major supplier to the eastern part of the nation. He invented a dripless

Opposite: *Meat packing was so important in 19th century Cincinnati that the city earned the nickname Porkopolis. Before Henry Ford made the assembly line famous, the device was developed in meat packing plants in Cincinnati, where overhead trolleys were used to transport the carcasses from worker to worker. After the Civil War, the Westward Movement of the population, expansion of the railroads, and the development of the refrigerated car led to Chicago replacing Cincinnati as "Hog Butcher to the World" (Library of Congress).*

One of the principal by-products of the meat packing industry was the production of lard, which was a widely used household necessity in the 19th century. One of Cincinnati's most prominent families, the Emerys, started in the lard business, expanded into real estate and other enterprises. John Emery was responsible for the construction of the multi-purpose Carew Tower. At 574 feet and 49 stories, it was the tallest building in the United States west of the Alleghenies when it opened in 1930 (Library of Congress).

candle and established the Emery Candle Company, which later metamorphosed into the nationally important Emery Chemical Company. Thomas Emery's greatest achievement, however, came in the real estate arena. He purchased large areas of what later became Cincinnati's downtown business district. His sons and grandsons consolidated the family's holdings and built substantial apartment houses, office buildings, and other structures in the center of the city. The most famous facility built by a member of the Emery family was the Carew Tower, a multipurpose building opened in 1930. At 574 feet and 49 stories, it was the tallest building in the United States west of the Alleghenies. Remodeled several times, the Tower is still in use. John Emery, grandson of Thomas, was responsible for the construction of the Carew Tower and was a major figure in the cultural life of the city for more than four decades.

In 1887 about 6,000 people earned their living in Cincinnati by working in meat packing. Slightly more than that were employed in related enterprises, such as leather making. By the 1880s meat packing had fallen to second place among the city's industries. In the last years of the 19th century, ironworking became Cincinnati's chief industry. Iron furnaces and forges proliferated in southern Ohio. The pig iron they produced was sent up and down the Ohio River to Pittsburgh and Cincinnati, where it was fashioned into products such as household utensils and tools, especially machine tools, which in turn could produce other products.

From the mid-19th century until closed by Prohibition in the early 1920s, breweries were among Cincinnati's principal claims to fame. Located mainly in the Over-the-Rhine area, the breweries provided employment to workers and profits to entrepreneurs, and contributed to the city's image as a free-wheeling, fun-loving place. Not the least, they played an important role in the establishment of baseball's American Association, the so-called Beer and Whiskey League. The number of breweries in Cincinnati was astonishing. In 1862, for example, there were 38 breweries in the city.[19] Some of them were small establishments, but several were large enterprises. Among the leading breweries were Kauffmann, Moerlein's, and J. G. Sohn and Company. All were located in the Over-the-Rhine area, and all were founded by immigrants. John Kauffmann was born in Alsace-Lorraine; Christian Moerlein and Johann Sohn were both born in Bavaria. These men and some of the other owners became wealthy. Known as Beer Barons, they tended to be involved in the cultural and civic life of Cincinnati, particularly in the Over-the-Rhine neighborhood.

The brewing industry affected the economy of Cincinnati in many ways. It was huge, not only in the number of people employed, but also in the number of other industries it supported. Among industries that expanded or otherwise profited from the breweries were:

Cooperages (manufacture of barrels)
Steel, brass, and copper (for use in kettles, vats, tubs, and tubing)
Canal boats (for transport)
Stables (for care of horses used in transport)
Grain (for use in manufacture of beer; most hops were imported
    from Germany; barley was grown by farmers in the area or
    imported from the West)
Storage (of grain, other materials, and the finished product)
Saloons (for sale and consumption of beer)

Saloons provided employment for owners, barkeepers, servers, security personnel, and often entertainers. The number of saloons in Cincinnati was astounding. Amazingly, in 1887 there were 1,837 saloons in Cincinnati, serving a population of 225,000. In 1890 there were 136 saloons on Vine Street alone. The amount of beer consumed in Cincinnati was incredible. In 1893 the per capita consumption of beer in the United States was 16 gallons. In Cincinnati 40 gallons were consumed for every man, woman, and child in the city.

Breweries and saloons played an important role in the history of 19th century baseball in Cincinnati. As noted elsewhere, the sale of beer in the ball park led to the expulsion of Cincinnati from the National League in 1880, followed by the establishment of baseball's American Association, the so-called Beer and Whiskey League, in 1882. Justin Thorner, who was connected to a local brewery, was one of the principal advocates of Cincinnati joining the new league. Thorner became president of the American Association Reds. The club was owned by Chris von de Ahe, a St. Louis saloonkeeper. After the Reds rejoined the National League, August "Garry" Herrmann served as president of the club from 1902 to 1927. He also served as president of the National Baseball Commission from 1903 to 1920, an apparent conflict of interest. (When he became Commissioner of Baseball while owner of the Milwaukee Brewers in the 1990s, Bud Selig was faced with a similar conflict of interest. He dealt with the situation by transferring ownership of the club to his daughter, Wendy Selig-Prieb, but many people believed he still kept his hand in the club's operations.) Although Herrmann had no direct connection with breweries, he was a great supporter of saloons. His biographer wrote that although Herrmann was financially successful, he entertained so lavishly at Vine Street establishments that he spent his entire fortune and left only a pittance in his estate.[20]

In order to understand the impact of saloons in Cincinnati, one must consider the lives of immigrants and second-generation Americans in Over-the-Rhine and other areas inhabited by workingmen. The saloon, sometimes called a tavern or a beer garden, was a place for residents to socialize. It was a neighborhood gathering place, a place where people learned what was going on in their community. Many of the establishments offered entertainment by musicians. Some provided free food; they made their profits from the beer they sold. In the days before radio, television, or movies, a saloon was an enticing place to spend time relaxing with family and friends.

Perhaps the most famous saloon in Cincinnati was Wielert's Café and Pavilion. Opened on West Vine Street in 1873 by a German immigrant named Heinrich Wielert, it was advertised as a strictly first-class family resort. In the rear of the saloon was a block-long beer garden, the largest in Cincinnati. On summer evenings, patrons of the beer garden were entertained by Michael Brand's 40-piece orchestra. (Brand's orchestra became a forerunner of the Cincinnati Symphony Orchestra.) The most famous customer of Wielert's was George "Boss" Cox, who met with his lieutenants every day at his personal table. Cox made no bones about being a political boss. "I am the Boss of Cincinnati," he said. "I've never dodged that statement in my life. I've got the best system of government in this country. If I didn't think my system was the best I would consider that I was a failure in life."[21] One of Cox's protégés was Garry Herrmann, who before entering the baseball arena held several minor political offices in the Queen City, such as managing the Cincinnati Waterworks, thanks to the Boss's support.

Most of the breweries in Cincinnati and throughout the country closed during the Prohibition era, costing jobs not only in the breweries but also in related industries. Most saloons survived the dry era, serving non-alcoholic beverages (or beer when they could escape the notice of law enforcement authorities). The term saloon fell into disrepute, and most neighborhood watering holes now call themselves bars. Upscale establishments prefer terms such as lounges and night clubs. Since repeal of Prohibition, new breweries have opened in Cincinnati (some even taking the names of historic businesses), but on a much smaller scale than in the halcyon days of the 19th and early 20th centuries. Several entrepreneurs are trying to revive brewing in the Over-the-Rhine area. Many of the former breweries have been demolished or converted to other uses. Over-the-Rhine was built during the streetcar era and has limited space for automobile parking. There is a movement afoot to restore streetcars to the area. The effort to revive brewing in Cincinnati is being pursued vigorously, but brewing is no longer a mainstay of the Cincinnati economy. When a contemporary person thinks of centers of brewing, he or she is more likely to think of St. Louis or Milwaukee.

David Stinton, who immigrated from Ireland in 1811, became the richest man in Ohio and one of the wealthiest people in the world. He made his fortune in the pig-iron industry during the Civil War. He owned furnaces in Lawrence County, Ohio, and in pre-war years stockpiled iron, waiting for wartime when he could sell his iron at inflated prices. His mansion on Pike Street in Cincinnati was considered one of the finest examples of Federal architecture in the country. The home is now the Taft Museum of Art. His name was preserved for many years by the Stinton Hotel. Located at Fourth and Vine in downtown Cincinnati, it was considered the city's most stylish hotel. It was at the Stinton Hotel that some of the visiting Chicago White Sox players allegedly conspired to throw the 1919 World Series to the Cincinnati Reds, resulting in a scandal that shook the baseball world. The hotel was demolished in 1969. Stinton's daughter married Charles Phelps Taft, brother of President William Howard Taft. It is reported that Stinton money helped finance Taft's presidential campaign.[22]

Three of the corporations most often associated by the public with Cincinnati—Procter and Gamble, Crosley, and Kroger—represent entrepreneurialism at its most successful level.

One of Cincinnati's early industries not only survived, but prospered and grew. Two immigrant brothers-in-law—William Procter, an English candlemaker, and James Gamble, an Irish soapmaker—formed a company which they called Procter and Gamble (P&G), in 1837. Twenty years later their sales reached $1 million annually. During the Civil War they secured contracts to provide the Union army with soap and candles.

In the 1880s, labor-management relations became acrimonious. In strikes, bloody confrontations sometimes occurred between workers and minions of their employers. In the hope that giving the workers a stake in the company would reduce the likelihood of strikes, P&G began a profit-sharing program for the company's workforce in 1887.

In the 1880s P&G began marketing a new product, called Ivory, a soap that floats in water. The slogan used in marketing the product was "99 44/100% pure." Outgrowing their facilities in Cincinnati, they began building factories in other locations, but kept their headquarters in the Queen City. The company diversified into other products, such as cooking oils, toothpaste, toilet paper, fabric softener, disposable diapers, and many other household products, including foods and beverages. With the growing popularity of radio in the 1930s, Procter and Gamble began sponsoring daytime serials, called soap operas, or simply soaps. The show *Ma Perkins,* sponsored by Oxydol, a P&G brand, was perhaps the first radio program to be called a soap opera. Among popular soaps, several of which were shown on television after that medium was introduced, were *As the World Turns, Guiding Light,* and *The Young and Restless.* Among dozens of brands marketed by P&G, some of the best-known in 1990 included: Bounty, Charmin, Crest, Crisco, Downy, Pampers, Prell, and Tide, as well as the iconic floating soap, Ivory.

In the 1980s the company faced two crises—one of their own making and the other due to irrational charges by religious fanatics. In 1980, 814 cases of menstrual-related toxic shock syndrome were reported, resulting in the deaths of 39 women. The majority of the women in these cases had used super-absorbent synthetic tampons, particularly the Rely brand manufactured by Procter and Gamble. In response to a report by the Centers for Disease Control, P&G voluntarily recalled the questionable tampons. The other controversy had to do with the company's logo. In the mid–1800s P&G had developed a trademark that showed a man in the moon overlooking 13 stars, said to represent the original 13 states of the Union. For over 100 years this logo had been used with no apparent ill effects, but in the 1980 rumors began to circulate that the moon-and-stars logo was a satanic symbol. Because of the controversy, P&G discontinued use of the logo in 1986. The company survived. In 1990 the P&G ranked 14th on Fortune's list of the 500 largest U.S. corporations.

Another Cincinnati industry worthy of note was the manufacturing and broadcasting empire of the entrepreneur Powel Crosley, Jr. Crosley first found success in the manufacture and sale of automobile accessories. In the early 1920s, he began building radios. By 1924, the Crosley Radio Corporation was the largest radio manufacturer in the world. In order to build the market for radios, Crosley went into the broadcasting business. He established WLW in Cincinnati, which for several years had the most powerful radio transmitter in the United States, until the Federal Communications Commission ruled that no transmitter could exceed 50,000 watts in power. Many of the nation's most famous entertainers performed live in WLW studios each week. Among them were such stars as Rosemary Clooney, Doris Day, Jane Frohman, the Mills Brothers, Red Skelton, Merle Travis, and Fats Waller. WLW called itself the "Nation's Station" and "Your Station of Stars." Crosley also developed some of the earliest soap operas sponsored by Procter and Gamble. In 1939 Crosley leased the 48th floor of the Carew Tower, Cincinnati's tallest building, in order to construct a television station. The Federal Communication Commission granted Crosley a license for experimental telecasts, one of the first to be approved in the United States. Commercial telecasts started on a regular basis in 1947.

In the 1930s Crosley had added refrigerators, freezers, dishwashers, and other household appliances to his product line. In 1939 he introduced the Crosley automobile, a small car that did not catch on with the public. The advent of World War II stopped its production in 1942.

In 1934 Crosley purchased the Cincinnati Reds. The name of the ball park was changed from Redland Field to Crosley Field, in his honor. The owner had electric lights installed and the first night game in major-league history was played there on May 24, 1935. Crosley Field was the home of the Reds until it was replaced by Riverfront Stadium in 1970.

In 1990 local heroes Marty Brennaman and Joe Nuxhall broadcasted Cincinnati Reds baseball games over WLW, the flagship station for one of the largest radio networks in professional sports, with affiliates in seven states. The games were telecast on WLW-TV by two former Reds players, Hall of Fame catcher Johnny Bench and pitcher Tom Hume, and carried on the Reds Television Network, which had 25 affiliates, ranging all the way from Ohio and Indiana to Florida. (WLW is no longer owned by the Crosley companies.)

The other company among Cincinnati's big-name three is Kroger. Now among the largest grocery chains in the nation, the company was founded in 1883, when Bernard "Barney" Kroger, a son of German immigrants, invested his life savings of $372 to open a grocery store on Pearl Street in downtown Cincinnati. Throughout the years Kroger has introduced many innovations into the grocery business. In 1972, for example, Kroger became the first grocery retailer in America to test an electronic scanner. It was installed in a store in a Cincinnati suburb, and visitors came from around the country to observe the device. Mergers have played a key role in Kroger's growth over the years. In 1983 Kroger merged with Dillon Companies to become a coast-to-coast operator of food and drug stores. Although Kroger owns dozens of food processing plants and operates over 2,400 stores in 31 states, its headquarters have remained in Cincinnati. In the 1990s Kroger climbed as high as 28th place on the Fortune 500 list, just a few spots below Procter and Gamble.

In 1990 Cincinnati's economy was in good shape. No longer dominated by meatpacking, breweries, or ironworking, Cincinnati had a diversified economy, featuring many small manufacturing plants as well as large commercial enterprises. Cincinnati was among the world's leading producers of machine tools, playing cards, and soap. The city's factories manufactured aircraft engines and parts, automobile bodies and transmissions, generators, and chemical products. The list goes on and on: athletic goods, leather products, metal cans, office furniture, pianos, radios and television sets, textiles, watches, and many other products.

The per capita income of Cincinnatians was slightly above the national average, and the unemployment rate was a little lower. Once known as a workingman's town, by 1990 skilled and unskilled workers still made up more than one quarter of the metropolitan areas work force, but they were no longer the most numerous class of workers. The 1990 census found that the largest employment category in the Cincinnati standard metropolitan area was in the executive, professional, and technical grouping. A cluster made up of precision workers, machine operators, and blue collar workers made up the second-largest occupational area. The rankings have not changed since 1990, but the distance between the two leading categories has increased. Manufacturing still employed more workers than any other industry group in 1990, but the census of that year was the last one to give first place to that domain. Since 1990 the service areas have grown at a faster rate than has manufacturing.

Cincinnati MSA Employment by Occupation in 1990

Category	Number	Percent
Total employed persons	872,258	100.0
Executive, professional, and technical	267,803	30.7
Sales	104,037	11.9
Administrative support, including clerical	149,892	17.2
Service	110,191	12.6
Precision workers, machine operators, and blue collar	240,534	27.6

Cincinnati MSA Employment by Industry in 1990

Industry	Number	Percent
Total employed persons	872,258	100.0
Agriculture, forestry, fishing, hunting, and mining	12,985	1.5
Construction	51,617	5.9
Manufacturing	181,917	20.8
Finance, insurance, and real estate	57,683	6.6
Educational, health, and social services	143,519	16.4
Professional and other services	129,864	14.9
Public administration	28,578	3.3
Wholesale and retail trade	165,729	19.0
Transportation, warehousing, and utilities	100,366	11.5

Regardless of how its residents earned their living, Cincinnati was still a baseball town in 1990.

Designed to Break
Your Heart

Baseball was shaken to its very roots in 1989, by one genuine tragedy and a series of events that, while not tragic in the Shakespearean sense, were serious enough to send tremors through the grand old game.

The real tragedy was the earthquake that struck California during the 1989 World Series. The quake struck the San Francisco Bay area on October 17 at 5:04 p.m., during the warm-up time for the third game of the World Series. Caused by a slip along the San Andreas Fault, the quake measured 7.1 on the Richter scale. It killed 63 people, injured more than 3,000 and left thousands homeless. The game was postponed indefinitely, but the World Series resumed ten days later. Another disaster occurred in 1989 when the tanker Exxon Valdez ran aground off the coast of Alaska, spilling 11,000,000 gallons of oil into Prince William Sound. Wildlife was devastated by this, the worst environmental disaster in United States history. This event had no direct effect on baseball, but was another thing that went wrong in that star-crossed year.

The earthquake and the oil spill were unforeseen future events when the baseball season got under way in the early spring of 1989. Coming off four consecutive second-place finishes, the Cincinnati Reds were picked by most prognosticators to be runners-up again, but some thought the Reds should be favored for the pennant. Peter Pascarelli wrote that the Reds could win it all, "if Benzinger can drive in runs the way a lot of people think he can and if certain other players have good years."[1] Benzinger was an interesting case. Although the youngster had not been very productive in his two seasons with the Boston Red Sox, Ted Williams, baseball's greatest living hitter, recommended him highly in a conversation with Pete Rose following the 1988 season. "Ted Williams told me he is the best young hitter he had seen in years," Rose said. "That was good enough for me.

The next week we traded for him."[2] (Although Benzinger played in the major leagues for nine years, he never became a superstar.)

Manager Pete Rose was eager to see his Reds take a flag after all those second-place finishes. He said, "Our important players ... have grown up. They know what it takes. It's time to quit knocking on the door. It's time to beat it down.... The only thing we want to do different this season is to move up one spot, just one, in the standings."[3] Although Charlie Hustle was already under investigation for allegedly betting on baseball games, he steadfastly denied charges. Apparently he thought he could beat the rap. If he had any doubts, he kept them to himself. In public he maintained his innocence and predicted he would be cleared of any wrongdoing.

Others were not so sanguine. Art Spander wrote, "For the baseball fan this has been a terrible spring, the scandal swirling about Wade Boggs merging with the hypocrisy engulfing Steve Garvey colliding now with the disgrace reaching out for Pete Rose."[4]

The scandals involving Boggs and Garvey were not baseball-related, but had to do with off-field activities. Both men were sued by women with whom they had affairs. Garvey's case was particularly galling because of the hypocrisy. He had gained the nickname "Mr. Clean" from the image he presented to the public. He was quoted as having said, "God has laid out the game plan. I walk around as if a little boy or little girl was following me and I don't do anything physically or mentally to take away from the ideal they might have for Steve Garvey."[5] A little boy or little girl following him around might have seen things not intended for the eyes of children. Steve Garvey was charged in paternity suits brought by two different women in 1989.

Spander could not have known it at the time, of course, but the summer was to bring even more bad news to baseball fans. Commissioner Bart Giamatti died suddenly from a heart attack; former Angels relief ace Donnie Moore committed suicide; pitcher Dave Dravecky was in the midst of a surprising comeback from cancer when he suffered a career-ending injury; and Rose was banned from baseball for life. To top it all off, one of the most fascinating men in all of baseball, Billy Martin, was killed in a truck crash in December. Indeed, 1989 was a terrible year for baseball fans.

The Cincinnati Reds got off to a good start in the 1989 season. During much of April and May the club was in first place in the National League West. After the games of June 10, the club was still in first place with a record of 35 wins and 24 losses. After that it was all downhill. The club won only nine of its next 30 games, falling below .500 for the first time on July 14. From June 10 to the end of the season the Reds were 40–63, ending the season in fifth place at 75–87 (.463), 17 games behind the San Francisco Giants. It was their worst finish since 1984.

Several factors contributed to Cincinnati's ills in 1989. Benzinger did not live up to expectations, hitting only .245 and driving in 76 runs. The turmoil around the Rose situation played a part. Injuries, however, were probably the major cause of the club's downfall. Injuries wreaked havoc upon the team. According to *The Sporting News*, every player in the Reds' regular lineup except Benzinger spent time on the disabled list during 1989.[6] That may have been a slight exaggeration, but it was not far off the mark. Greg Hoard of the *Cincinnati Enquirer*, writing in Athlon's 1990 baseball guide, put the number of different Reds players on the 1989 disabled list at 13, including seven starting position players.[7] Apparently, different writers have differing interpretations of the term "starting players." The *New York Times* reported that 12 Reds had been on the disabled list by early August in that season, but only three of them were regular position players—Larkin, O'Neill, and Sabo. The *Times* quoted Pete Rose: "Injuries are part of the game, and we've had our share, and someone else's share.... I'm sorry to make excuses, but anybody who knows anything about baseball knows we've been asked to overcome too much. It's impossible."[8]

The most serious injury was to Barry Larkin, the club's shortstop and probably its most valuable player when healthy. Named to the National League All-Star team for the second year in a row, Larkin was participating in skills competition the day before the game. While making a throw he tore the medial collateral ligament in his right elbow. Doctors said he had come within a centimeter or two of suffering a career-ending injury. During the second half of the season he was limited to only a few pinch-hitting appearances.

Third baseman Chris Sabo was on the disabled list with a knee injury for more than two months. "The entire 1989 season was a disaster any way you want to look at it," said Sabo.[9] Infielder Mariano Duncan missed the final week of the season with a pulled hamstring. Right fielder Paul O'Neill missed six weeks with a broken thumb. Center fielder Eric Davis was out for more than 30 games due to a variety of injuries. Bo Diaz had been expected to be the Reds' number one catcher, but he missed most of the season with an injury to his left knee. The pitching staff also was beset by injuries. Starting pitchers Danny Jackson, Jose Rijo, and Ron Robinson spent a combined 38 weeks on the disabled list.

Rose's problems also contributed to the club's lack of success in 1989. The players could not help being distracted by the manager's troubles.

Rose himself probably gave less than full attention to his managerial duties. Whether his mind was on other things or it was just his style of managing, Rose took a decidedly hands-off approach. Vice-president Jim Ferguson said, "Pete's theory of managing is more or less to leave the players alone, just like he wanted to be left alone when he was playing."[10]

Rose may have allowed his younger players too much latitude. It was also charged that he bent over backwards to avoid ruffling the feathers of the veterans. Ron Oester observed: "The team lacked discipline under Pete. He was too nice. He didn't have many rules and those he had were not enforced.... People took advantage of him."[11] Too nice? That doesn't sound like the Pete Rose of the Big Red Machine. For the hard-driving competitor that Charlie Hustle was in his playing days, it seems surprising that he did not push his players to exert their utmost efforts. Yet Lou Piniella said, "When I agreed to take on the Reds' job, I was given the distinct impression that Pete had been running a country club in Cincinnati."[12]

It cannot be denied that the gambling charges against Rose weighed heavily on his mind. The accusations had to affect his demeanor on the field and in the clubhouse. If the personality of the manager affects the attitude of the players, the 1989 Reds were not candidates for a championship. The commissioner's office had announced on March 20 that it was investigating complaints that Rose had bet on baseball games. A Washington lawyer, John M. Dowd, was appointed special counsel to the commissioner and headed up the investigation. For months Rose denied the charges. But he had been under a cloud of suspicion ever since spring training. The Dowd Report contained such convincing evidence that Rose accepted a plea agreement in August, which called for his lifetime suspension from baseball. He expected to ask for and receive reinstatement in one year. However, one week after announcing the suspension, Commissioner Giamatti died of a heart attack. Giamatti's successors have refused to lift the ban. The severity of Rose's punishment is controversial. Two of the biggest stars in baseball, Ty Cobb and Tris Speaker, probably bet on at least one game and were accused of conspiring to fix a game. Commissioner Kenesaw Mountain Landis relieved them of their managerial assignments but did not ban them from the playing field. They were among the first players elected to the National Baseball Hall of Fame in Cooperstown, from which Rose is permanently excluded. However, the evidence against Rose was much stronger than that against the two earlier stars.

Tommy Helms was appointed interim manager on August 25 and led the team to a 14–21 mark the rest of the way. The club had been 59–68 under Rose, so for the season it went 73–89 and finished a disappointing next-to-last in the National League West. The California earthquake helped put the Reds' woes in perspective, but still it was a dismal season for the Cincinnati club. The thing about baseball is that there is always a next year, or so it was thought. Fans and players will endure a long winter, but spring will come and with it a new baseball season and hope for a better day. "I know fans are tired of the wait until next year garbage," said Paul O'Neill. "But right now what else is there?"[13]

During the off-season a new general manager, Bob Quinn, and a new field manager, Lou Piniella, took the reins. Despite her well-deserved reputation as a penny-pincher, owner Marge Schott was prepared to loosen the purse strings if additional players were needed.

The stage was set for the 1990 season.

A Personnel Matter

Building a baseball club requires the efforts of many people—scouts, coaches, managers, player development personnel, general managers, club executives, and owners, among others. The vast majority of the 1990 Reds players were acquired during the time the club was under the ownership of Marge Schott. Schott was very much a hands-on proprietor, one of the most visible owners in all of sports. From 1985 to 1990 and beyond, she was president and CEO of the Reds, very much involved in the day-to-day affairs of the club. She was one in a long line of German-American owners of Cincinnati baseball clubs, stretching all the way back to the Reds' Justin Thorner and the Porkers' Chris von der Ahe, both of whom were born in Germany. Born Margaret Unnewehr in Cincinnati on August 18, 1928, she was the daughter of a wealthy Cincinnati businessman of German extraction. She thought her father had always wanted a son instead of a daughter, so she became a tomboy in an attempt to please him. Marge attended Catholic parochial schools, where her classmates, focusing on the name Unnewehr, quite naturally nicknamed her "Underwear." Her father called her "Butch."

In 1952 Marge married Charles Schott, also a wealthy Cincinnatian of German ancestry. When Charles Schott died of a heart attack in 1968, Marge inherited his automobile dealership and other enterprises. A longtime Reds fan, she bought a minority interest in the club in 1981. She purchased controlling interest in 1984 and became president and CEO of the club the next year. She kept ticket and concession prices low. She watched many Reds games from her regular box seat at Riverfront, sometimes accompanied by her Saint Bernard, Schottzie. She allowed the dog free access to the field before games, leaving deposits on the Astroturf for players to dodge. Just before game time, she would send an assistant with a pooper-scooper to remove the debris from the field.

Often criticized for her frugal ways, her limited knowledge of baseball, her insensitivity to fellow humans, and countless other faults, Schott nevertheless helped bring a world championship to the Queen City within five years of taking the helm. This was accomplished with a mid-market club with the second-lowest payroll in the National League.[14] She must have done something right. She also did a lot of things wrong.

Rick Riley wrote in *Sports Illustrated* that Schott was "tighter than shrink wrap."[15] One way to save money was to fire all the scouts because, she said, "All they do is watch ball games.[16] Yes, scouts

Brash, outspoken, and opinionated, Marge Schott was a controversial figure. Within five years after assuming control of the club, she helped bring a championship to the Queen City. Among her most successful actions were the employment of Bob Quinn as general manager and Lou Piniella as field manager (National Baseball Hall of Fame Library).

watch ball games, sometimes as many as 200 games in a year. They watch the games with a practiced and intensely focused eye, take copious notes, and establish relationships with players, coaches, and managers that may lead to a top young prospect signing with the club. Then they move on to the next town. Some drive thousands of miles a year and sleep in dozens of different motel rooms. Called ivory hunters, they perform an invaluable service. Lou Gorman, general manager of the Boston Red Sox, winners of the American League East in 1990, said, "I don't think you could ever get away from having good scouts. You don't win without good scouts."[17]

Roland Hemond, a long-time, highly respected baseball executive and winner of a Lifetime Achievement Award from the National Baseball Hall of Fame, wrote: "Having been in the game since 1951, I realize that organizations will fail without competent scouts who possess the ability not only to sign players, but to project the eventual development of their candidates."[18] Some say the job of the scout is to find a diamond in the rough.

Among prominent players who disagreed with Schott on the importance of scouts, perhaps the most outspoken was Joe Morgan. The great second sacker said he would never have made it in professional ball if it were not for baseball scouts. "I never would have gotten a chance. I was 5 foot five, 140 pounds. No computer would give me a look. Without a scout, a man named Bill Wight, I wouldn't have gotten a shot."[19]

How did Marge Schott reward her scouts? No, she didn't fire them all. But Cincinnati sportswriter Paul Daugherty thought she owed an apology to every scout "who watched ball games … and who, when traveling for the club, had to wash their clothes in a laundromat and plop quarters into motel pay phones because Schott wouldn't pay for in-room local calls."[20]

For the owner of the ball club, who described herself as a long-time rabid Cincinnati Reds fan, it is surprising how ill-informed she was about the history of the club. For example, she had no awareness of Edd Roush, the Hall of Famer who is generally regarded as the greatest Reds player of the first half of the 20th century. The story is told that Schott was once approached by a woman introducing herself as Edd Roush's granddaughter. "That's nice, hon," Schott replied. "What business is he in?"[21]

Schott deserves credit for helping make the 1990 season so successful, but her sometimes outrageous behavior brought about her downfall. She was accused of making racist slurs, anti–Semitic remarks, and homophobic comments. Among comments attributed to her were: "Sneaky goddamn Jews are all alike," "Never hire another nigger. I'd rather have a trained monkey working for me than a nigger," "Only fruits wear earrings," and "Everybody knows Hitler was good at the beginning, but he just went too far."[22] In 1993 Schott was fined $25,000, banned from baseball for a year, and ordered to attend multicultural training programs. The programs did not change her behavior. In *Sports Illustrated* Rick Riley wrote: "Sending Schott to sensitivity training is like sending a pickpocket to a Rolex convention."[23] Marge Schott loved children and animals, but she had little use for most people.

Schott imposed a strict dress and grooming code on players and other employees alike. Riley quoted her as saying, "If nothing else, the one thing I am most proud of is no facial hair and earrings." He further reported a conversation allegedly held between the club owner and baseball commissioner Bart Giamatti when Schott spotted a long-haired ballboy:

SCHOTT: "Is this a girl or a boy that needs a goddamn haircut?"
GIAMATTI: "It's a young man with a modern haircut."
SCHOTT: "Well, he'll never be out here again with long hair like that."[24]

Schott's objection to long hair grew out of her social conservative values. She associated long hair on men with hippies and the counter-culture, which she detested. She was not the first Cincinnati official to ban long hair. Schott simply enforced the policies established by fellow social conservatives Bob Howsam and Sparky Anderson. However, many ballplayers had for years voluntarily kept their hair short for reasons having nothing to do with cultural symbolism. Summertime is hot in Cincinnati. It can get quite warm in St. Louis and other baseball cities as well. Before the prevalence of night games, most games were played under a hot sun, causing players' heads to sweat profusely. Bill Werber wrote that it was easier to shower out the sweat and dirt if the hair was short. Of course, that mattered not a bit to Schott. She simply did not like long hair on men. Werber also related that ball clubs kept a large bucket of ice water in the dugout, so players could sponge their faces and get the sweat off their hands. By the end of the game, the water would be too muddy for the players to use in washing their hair, of course. However, he admitted once dumping a bucket of muddy ice water on the head of a heckling fan.[25]

Two examples suffice to show Schott's lack of concern for her fellow humans. In Game 4 of the 1990 World Series, Eric Davis lunged to try to catch a ball driven to the outfield. When he positioned his right arm to break the fall, the arm plunged into his ribcage, causing piercing pain. He was rushed to an Oakland hospital, where X-rays showed a severely bruised right kidney. After a week in intensive care he was permitted to fly home, but he was told he would have to stay in a prone position on the flight, so he would have to take a charter flight. Davis's agent called Quinn and asked him to set up a charter flight back to Cincinnati. Quinn reportedly replied, "Davis makes three million a year. He can set up his own flight."[26] (Actually Davis was paid $2,100,000 in 1990, the second-most on the payroll, $25,000 less than club leader Tom Browning.) The outfielder then called Schott directly, asking for help. She told him she didn't know anyone with a private jet. Davis made his own arrangements for the flight home. He and the Reds battled over who should pay the $15,000 bill for the charter. Schott eventually reimbursed Davis for the flight. Many fans and Davis's teammates though the owner had treated Davis shabbily. Jose Rijo said, "It's wrong. He deserves better, and not just because of who he is, but because he is a human being."[27]

More tragic than the injury to Davis was the death of umpire John

McSherry six years later. On Opening Day 1996, the weather was cold and blustery. It had snowed earlier in the day. Shortly after the game began McSherry, the home plate umpire, called time out and motioned towards the Reds dugout, perhaps intending to ask for medical help. After taking a few steps, he collapsed face-down on the Astroturf. Attempts to revive him were fruitless. An hour later he was pronounced dead of a heart attack. The other umpires decided to postpone the game, much to Schott's displeasure. Apparently, she was more concerned about the postponement than about the stricken umpire. Schott said, "Snow this morning and now this. I don't believe it. I feel cheated. This isn't supposed to happen to us, not in Cincinnati. This is our history, our tradition, our team. Nobody feels worse than me."[28]

In 1993 a committee appointed by Major League Baseball found that Schott commonly used language that was racially and ethnically insensitive, offensive, and intolerable. Her behavior was said to have brought substantial disrepute and embarrassment to the game and was not in the best interests of baseball, resulting in a fine of $200,000 and suspension from day-to-day operation of the club during the entire season.[29]

Although proud of her German heritage, Schott denied being a Nazi sympathizer. She shared their homophobia, racism, and anti–Semitism. But guilt by association is not appropriate. She explained that she kept a Nazi swastika at her home because her husband had brought it home as a souvenir from fighting against the Nazis in World War II. She kept it in memory of her husband's bravery and service to his country.[30]

Nevertheless, her praise of Hitler was one of the factors leading to another suspension from Major League Baseball in 1998. She sold her controlling interest in the Reds in 1999. She devoted her last years to giving away a considerable portion of her fortune. Among beneficiaries of her generosity were St. Ursula Academy, the Boy Scouts, the Cincinnati Zoo and Botanical Gardens, and the Cincinnati Humane Society. She maintained her love for children and animals to the end. Marge Schott died on March 2, 2004.

Among Schott's chief contributions to making the Reds a championship club were the selections of Bob Quinn as general manager on October 15, 1989, and Lou Piniella as field manager on November 3. The vacancy in the general manager's position occurred on October 13, when Schott fired Murray Cook. When asked what Cook had done wrong, Schott replied, "Nothing. It was just time for a change."[31] Asked whether Cook resigned or was fired, Schott told reporters, "I don't think that needs to be said."[32] She felt that her action needed no explanation or justification.

In her view, replacing general managers was one of the prerogatives of ownership. After all, Schott's hero, George Steinbrenner, frequently changed managers and general managers, sometimes for no apparent reason.

Schott never announced publicly why she chose Quinn for the position, but it may have had something to do with the fact that Quinn had worked for Steinbrenner. Schott had tremendous admiration for the Yankees owner. He had an outsized personality; he did things his way; he had no compunctions about firing people; and he made his office people, his managers, and his players squirm. It was said that Schott liked that last part best of all.[33] Another reason for hiring Quinn was that he was a very good baseball man.

Quinn was a third generation baseball executive, the grandson of an earlier Bob Quinn, who had been a baseball owner and general manager, and served in other executive positions, such as president of the National Baseball Hall of Fame. The elder Bob Quinn's son John was employed as general manager of two major league clubs. John's son Bob was born in Boston in 1936, when John was general manager of the Boston Braves. Bob moved with the family to Wisconsin when the Braves moved from Boston to Milwaukee. From the time he was in high school, Bob wanted to follow in his father's and grandfather's footsteps. "Dad encouraged me, but only if I wanted to go out and learn the business at the minor league level," he said. "He didn't feel it was appropriate to summarily give me a job in the Braves' front office. He wanted me to learn the business from the ground up." Learn the business is what Bob Quinn did. In 1971 he became director of minor league operations for the Milwaukee Brewers. Later he served in the same position for the Cleveland Indians, who promoted him to vice president in 1981. In 1987 he joined the New York Yankees as a vice president. He served as general manager for the Yankees in 1988 and 1989. Bob Quinn knew his way around the world of baseball. His recommendation carried a lot of weight with Marge Schott.

One of Quinn's first jobs was to help Schott find a field manager. When Reds manager Pete Rose was banned from baseball in August 1989, then-general manager Murray Cook named Tommy Helms interim manager. Helms was given a contract through the end of the season. He was told he would be considered for the position in 1990. *The Sporting News* quoted several Reds players who openly expressed support for Helms getting the job.[34] Among those quoted was Todd Benzinger: "They can save a lot of grief by hiring Tommy. He knows the personalities and we all respect him. If he has done anything right, it was earning the respect of all the players, and that's half the battle." Eric Davis stated his position:

"Because this team was under adversity all year, Tommy never got a legitimate opportunity. He deserves to start from scratch. He had good rapport with all the players, and I was real impressed with the way he took control." Paul O'Neill observed: "We all know there will be some changes, but I hope they give Tommy a chance. Tommy was thrown into the fire and was expected to turn things around when they were too far gone."

Other candidates, including former major league managers Hal Lanier and Chuck Tanner, announced their interest in the position, but weeks went by with Helms receiving no news about his future with the club. After being kept in limbo for six weeks, Helms learned he would not be hired for 1990. He said the front office treated him like dirt: "I don't want to be around Marge Schott no more. I've been kicked around enough, and I don't want to be kicked any more. If the ball club is ever sold, I would like to come back as manager, but not as long as she is here."[35] He was not the first nor the last disgruntled Red who had harsh words for Marge Schott.

Schott wanted a tough guy for field manager. When she asked, "Who is the toughest guy in baseball?" the answer came back: Dallas Green.[36] "I express my thoughts," Green said. "I'm a screamer, a yeller, and a cusser. I never hold back."[37] Along with other positions in baseball, Green had managerial experience, leading the Philadelphia Phillies to the World Series title in 1980. He managed the Yankees for most of the 1989 season before being fired by Steinbrenner, perhaps for not showing enough deference to the Boss. So Schott's first choice for the field manager's position became Dallas Green. Of course, Quinn had known Green when both were with the Yankees, and he approved of the owner's choice. Green had doubts about accepting the post. He was concerned whether the Reds would make the necessary monetary expenditure to build a winning club. Schott wanted Green to retain some of the coaching staff to maintain a connection with the Big Red Machine. (Obviously she meant Tony Perez, as he was the only former member of the Machine on the coaching roster.) Green insisted on carte blanche to hire an entirely new staff. Eventually, Green turned the job down. As no formal announcement had ever been made that the position was actually offered to him, it was reported that Green withdrew his application.

With Green no longer in the picture, Quinn recommended that Schott consider Lou Piniella. Lou who? Quinn said, "Marge didn't know Lou Piniella from a Puerto Rican rum drink, but that's who I wanted. Lou was the perfect fit."[38] Quinn had to convince Schott to allow him to offer the job and then persuade Piniella to accept it. Quinn was successful on both counts. Piniella was under a personal service contract to George Steinbrenner. When the Cleveland Indians wanted permission to talk to Piniella about a managerial post, the Yankees' owner had turned them down. He didn't want Piniella managing another team in the same league as the Yankees. When it came to a National League team, that was a different matter, and Steinbrenner released Piniella from his contract.

The Sporting News reported that the owner and her new manager were on the same wavelength. They were both into winning. However, Piniella let it be known that he, not Marge Schott, would be in charge of the club. "I told Mrs. Schott that I won't disappoint her. She's a friendly lady and, uh, interesting. I know she's dead set on bringing a winner to Cincinnati. I don't know anything more about her, but I do know the baseball people should run the baseball operation."[39]

For her part, Schott made the point that she expected the manager to deliver wins. "I'm the type who expects results immediately. I have a man who wants to win as much as I do. And when I say it's a whole new ball game for the Reds, it's a whole new ball game."[40]

Lou Piniella was born in Tampa, Florida, to Spanish-speaking parents, on August 28, 1943. He won All-American honors in baseball at the University of Tampa, signed as an amateur free agent with the Cleveland Indians in 1962, and made his major league debut on September 4, 1964, a few days after his 21st birthday. During the next few years he played mainly in the minor leagues, and was named American League Rookie of the Year in 1969. How could he be considered a rookie five years after playing his first major league game? He played only ten games in the majors from 1964 through 1968. In 18 seasons in the majors, he made the All-Star team once, but earned a

By the time he joined the Reds, Lou Piniella had more than 20 years of experience as a major league player or manager, all of it in the American League. In his first season in the National League—1990—he led the Cincinnati Reds to a World Series title. "Sweet Lou" deserves a great deal of credit for the success of the 1990 Reds (National Baseball Hall of Fame Library).

reputation as a scrappy player. After retiring as a player, Piniella joined the New York Yankees as a hitting coach. George Steinbrenner twice hired Piniella as manager of the Yankees and fired him both times. Of course, getting fired by Steinbrenner was no disgrace. In his two-plus years as Yankees manager, Piniella won 224 games and lost 193, for a winning percentage of .537. In his two full seasons as Yankees skipper, the club finished second and fourth. In between his managerial stints he served briefly as the Yankees' general manager.

By the time he joined the Reds, Piniella had accrued more than 20 years of major league experience as a player or manager—all of it in the American League. Not one day in the National League. He saw the move to a different circuit as more of an opportunity than a problem. "It is a tremendous challenge. I have to acquaint myself with the talent on the ball club, and I'm looking forward to all the new cities and new ball parks."[41] He thought the difficulty of changing leagues was overrated. "It's still the same game, and the players have to hit the ball, catch the ball, and throw it," he said. "My job is just to provide leadership on the field and in the clubhouse and set a good positive tone for the club. I have to get the players to play hard. I don't anticipate problems."[42]

Events proved that Piniella did his job well. He took over an underachieving team, beset with turmoil that came from the Rose situation, and distressed by their losing record in 1989. From the very beginning he said he was not worried about taking over a "troubled" team. "Not at all. It's a new start. The most important thing is to go into spring training and instill a positive attitude. I don't think we'll have an attitude problem."[43] In his first press conference, Piniella said, "I didn't come here just to manage. I came here to win."[44] Paul Daugherty quoted pitching coach Stan Williams as saying, "A refusal to be a happy loser. That's what he brought. He harped on it, beat on it, insisted upon it."[45] By the end of the season the players were as dissatisfied with losing as the manager was. His leadership spurred the players on to success. The sense of impending failure disappeared from the clubhouse. Players who had formerly been accused of being selfish or lackadaisical were instilled with a team spirit and exerted greater effort to win, not just for themselves, but for the team and for the manager. Barry Larkin said, "I think every year you play for your teammates. But I was playing for Lou."[46]

Within a few days of accepting the Cincinnati managerial post, Piniella named his coaches for the coming season, apparently without any interference from either Schott or Quinn. One of his first announcements was his decision to keep Tony Perez as hitting coach. Was Perez retained to placate Marge Schott? "Not so. No way. One condition I made before coming here was that I would select all of my coaches. Repeat, all of them," he said. "Look, I wanted to keep Tony because he knows the talent levels of this team and because we have the same teaching philosophies.... We work hand in hand."[47] Piniella spoke of his coaches in terms of their teaching abilities. When asked if his emphasis on teaching indicated that he thought the team was weak in fundamentals, he replied, "Let's just say that with a young club, you can never have too many teachers. Maybe others before me thought that all the fundamentals should have been taught in the minors. But it just doesn't work that way anymore."[48] Piniella was not content to leave the teaching to his coaches. He was personally involved. "I think it's good for the players to see their manager on the field daily before a game," he said. "Besides, I enjoy working with the hitters because it gives me a better perspective. It gives me a chance to know the players, to talk with them and learn their thinking."[49]

Cincinnati fans welcomed the retention of Perez. Born in Cuba in 1942, Perez was signed as a teenaged amateur free agent by the Reds in 1960 and played in the major leagues for 23 years. The Big Dog, as he was called, was one of the most productive members of the Big Red Machine and one of the most popular players ever to ply his trade on the banks of the Ohio. His trade away from the Reds after the 1976 season was considered by some fans as one of the main reasons that the Reds fell upon hard times shortly thereafter. He returned to Cincinnati in 1984. Immediately upon his retirement at the age of 44 in 1986, manager and former teammate Pete Rose appointed him first base coach, and later shifted him to hitting coach. Perez later managed the Reds in 1993 and the Florida Marlins in 2001. He was inducted into the National Baseball Hall of Fame in 2000. In 2014 he was a special assistant to the general manager of the Miami Marlins.

None of the other coaches employed by Piniella had strong major league playing careers, but all of them were very competent baseball men. Third-base coach Sam Perlozzo, bench coach Jackie Moore, bullpen coach Larry Rothschild, and pitching coach Stan Williams were not well known to the casual baseball fan, but their abilities were highly respected by Piniella, and for good reason. Early in Piniella's tenure it was rumored that former Reds pitching ace Don Gullett was in line for the bullpen coaching job, but that did not work out, and the new manager turned to Rothschild.[50]

Sam Perlozzo was born in Cumberland, Maryland, in 1951 and was signed by the Minnesota Twins as an amateur free agent out of George Washington University in 1972. He played eight seasons in the minors and one season in Japan, but played only 12 games in the major leagues. In 1981 Perlozzo retired as a player and managed in the New York Mets farm system for five years. From 1987–1989 he was third-base coach for the Mets, until Piniella brought him to Cincinnati. After the 1992 season, he left with Piniella to go to Seattle. He has since coached for several different clubs and has managed the Baltimore Orioles. Despite minimal major league playing experience, Perlozzo has coached or managed in the big leagues for more than a quarter-century. In 2014 he was the minor league infield and base-running coordinator for the Minnesota Twins.

Jackie Moore is similar to Perlozzo in having limited major league playing experience but still carving out a successful career in The Show as a coach and manager. Moore was born in Florida in 1939 and signed with the Detroit Tigers as an amateur free agent in 1957 at the age of 18. He spent eight years in the Tigers' farm system, as an outfielder and catcher, before making his big league debut in 1965. He appeared in only 21 games for the Tigers. After one season back in the minors, he retired as a player. Since then he has spent more than 40 years as a coach or manager, most of it at the major league level. Included were one full season and parts of two others as skipper of the Oakland Athletics. He was the third-base coach for the Montreal Expos when Piniella brought him to Cincinnati. When Piniella left the Reds after the 1992 season, Moore also moved on. He was the Texas League "Manager of the Year" three times (2000, 2001, and 2004) before returning to the majors as a coach. In 2013 he was the bench coach for the Texas Rangers.

Larry Rothschild was born in Chicago in 1954. He was signed by the Cincinnati Reds as an amateur free agent out of Florida State University in 1975. Like Perlozzo and Moore, he had an undistinguished major league playing career, appearing in only seven games as a relief pitcher, winning no games, and securing one save. In 11 seasons in the minors he won 66 games and saved 50. Pete Rose brought him to Cincinnati as a bullpen coach in 1986. Rothschild was the Reds' minor league pitching instructor for four seasons until Piniella fetched him back to the parent club. He left the Reds after the 1993 season. He was a pitching instructor for the Atlanta Braves in 1994 and spent the next three years with the Florida Marlins. In 1998 he was named manager of the Tampa Bay Devil Rays for their inaugural major league season. The neophyte Rays were unable to post a winning record under Rothschild's leadership. He was fired in 2001, but has remained in the major leagues since in various capacities. In 2014 he was the pitching coach for the New York Yankees.

Piniella rounded out his coaching staff by bringing a former colleague to the Queen City. Stan Williams was born in New Hampshire in September 1936. As a 17-year-old high school pitcher, he was drafted by the Brooklyn Dodgers in 1954. After a little more than three years in the minors, he made his big league debut in 1958. His major league career lasted 14 seasons, in which he pitched for six different clubs and won 109 games. After retiring as a player, he spent another 14 years as a pitching coach and several years as a scout. Williams was a pitching coach for the Yankees from 1980–1982 when Piniella played for the club and in 1987–1988 when Sweet Lou managed the Yankees. In 1989 he was serving as a scout for the Pinstripers when Piniella tapped him for the Cincinnati job. In 2014 he was a scout for the Washington Nationals.

From his New Jersey home, Piniella watched videos of the 1989 Reds. He liked much of what he saw, but he was bothered by excessive strikeouts: "One of the things I'm most concerned about, and one of the things our club will work on this spring more than anything, is to cut down the strikeouts. We have talent here, and I don't see why our hitters strike out as much as they have. We have to make our hitters attuned to the fact (that) if you make contact, you can score runs. A strikeout does nothing."[51] The new manager's concern about strikeouts was well founded. Todd Benzinger and Eric Davis had both fanned more than 100 times, and Rolando Roomes had struck out 100 times in only 334 times at bat.

Piniella was intrigued by Roomes: "He is a hell of a player. I think I can help him. I like young players and if they can play or pitch, they'll be on the field."[52]

Rolando Roomes was born in Kingston, Jamaica, on February 15, 1962. The family moved to Brooklyn in 1969. Young Roomes first became exposed to baseball by watching as his father viewed Mets games on television. He played stickball in the streets, but did not take up baseball seriously until his senior year in high school.[53] Luckily, baseball scouts watched some of his high school games and were impressed by his potential. The Chicago Cubs signed the 18-year-old pitcher-outfielder as a free agent on July 14, 1980. (As he was not yet a United States citizen, he was not included in the amateur draft.) The youngster turned down an offer to play college football in order to join the Cubs organization. After nearly eight years in the minors, it was starting to appear that he would be a career minor leaguer. Finally, he was brought up to the parent club and made his major league debut on April 12, 1988. He got into only seven games before being sent back to the minors. He hit well at Class AAA Iowa and was called back up in September, getting into ten more games for the Cubs.

After the season, Roomes went to Puerto Rico to play winter ball. While he was there on December 8, 1988, the Cubs traded him to the Cincinnati Reds for Lloyd McClendon. The Reds sent him to their Class AAA affiliate in Nashville, but brought him back up after an injury sidelined Eric Davis in May. Roomes played in 107 games for the Reds in 1989. He hit a respectable .263 and appeared to be ready to take over as the Reds' regular left fielder in 1990. However, when spring training finally arrived, Roomes struck out nine times in 15 at-bats. Just before the end of spring training the Reds obtained Billy Hatcher, relegating Roomes to a back-up role. On June 5 the Reds acquired Glenn Braggs, ending any chance for Roomes to play regularly in Cincinnati. Piniella said, "Braggs is a heck of a lot better than Rolando Roomes, isn't he?"[54]

On June 18 the Reds waived Roomes to Milwaukee. He got into 16 games for the Brewers before making his final major league appearance on September 30, 1990, at the age of 28. Roomes played one more year in the minors before retiring to his home in Mesa, Arizona. In 2007 he became a United States citizen.[55]

Before and after his tenure with the 1990 Reds, Lou Piniella was noted for his run-ins with umpires. Ballplayers and managers expect every close call to go their way. In order to make sure this happens, novices may try to intimidate the umpire. This doesn't work. Big league umpires cannot be intimidated. If they could be, they would never have made it to the majors. They know if they give an irate manager an inch, he'll take the proverbial mile. As veteran umpire Ken Kaiser put it, "You give a manager like.... Lou Piniella one little inch and they'll take your house, your car, and your next-born child."[56]

Piniella was experienced enough and intelligent enough to know that attempted intimidation would not work. So why did he engage in so many confrontations with the arbiters? Depending on the circumstances, there were three possible explanations. One, to protect a player. If a player was losing his cool in an argument with an umpire, Piniella would step between the two antagonists and take the heat in order to prevent his player from being ejected from the game. Two, in order to inspire his team. He believed that by showing his players that he was fighting for them, he might spur them on to greater effort. Three, sometimes he was genuinely angry and had to vent his ire.

Piniella was called "Sweet Lou." He must have been given the nickname on Opposite Day, for his disposition was anything but sweet. Ill-tempered might be a more accurate description. He was loud and brash and sometimes intemperate. When he was unhappy, he let everybody know it in no uncertain terms. In confrontations with umpires he often was belligerent, getting in their faces and kicking dirt on the plate. He would throw his cap down in the dirt, stomp on it, and kick it around, while screaming about how he was being cheated. Once he picked up a base and threw it. If he was really angry his face would turn red, and the veins on his neck would stand out. Kaiser said that no one threw a better tantrum than Lou Piniella when he disagreed with a call. If throwing a tantrum were an Olympic event, Piniella would win the gold medal.[57] Some of his displays of temper may have been exaggerated for effect. Sweet Lou was an actor. He was also precisely the manager that the Reds needed in 1990.

Piniella was instrumental in the Reds winning the 1990 pennant. He brought to the team a sense of determination and a winning attitude that had been in short supply in 1989. Another attribute of a successful manager is gaining the trust of his players, convincing them that he is a straightforward, stand-up guy who says what he means. Larkin said of Piniella; "The first day of spring training, Lou said that this was his ball club, that he was going to run it his way and that if we had any questions all we had to do was ask. If Lou has anything to say to you, he will say it to your face. You don't have to read about it in the newspaper the next day."[58]

(Trades negotiated by Bob Quinn plus the inspiration and guidance of Lou Piniella helped bring a world championship to the Queen City in the magical year of 1990. Alas, the magic did not linger. Both men moved on after the 1992 season. Marge Schott had hired them, and she saw them leave. After leaving Cincinnati, Piniella twice won the American League Manager of the Year Award.)

Of the 40 players who appeared in Reds games during the 1990 season, 27 of them had been acquired by the club before Quinn accepted the general manager's position. They had found their way to Cincinnati through a variety of routes. Thirteen had been acquired through the Rule 4 draft of eligible high school and college free agents. Of these 13, five (Jack Armstrong, Rob Dibble, Barry Larkin, Ron Robinson, and Scott Scudder) were drafted in the first round. The other eight were taken anywhere from the second round (Chris Sabo) to the 21st (Keith Brown). Paul O'Neill was drafted in the fourth round. Tom Browning, Eric Davis, Terry McGriff, and Ron Oester were all eighth- or ninth-round draftees. One player, Joe Oliver, was acquired in a supplemental round, as compensation for the Reds having lost a player to free agency.

Two players, Gino Minutelli and Rosario Rodriguez, were signed as undrafted free agents. As a Mexican citizen, Rodriguez was exempt from the Rule 4 draft. Although eligible, Minutelli had not been selected in the draft.

Two players, Rick Mahler and Ken Griffey, were signed as free agents after being released by the Atlanta Braves. Griffey was a special case. Born in Donora, Pennsylvania, on April 10, 1950, he had been drafted by Cincinnati in the 29th round of the 1965 Rule 4 draft, played an important role in the Big Red Machine, and was traded to the New York Yankees in 1981. From New York he went to Atlanta and was released by the Braves in 1988. He then returned to Cincinnati. He was the only player from the 1975–1976 championship clubs to play for the Reds in 1990. (Tony Perez, another veteran of the Machine, was the first base coach in Cincinnati in 1990.) Griffey did not last the full 1990 season with the Reds, securing his release on August 24. He signed with the Seattle Mariners and became a part of baseball lore, when he and Ken Griffey, Jr., became the first father and son combination to hit back-to-back home runs for a major league club. He played his last game for Seattle on May 31, 1991. In 2011 he was appointed manager of the Bakersfield Blaze, Cincinnati's affiliate in the Class A California League.

Ken Griffey was the only player from the 1975–1976 championship clubs to play for the Reds in 1990. He was released by the Reds in August and joined the Seattle Mariners, where he played alongside his son, Ken Griffey, Jr. In 1991 the Griffeys became the first father-and-son combination to hit back-to-back home runs for a major league club (National Baseball Hall of Fame Library).

Quinn inherited ten players whom the Reds had obtained through trades: Todd Benzinger, Tim Birtsas, Norm Charlton, Mariano Duncan, Danny Jackson, Luis Quinones, Jeff Reed, Jose Rijo, Rolando Roomes, and Herm Winningham.

Upon the advice of Piniella and approval by Schott, 13 players were acquired by Bob Quinn for the 1990 pennant race after he assumed the general manager's position in October 1989.

Quinn's first acquisition was Tim Layana through a Rule 5 draft, which was intended to prevent wealthier clubs from stockpiling prospects in their minor league systems. A right-handed pitcher, Layana lived a short, but eventful, life that ended in tragedy. Born in Inglewood, California, on March 2, 1964, he was drafted out of Loyola High School in Culver City, California, by the Chicago White Sox in the 28th round of the 1982 amateur draft. Opting instead to attend Loyola Marymount University, Layana did not sign with the Sox. In 1985 the Mets drafted him in the fifth round, but Layana still declined to sign. His waiting game paid off, and he was taken by the New York Yankees in the third round of the 1986 draft. The Yankees sent him to the minors, where he compiled a 28–32 record in four seasons. When the Yanks failed to promote him to the big leagues, he was taken by the Reds in the Rule 5 draft on December 4, 1989. Although he had been primarily a starting pitcher throughout his career, the Reds planned to use the 25-year-old hurler in long relief.

Layana made his major league debut with the Reds on April 9, 1990. He was an important contributor to the team's pennant chase, winning five games while losing three, all in relief. He picked up two saves. Despite this success, he was used sparingly in 1991 and was released at the end of the season. He spent most of the next five years in the minors, although he returned to "The Show" for a final big league appearance on July 26, 1993. After retiring as a player, Layana returned to California. In 1999 he was coaching high school baseball in Santa Monica. Returning from a golf tournament held in Arizona to raise funds to fight juvenile diabetes, his sports utility vehicle was broadsided by another car. Layana died from his injuries on June 26, 1999, at the age of 35.

Two days after acquiring Layana, Quinn negotiated a major trade which raised the hackles of Cincinnati fans. He sent John Franco, the Reds' highly popular closer, and minor league outfielder Don Brown to the New York Mets in exchange for reliever Randy Myers and minor league pitcher Kip Gross. According to writers John Erardi and Joel Luckhaupt, Quinn and Piniella wanted to put their own stamp on the ball club by making a major change that would attract the attention of the baseball world.[59] The trade certainly did that.

Not only were the fans angered by the deal, but Cincinnati's sportswriters and many of the Reds players were upset. Almost everyone appeared to believe that the deal was another action of "penny pinching Marge Schott" to save some big bucks. Franco had been paid $1,067,500 by the Reds in 1989; Myers had received $300,000 from the Mets. Quinn said money had nothing to do with the trade, but few people believed him.

Writing in *The Sporting News,* Peter Pascarelli opined: "Sure, money was a big reason why the Mets traded Randy Myers to Cincinnati for John Franco. Franco would have been very expensive for Cincinnati to re-sign…. Meanwhile, Myers is still three years away from free agency. But from a baseball standpoint, there is little debate that most NL managers would prefer having Franco in their bullpen."[60]

At first Norm Charlton didn't like the trade. "Johnny was a popular guy in the clubhouse. He was good to me, had taken me under his wing, explained things to me. I liked him immensely. He was a good guy and a hell of a closer, and I was upset that he was traded." Later, Charlton had second thoughts. "But you know what? Trading him for Myers allowed me and Dibs to blossom. It allowed us to be the idiots we were. And it gave us a persona [the Nasty Boys]."[61]

Danny Jackson said, "I don't put Myers in Franco's category. He can be, but he isn't right now. For three and a half years, Johnny was the best in the National League and one of the two or three best in baseball." Chris Sabo stated his perspective bluntly. "It seems pretty obvious what the intent was. Why do you trade the best for another left-hander? Sure it's obvious what they are doing. It's money; that's all it is." Larkin agreed with Sabo, but was a bit more circumspect in his comments. "What did we get, a lefty for a lefty? I think it's pretty obvious what's going on. I will let the obvious speak for the obvious." Was it really to save money? Paul O'Neill hoped it wasn't. "I hope it's not like that. When you start looking at things like that, people start wondering if you really want to win."

There should have been no doubt that Piniella wanted to win. He probably thought he had a better chance with Myers than with Franco. "The way I work, I like a left-right combination," the skipper said. "Franco always did it all for the Reds, and I don't think he would accept sharing that role with Dibble. With Myers and Dibble both close to 100mph, we'll have the hardest throwing combination in baseball. Money was no factor. This was a baseball trade."[62]

The deal turned out to be not as lopsided as it first appeared. The two principals had nearly identical records in 1990. Franco had 33 saves in 39 chances; Myers had 31 in 37 opportunities. Myers actually had a lower earned average than Franco. Myers won over some fans in the first game of the season. He was the winning pitcher in relief as the Reds defeated the Astros on Opening Night. "Nasty Boy" Myers provided an intimidation factor to the bullpen that the more gentlemanly Franco lacked.

A native of Washington State, born in Vancouver on September 19, 1962, Myers played baseball at Evergreen High School and Clark College, a community college in his home town. Baseball-reference.com reports that he attended Eastern Illinois University in Charleston, Illinois, but this is almost certainly incorrect. Eastern Illinois does not list him among its notable athletes or notable alumni, and Baseball Almanac does not include him among Eastern Illinois alumni who reached the major leagues. The Cincinnati Reds had their eye on Myers while he was still at Clark College. The Reds drafted the 19-year-old pitcher in the third round of the January 1982, amateur draft, but he did not sign. He waited until the June secondary draft, when he was taken by the New York Mets in the first round. After he toiled several years in the minors as a starting pitcher, the Mets converted him into a reliever. Myers made his major league debut in 1985 and was used by the Mets exclusively as a relief pitcher. The brash, feisty lefty enjoyed promoting his image as a "tough guy." In New York he was given the nickname "Psycho." Occasionally he wore a scarf tied around his brow and a black T-shirt with the inscription "Gun control is holding it in both hands."[63] He dressed in army fatigues—camouflage shirts, hats, and pants. In his locker at Riverfront Stadium he stored two metal olive-drab ammo boxes, two defused hand grenades, and two large Bowie knives.[64]

It was expected that Myers, two years younger than Franco, might yield more to the Reds over the long run than Franco would for the Mets. This did not prove true. Myers spent only two seasons with the Reds before moving on, whereas Franco anchored the Mets' relief corps year after year. Over their careers Franco notched 424 saves, compared to 347 for Myers. But for the championship year of 1990, Myers made quite a contribution. Perhaps he was even more valuable to the Reds in 1990 than Franco would have been.

All of the talk about the big trade concerned Myers and Franco. To most people Brown and Gross were inconsequential. Keith Brown never played a game in the majors, but Kip Gross pitched in the big leagues for parts of six seasons. Gross was born in Scottsbluff, Nebraska, on August 24, 1964. He was drafted by the St. Louis Cardinals in the third round of the 1985 amateur draft out of Murray State (Murray State College, a community college in Tishomingo, Oklahoma, not the more famous Murray State University in Kentucky). However, he did not sign with the Cardinals and played one year for the University of Nebraska. When the New York Mets drafted him in the fourth round of the 1986 draft, he did not sign immediately, as he wanted to play in the Alaskan League that summer. Later, he signed a contract and remained in the Mets' farm system until traded to Cincinnati. He did not make a large contribution to the Reds in 1990, but posted a 6–4 record in 1991, his most successful major league season. After the trade to Cincinnati he made his major league debut on April 21, 1990, at the age of 25. He spent most of the season in Nashville, but appeared in six games for the Reds, with no wins, no losses, and no saves. After the 1991 season he was traded to the Los Angeles Dodgers along with Eric Davis for Tim Belcher and John Wetteland. In May 1994 he was purchased by the Nippon Ham Fighters of the Japan Central League. He was a huge success in Japan, leading the Central League in wins in both 1995 and 1996. He said he loved playing in Japan. The language was not a big problem because most everyone in Tokyo spoke English, and interpreters traveled with the team on the road. Gross played in Japan for four years until he returned to the United States in 1988 to undergo surgery. He had a couple more trials in the big leagues, with Boston in 1999 and Houston in 2000, but was unable to win a game for either club. His final game was on May 29, 2000. He pitched in the minor leagues in 2000 and 2001 before calling it quits as a player. Since retiring he has been unable to secure a coaching job in Organized Baseball, although he managed an independent team in 2010, the victorious Seals in the Golden Baseball League.

Gross told an interviewer that Lou Piniella was his favorite major league manager, Dodger Stadium was his favorite ballpark, and Cincinnati was his favorite city in which to play. He said one of his favorite times in his playing career was being with the Reds in the 1990 World Series. "Although I didn't pitch in the playoffs or the Series.... I still have my ring. Playing in Japan was also a huge deal for me. I always told myself that if I ever got a chance to play over there that I would go under the right circumstances."[65]

If Quinn's first trade was a near standoff, his second was a clear win for the Reds. On December 12, he traded Tim Leary and Van Snider to the New York Yankees for Hal Morris and Rodney Innes. Neither Snider nor Innes played a game in the major leagues, so in effect the trade was one-on-one—Leary for Morris. The veteran Leary was expendable, having won only two games for the Reds in 1989. Desperate for pitchers, the Yankees were willing to gamble on the hurler. They lost their bet. Leary went 9–19 in the Bronx in 1990 and posted a lifetime 78–105 record. In return they had given up their top prospect.

Hal Morris was born in Fort Rucker, Alabama, on April 9, 1965, went to high school in Munster, Indiana, and played baseball at the University of Michigan. Drafted by the New York Yankees in the eighth round of the June 1986 amateur draft, he immediately established his reputation as a coming star. He won the International League batting title in 1989 and was voted the Yankees' minor league player of the year. The left-handed hitting first baseman-outfielder was coveted by several big league teams, and the Reds were thrilled to get him. Moss Klein wrote that Morris would become another "Yankee Who Got Away."[66] Quinn said, "Morris could be an important part of our 1990 season. His ability to play first and left gives Lou flexibility in his lineup. We have high aspirations for Morris."[67] Piniella planned to platoon Morris and Roomes in left field, although he toyed with idea of shifting Benzinger to the outfield and installing Morris at first base. The acquisition of Billy Hatcher shelved those plans. Hatcher became a regular outfielder, playing in both center and left; Benzinger and Morris shared first base; and Roomes became the odd man out. Morris hit .340 in 107 games in 1990 and starred for the Reds at first base for the next several years. He compiled a .304 batting average in 13 big league seasons.

On January 5, 1990, the Reds signed free agent Paul Noce, an infielder who had been released by the Seattle Mariners. Noce attained the highest batting average of any Reds player in 1990, hitting a perfect 1.000. (He hit a single in his only time at bat.) Musicians who have only one successful record are called "one-hit wonders." Noce was truly Cincinnati's one-hit wonder in 1990. A native of San Francisco, Noce was drafted by the San Diego Padres out of Sequoia High School in Redland City in 1978, but did not sign, preferring to attend Washington State University. San Diego tried again in 1981 and was successful on this attempt. The youngster played for various minor league clubs until making his major league debut for the Chicago Cubs in 1987. He hit only .228 for the Cubs and was returned to the minors. In 1988 and 1989 he played at times for farm clubs of the Cubs, Montreal, and Seattle. After securing him from Seattle, Cincinnati assigned him to their Nashville affiliate, called him up for the one game, and then returned him to the minors. After playing 24 games for Phoenix in the Pacific Coast League in 1991, Noce retired from professional baseball.

At the very end of spring training the Reds made a move to strengthen the left field position. None of the three holdovers from the 1989 squad seemed to fill the bill. Forty-year-old Ken Griffey was winding down a long and distinguished career. Neither Rolando Roomes nor Herm Winningham impressed the new manager. Piniella had considered converting Benzinger into an outfielder, but the first sacker had not yet recovered from his recent injury. Hal Morris was another possibility, but Morris had very little major league experience.

Piniella still needed a right-handed-hitting outfielder. He was pleased with the trade for the lefty Morris, but that did not fulfill his needs. The

Reds had tried to acquire an outfielder who could hit from the right side, but the asking price was too high—pitchers Scott Scudder and Jack Armstrong. Piniella said, "If we had wanted to trade one of those two, we could have obtained a right-handed hitter, but we're not going to do it right now."[68]

Piniella got his righty without giving up a prize pitcher. Bob Quinn came to his manager's rescue. On April 3 Quinn traded Jeff Richardson and pitcher Mike Roesler to the Pittsburgh Pirates for outfielder Billy Hatcher. What a deal! Hatcher filled the bill remarkably well. He could bat in the number two spot in the lineup, could play in either left or center, could run the bases well, and brought a can-do spirit to the Reds. Richardson was a weak-hitting shortstop who played less than 100 games in his major league career, while compiling a lifetime .176 batting average, far below the Mendoza line. Roesler spent parts of three seasons in the majors, winning one game and saving none.

On the other hand, Hatcher was just what the Reds needed in their hunt for a Reds October. Born in Williams, Arizona, on October 4, 1960, Hatcher pitched an 11-inning no-hitter as a high school junior in his home town. Montreal drafted him in the 30th round of the 1979 draft, but Hatcher rejected the Expos in order to attend college. At Yavapai Community College in nearby Prescott, he switched to the outfield and became a junior college All-American. He was drafted by Houston in 1980, but refused to sign. He was selected by the Cubs in the sixth round of the 1981 draft and began his professional career in the Cubs' farm system. He made his big league debut with the Cubs on September 10, 1984. Following the 1985 season, Hatcher was traded to Houston. In the 1986 National League Championship series, he hit one of the most dramatic post-season home runs ever. In the 14th inning of Game 6, he hit a game-winning blast off the Mets' Jesse Orosco to keep the Astros' pennant hopes alive. In 1987 he was suspended for ten games in a bat-corking incident. Maintaining his innocence, Hatcher claimed the doctored bat was one he had borrowed from a teammate. Near the end of the 1989 season, he was traded to Pittsburgh, from whom the Reds acquired him.

Quinn exulted about the trade. "We're adding a player who can help for 1990 for two players who don't figure in our immediate plans.[69] Piniella was equally enthused. "Hatcher gives us speed, depth, and versatility. He is a guy who can bat leadoff."[70] Sweet Lou's facetious response when he was told about the bat-corking incident: "Oh, he's a cheater. I like that, too."[71] Quinn and Piniella were vindicated in their enthusiasm for the acquisition of Hatcher. A solid performer, playing left field or center field as needed, Hatcher was an important cog in the 1990 machine. Although he did not win a Gold Glove Award, he was an excellent fielder at either position. Of course, his record-setting performance in October against Oakland in the World Series will long be remembered in Reds Country. Following a 12-year playing career, Hatcher entered the coaching ranks. After spending several years in the Tampa Bay organization, he returned to the Reds in 2006. He has coached third base and served as bench coach since then, but his most frequent role is first base coach.

With Hatcher in the fold, the Cincinnati Reds were now ready for the 1990 season to begin. The addition of Hatcher readied the Reds for the pennant chase, but Quinn was not through dealing. During the season, Chris Hammond, Terry Lee, and Glenn Sutko were called up from the minors. Alex Trevino was signed as a free agent. In trades Quinn acquired Billy Bates and Glenn Braggs on June 9 and Bill Doran on August 31. Details of these transactions will be provided as the story of the 1990 season unfolds.

At the end of the 1990 season, Bob Quinn was selected by *The Sporting News* to receive the Major League Executive of the Year Award. For his part in making the deals that led to a world's championship, he was a worthy recipient of the honor.

Can Hope Spring Eternal?

The Lockout

Would the lockout of baseball players from spring training camps lead to cancellation of the 1990 season? Would a settlement be reached soon enough that some part of the regular season could be played? Would there be a World Series? Fans were understandably frustrated. This was the fifth work stoppage since 1972. Would adversarial relationships between players and owners destroy the national pastime? The frustration may have been justified, but the fears turned out to be unfounded. Baseball would survive.

Conflict between players and owners was not new; it had gone back well more than a century. Indeed, confrontation between workers and management may be inevitable in a society that professes a belief in both constitutional law and capitalism. Much of the contention had involved salaries and the reserve clause. As early as the 1880s, players were claiming their reputations, abilities, and drawing powers entitled them to higher salaries. Why should management make all the money when the players were the ones who drew the crowds through the gates? The players could not sell their services to clubs willing to pay higher salaries because their playing was restricted to one club by the reserve clause. Adopted by the National League in the 1870s, the provision bound players to one club as long as the club wished to employ them. They could play for no other. As the price for playing professional baseball, the player had to accept involuntary servitude. The club had a weapon to keep salary demands and player conduct in line. Clubs had a property interest in their players, and as property, players could be bought and sold at the whim of their employers.

To fight back, players formed new leagues, but the new circuits always failed or were co-opted into the establishment. The Union Association was formed by owners who objected to the reserve clause. It lasted one year, 1884. The Players' League, formed by the Brotherhood of Professional Baseball Players under the dynamic leadership of John Montgomery Ward, also survived for only one year, 1890. Organized Baseball had a monopoly, and there was no escape from the rule.

The Federal League fared little better, lasting for two season, 1914 and 1915. It was formed by capitalists who wanted a vehicle to share in the profits of the two major leagues. The Federal League ignored the reserve clause and raided the established leagues to woo away some of the game's biggest stars. When Organized Baseball used the reserve clause, among other weapons, to destroy the upstart league, the Baltimore club brought suit in the federal courts, basing their claim upon the Sherman Anti-Trust Act, which used the Interstate Commerce Clause to prohibit unfair competition in restraint of trade. However, in 1922 the Supreme Court of the United States, ignoring evidence to the contrary, ruled that baseball was not involved in interstate commerce.[1]

Efforts by the players to organize yielded few positive results. The Players Protective Association in 1900, the Fraternity of Professional Baseball Players in 1912, and the National Baseball Players Association of the United States in 1922 all failed to achieve much success. The Major League Baseball Players Association, created in 1953, had slight impact during its early years.

Veteran ballplayer Curt Flood mounted a challenge to the reserve clause in 1969. Calling himself "a well-paid slave," Flood said in a letter to the commissioner, "I do not feel I am a piece of property to be bought and sold irrespective of my wishes." A deeply divided Supreme Court ruled against Flood in 1972.[2] The player had lost in the court of law, but he eventually won in the court of public opinion.

By the 1960s, a time of social unrest in the United States, baseball players had tired of waiting for their employers and an unresponsive government to correct what they considered to be economic injustice. Taking a cue perhaps from protest movements in the larger society, they resolved to take action and do something for themselves. In 1966 Marvin Miller, an economist for the United Steel Workers of America, was hired as the executive director of the previously ineffective Major League Baseball Players Association (MLBPA). Miller transformed the association into a genuine labor union. At first, some players were reluctant to unionize. "I didn't think we really realized how strong being united is and how fighting for everyone makes sense," said Darrell Evans. "It took a lot of talking to convince people that we were like everyone else in the workforce. The union was a new thing, and when you try something new, usually there's a lot of opposition to it. We had to get everyone involved enough to realize it was good for everybody."[3]

In 1968 the MLBPA negotiated the first collective bargaining agreement in the history of professional sports. In 1970 the union won an important advance when the next agreement included the used of arbitration to settle disputes. Miller and others were determined to end the reserve clause. The demise of the rule came, not by a lawsuit, but by the actions of two players. Andy Messersmith and Dave McNally, played a full season without contracts, after which an arbitrator ruled them to be free agents. What Messersmith and McNally had done could be emulated by any other player. The reserve clause was dead.

The death of the reserve clause did not end conflict between players and owners. Since Miller's arrival, the players had achieved great advances in the conditions of their employment, but at a cost. These advances came as the result of work stoppages in 1972, 1976, 1981, and 1985. Following the settlement of the 1985 strike, owners reduced their signing of free agents. In 1987 arbitrators found that the owners had engaged in illegal collusion to keep the cost of free agency under control. The adversarial relationship between owners and the union worsened. The current Basic Agreement was scheduled to expire at the end of 1989. Negotiations began on November 29. Little progress was made in the early days of the process. This seems to be the model for negotiations in professional sports. Often they wait until the regular season is almost upon them before the negotiators become serious about their task. On February 15, 1990, the lockout occurred when owners refused to open spring training camps.

The owners came to the negotiations with three proposals:

1. Players would be guaranteed 48 percent of the revenue from ticket sales and radio and television contracts.
2. A pay-for-performance system in which players with less than six years of experience would be paid on the basis of seniority and performance based on statistical formulae.
3. A salary cap limiting the total amount of salary any team could pay to players.

The players came to the table with five proposals:

1. Eligibility for salary arbitration would be restored to players with only two years of major league experience.

2. A raise in the minimum salary from $68,000 to $125,000.

3. Continuation of the current formula fixing owners' contributions to the fund for pensions and health insurance.

4. Triple damages for collusion by the owners and language protecting the union against charges of collusion.

5. An increase in roster size to 25 from the current 24.

As negotiations dragged on, Don Fehr, the union's executive director, complained:

> Some players won't have enough spring training; some won't have enough of a chance to make the team; managers won't have enough time to look at some players.... We were told this was for the fans. Which fans were they thinking of 10 months ago when they decided to have the lockout? And on February 9 when they met in Chicago and decided to go ahead with the lockout, and when it started on February 16? Do the owners really intend to shut this industry down to break the players over half a year of salary arbitration? If the answer is yes, then the whole negotiation has been a charade. If the answer is no, enough already. Let's end it.[4]

Lou Piniella, new manager of the Cincinnati Reds, was distressed about the effect that the lockout would have on spring training and his club's preparation for the 1990 season. "We had planned a lot of fundamental work because I plan to utilize the hit and run, the suicide squeeze, the delayed steal. We might have to work on fundamentals after the season begins."[5]

Bud Selig, chairman of Organized Baseball's Player Relations Committee, responded that the lockout was implemented because of persistent rumors that players would strike during the regular season if a new agreement was not reached. "The lockout was designed to produce an agreement," Selig said.[6]

On March 19, an agreement was reached on a compromise, with both sides making some concessions and both achieving some of their goals. An outsider looking at the terms of the agreement would probably conclude that the union was more successful than the owners. The main points in the agreement were as follows:

1. Eligibility for salary arbitration had become one of the main sticking points. A compromise was eventually reached making about 17 percent of the players with between two and three years of service eligible for arbitration.

2. Minimum salaries were raised to $100,000.

3. The amount of the owners' contribution to the benefit fund was increased.
4. The union demands on collusion were accepted.
5. The roster size was increased to 25.
6. A six-member commission was appointed to study revenue sharing and baseball economics.

The owners lost revenue due to cancellation of half the spring training games and suffered an increase in ill-will by the public, fed up with work stoppages in the national pastime. The players individually lost whatever advantages accrue from a full period of spring training. Sometimes labor strife produces winners and losers. Reds player representative Danny Jackson said the lockout resulted in no winners: "There were no winners or losers. Everyone was a loser. The ones that lost the most were the fans. They're missing baseball."[7]

Many fans agreed that there were no winners, only losers. Disgusted with both the players and the owners, they would agree with the sentiment attributed to Mercutio by Shakespeare, "A plague on both your houses."[8] The reaction of Jacques Barzun to recent work stoppages was perhaps atypical, but certainly illuminating. The reason why one of the game's most eloquent supporters turned against baseball is instructive. In 1954 Barzun had written one of the most lyrical tributes to baseball ever penned: "Whoever wants to know the heart and mind of America had better learn baseball." The cultural historian compared Brooklyn's loss of the 1951 pennant on Bobby Thomson's game-ending home run to a Greek tragedy. "Baseball is Greek in being national, heroic, and broken up in the rivalries of city-states.... That baseball fitly expresses the powers of the nation's mind and body is a merit separate from the glory of being the most active, agile, varied, articulate, and brainy of all group games."[9]

Writing in 1954, Barzun confined himself to the aesthetics of the game on the field. He made no mention of the reserve clause, the trading of players, the power of the owners, the league system, the structure of the game's governance, or any labor-management issues. It seems odd that this very learned man ignored those vital aspects of the sport he idolized. However, Barzun changed his mind about baseball. The strikes and other labor stoppages of the 1970s, 1980s, and 1990s, the use of steroids, and perhaps even the abandonment of Brooklyn by the Dodgers for Los Angeles, fueled his disenchantment. "I've gotten so disgusted with baseball, I don't follow it anymore. I just see the headlines and turn my head in shame from what we have done with our most interesting, best, and healthiest pastime."[10]

Barzun attributed his disappointment with baseball to one thing—greed. "The commercialization is beyond anything that was ever thought of, the overvaluing, really, of the game itself. It's out of proportion to the place an entertainment ought to have," Barzun said. "Other things are similarly commercialized and out of proportion, but for baseball, which is so intimately connected with the nation's spirit and tradition, it's a disaster."[11]

Support for Barzun's views about overcommercialization can be found by observing the actions of Commissioner Fay Vincent, who, fearing that the work stoppage would jeopardize the newly signed television contract, used his influence to end the lockout on terms that the owners believed were unfavorable to them.[12] The 1990 agreement was a stopgap measure. It did not resolve the animosity between owners and players, nor did it insure lasting peace or prevent future work stoppages. A devastating strike was to occur just four years down the road.

Barzun was not the only person disappointed by the lockout. For a century spring training had been the harbinger of springtime for Americans. With the lockout came the probability of no spring training and the possibility of no baseball season to replace the dreary months of winter. In commenting on the seasonal nature of baseball, Bart Giamatti wrote, "Baseball breaks your heart. It is designed to break your heart. The game begins in the spring when everything begins again and it blossoms in the summer, filling the afternoons and evenings, and then as soon as the chill rains come, it stops and leaves you to face the fall alone You can count on it, rely on it to buffer the passage of time, to keep the memory of sunshine and high skies alive, and then just when the days are all twilight, when you need it most it stops. And summer is gone."

So baseball breaks your heart. How do you deal with a broken heart? Like Rogers Hornsby, you look out the window all winter and think about baseball. For this lockout will end. Spring will come again. There will be another baseball season. Lockouts and strikes may mar the horizon, but baseball will be back. Wait 'til next year! There will be another "season of love and laughter, of light and life, and pleasure and pain." For the Bible tells us (with the substitution of but one word) that when "the winter is past, the rain is over and gone, the flowers appear on the earth, the time of the singing of birds is come, and the voice of the umpire is heard in our land."

At least one player was a casualty of the lockout. Cincinnati's first baseman, Todd Benzinger, the only Reds regular not to be on the disabled list in 1989, broke the little finger on his left hand while hitting against a pitching machine in Cincinnati on March 2. Had it not been for the lockout, he would have been in spring training in Plant City, Florida, on that date. To add insult to injury, the Reds refused to pay for the medical expenses resulting from the injury. The club claimed that it was not liable, as the player was working out on his own. "What did the Reds want me to do?" he asked, "report to camp fat and sloppy? I was working to stay in shape for them."[13] Don Fehr had told the players to go hunting and fishing during the lockout, but Benzinger said he had never caught a fish in his life. Benzinger was a native of Dayton, Kentucky, just across the Ohio River from Cincinnati. He played high school baseball in New Richmond, Ohio, and was drafted from there by the Boston Red Sox in the fourth round of the 1981 draft. He spent nearly six years in the Boston minor league system, mostly as an outfielder, before making his major league debut on June 21, 1987. He was traded with Jeff Sellers and minor leaguer Vasquez to Cincinnati on December 13, 1988, in exchange for first baseman Nick Esasky and pitcher Rob Murphy. In 1989 he played 158 games for the Reds, all at first base. He expected to have his finger in a cast for three or four weeks. Whether he would miss any regular season games depended on when (or if) the major league season had an Opening Day.

Several other Reds players turned up early in Plant City. Locked out of the club's facilities, they worked out on the Plant City High School field, always during school hours, so as not to interfere with high school practice.

The regular season was salvaged when agreement was reached to delay its start from April 2 to April 9. In order to get in the full 162 games, the starts of the League Championship Series and World Series had to be delayed. The power of commercialization is illustrated by the necessity of Organized Baseball getting permission from CBS to make this change. After 32 days, the second-longest work stoppage in major league history was finally over.

Baseball is resilient. The game has survived the Black Sox scandal of 1919, strikes and the lockout, the downfall of Pete Rose, and more recently the steroid era.

Ready or not, it was time to start the hunt for a Reds October.

Spring Training

As 1989 calendars were discarded and a new year dawned, baseball publications began making predictions about the 1990 season. The prognosticators, writing in *Athlon's Baseball, The Sporting News Baseball Year-*

book, and *Inside Sports Baseball Preview,* agreed that San Diego would be favored to win the National League West. The consensus was that Cincinnati would finish third, behind either Los Angeles or San Francisco. (In the 1991 edition of Street and Smith's *Baseball Yearbook,* Maury Allen still wondered how the Reds had won in 1990. "The Reds really aren't that good," he wrote.)[14] Most writers agreed that the Reds had a world of talent, but there were too many unanswered questions for the club to be viewed as a legitimate championship contender.

One set of questions had to do with injuries. "Barring injuries the Reds' starting eight is solid though unspectacular," wrote Hal McCoy in the *Dayton Daily News,*" and the pitching is as sturdy as the Berlin Wall, circa 1961."[15] During 1989 the Reds had 13 different players on the disabled list— two of them twice. Seven of the eight starting position players made that

The World Champion 1990 Cincinnati Reds. In front: Team mascot, owner Marge Schott's St. Bernard, Schottzie. Front row: Chris Sabo, Billy Hatcher, Luis Quinones, coach Jackie Moore, coach Tony Perez, manager Lou Piniella, coach Sam Perlozzo, coach Stan Williams, coach Larry Rothschild, Bill Doran, Todd Benzinger. Middle row: Equipment manager Bernie Stowe, batboy Dave Reynolds, Danny Jackson, Hal Morris, Jose Rijo, Terry Lee, Rob Dibble, Glenn Braggs, Paul O'Neill, Joe Oliver, Norm Charlton, Jeff Reed, Eric Davis, traveling secretary Joe Pieper, trainer Larry Starr. Back row: Randy Myers, Tim Layana, Scott Scudder, Jack Armstrong, Ron Oester, Rick Mahler, Keith Brown, Herm Winningham, Mariano Duncan, Barry Larkin, assistant trainer Dan Wright (National Baseball Hall of Fame Library).

list. (The only exception was first baseman Todd Benzinger, and he was injured in a freak accident during the 1990 lockout.) Injuries and distractions caused by the Pete Rose betting scandal were blamed for the Reds' collapse to a 75–87 finish in 1989, their worst record in half a decade. The 1989 Reds were likened to a MASH unit. They had suffered so many injuries that *The Sporting News* quipped: "Hawkeye Pierce might have been able to keep the Reds in contention, but not a Pete Rose or even a Lou Piniella."[16] Rose was gone, but had the players recovered from their injuries? Were key infielders Chris Sabo and Barry Larkin back at full strength after their respective knee and elbow injuries? Benzinger would probably not be available full-time until early May. The club's leading pitcher, Danny Jackson, underwent off-season shoulder surgery and was expected to miss six to eight weeks. Jose Rijo was another question mark on the pitching staff.

The other set of questions had to do with the new manager—Lou Piniella. Although he had undergone two stints as manager of the New York Yankees under George Steinbrenner, and been fired twice, Piniella was new to the National League. He didn't know his players, nor did they know him. Abbreviated spring training did not give Piniella enough time to learn his players' capabilities. *The Sporting News* said "It's a little difficult to go to war when you still aren't sure if you're packing rifles or peashooters."[17]

With the lockout finally over on March 19, 1990, the Cincinnati Reds opened their spring training facility at Plant City, Florida, for the third consecutive year, having moved over from Tampa's Al Lopez Field in 1988. New manager Lou Piniella addressed his players for the first time on March 23. "There are only three things you need to do," he said. "One, show up on time. Two, listen to everything I say. And three, play like hell." He added, "You've got too much talent not to have won by now.... I want to win, too.... And I don't care if you like me."[18]

Todd Benzinger told Cincinnati radio station WLW about the new manager. "Lou has three rules for us—be on time, play heads up, and, uh, I forget the third."[19]

By 1990 spring training had been an annual rite of the season for more than 100 years. Baseball historians disagree about when the practice started. Popular radio commentator Bill Stern was no baseball historian, but he had a story about almost everything. According to Stern, Cap Anson, manager of the Chicago White Stockings, invented the spring training camp in the 1880s.[20] In those days players did not earn enough money from baseball to support themselves all year. Some of the off-season jobs, such as saloon keeping or bartending, did not enhance the physical conditioning of the practitioners. Anson grew tired of seeing his players report in the spring, fat, heavy, and sodden. One spring he ordered his men to report to him in Hot Springs, Arkansas, to "boil out." He put his players, grumbling and complaining, through rigorous physical conditioning. Thus, according to Stern, the ritual of spring training was born.

By 1990 most players kept themselves in physical condition all year. Columnist George Will wrote in 1990 that "the team bends and stretches and generally works on baseball's latest fetish—flexibility."[21] Spring training still has a role in getting bodies ready for the demands of the game.

However, conditioning is but one aspect of spring training. Six weeks from mid–February until Opening Day provides an opportunity for new players to try out for roster spots, for the managers to determine the starting lineups, and for building the disparate players into a cohesive unit. Pitchers and catchers normally arrive about a week or more before the other players, because it takes hurlers longer to get their arms in shape. Hitters need to take batting practice to regain their timing. Infield practice is one of the most important parts of pre-season. Infielders are constantly told: "Don't mess up a play by thinking about it. Let your instincts take over." Actually, making the right play is not instinctive. It is learned behavior, learned by taking "reps" over and over again during spring mornings. Pitchers learn how to cover first base, and fielders learn which foot to put on the bag, how to make a throw to the right side of the base, and a myriad other things by constant practice.

For the Cincinnati Reds in 1990, spring training served another very important function. It gave the players an opportunity to adjust to a new manager, and the manager a chance to adjust to new players and to a new league. Lou Piniella had played major league baseball and had managed before, but never in the National League. With spring training reduced from its normal six weeks to a mere 3 weeks and the exhibition schedule slashed from 30 games to 16, would the players and manager get to know each other?

Piniella said the loss of spring training time was a severe blow to the Reds. "Losing time really hurts us because as a new manager I planned to have my players get acquainted with me and my system," he said. "It is important for us to get off to a good start. I wanted our players to realize they have a good ball club here and can win this division. With a fast start, we could run away with it. Now we might still be working on fundamentals when the season begins."[22]

In assessing his club, Piniella said," It might look like we are a little thin at catching, but we are not going to go looking for anyone. Oliver proved a thing or two last year, and we can depend on Jeff Reed to do a steady job."[23] The veteran Reed had earned a reputation as a solid defensive catcher. Born in Joliet, Illinois, on November 12, 1962, he was drafted out of high school by the Minnesota Twins in the first round of the 1980 amateur draft. At the age of 17, he played his first professional game for the Elizabethton (Tennessee) Twins in the Appalachian Rookie League. Five years later he made his big league debut with Minnesota. He was traded to Montreal and acquired by Cincinnati in 1988. The Reds released him after the 1992 season. Reed then played for several different clubs in the majors and minors. During his career of more than 20 years, he was mainly a backup catcher. By 2014 he was a coach back where his professional career started, in Elizabethton.

Players who allowed themselves to be quoted were supportive of the new manager. No surprise there. Rick Mahler ventured an opinion: "Last night I got to watch him in the dugout. I was impressed because he noticed everything. He was into the game.[24] A lot of managers let their coaches move people around. He seemed to control the game." Other players compared the 1990 clubhouse to that under their departed manager, Pete Rose. Rolando Roomes said: "Things are real loose. You don't have that Pete Rose thing going on. That's the biggest reason."[25] Ron Oester chimed in: "It's just baseball this year. There are no distractions. It's easier to get your work in. Everybody wants to talk about baseball this year. They don't want to talk about Pete."[26] Later Oester observed, "The team lacked discipline under Pete. He was too nice. He didn't have many rules and those he had were not enforced…. People took advantage of him."[27]

For players who didn't want to talk about Pete, a lot of them talked about Pete. Shortly after the season began, Rob Dibble said: "For a change, this year we are a team. We are the Reds. We finally have our own identity. When Pete was the manager, we were always known either as Pete Rose and the Reds or as Pete Rose's Reds. Now Lou is the manager. He's not a hero. He's not a legend. He's just the boss."[28] Chris Sabo opined that the biggest difference in the approaches of Rose and Piniella was that one of them used a "hands-off" approach, and the other one was now using a "hands-on" approach. "There's not a bit of malice in what I have to say, but, simply, Rose, who was a great hitter—had trouble teaching others how to hit. Lou is able to analyze hitting and he can teach you how to relate to other things you might do…. He can show you how you're back too far in the box, or if you're off-balance … things like that."[29]

Things did not always go smoothly between Piniella and his players during spring training. During the winter Ron Oester read in a newspaper that Piniella had awarded the second base job to Mariano Duncan. Oester was understandably miffed. "What really ticks me off is that he hasn't seen either of us play and he makes a decision like that. I'd like to know how I lost my job."[30] No reports ever surfaced as to how Piniella mollified the veteran second sacker. Duncan started at second base on Opening Day. Oester replaced him in the eighth inning. During the season, Duncan appeared in 125 games, Oester in 64.

Ron Oester was born in Cincinnati on May 5, 1956. After playing baseball at Withrow High School, the 18-year-old shortstop was drafted by the Reds in the ninth round of the 1974 amateur draft. His professional career started in Billings of the Pioneer Rookie League that summer, and he played in Tampa and Trois Rivieres before being promoted to the Reds' 40-man roster in November 1976. "The kid has a great arm and great hands," said farm director Joe Bowen. "He has developed into an even better prospect than we originally thought he'd be."[31] Being on the roster didn't mean he would play in the majors right away, but it proved the club thought enough of him to protect him from being drafted. He was thrilled to be assigned to Indianapolis in the Class AAA International League in 1977. The switch-hitter spent most of the next three years in the Indiana capital. In 1978 Oester was a September call-up. The 20-year-old rookie made his major league debut on September 10. Oester played only six games for the Reds that season and six games again in 1979. He became a regular with the Reds in 1980 and spent the rest of his 13-year major league career with his home town club, playing second base most of the time, with occasional stints at shortstop or third base. He played his final game on October 3, 1990, at the age of 34.

After retiring as a player, Oester remained in the Reds' organization for many years, serving in various capacities. He managed the Reds' farm club in Chattanooga in 1992. He was a member of the coaching staff in 1993 and again from 1997–2001. He was working in the Phillies' player development program in 2003, when the Reds brought him back as coordinator of the on-field minor league operations. Later Oester was employed as an infield instructor for the Chicago White Sox. In 2014 he was elected to the Cincinnati Reds Hall of Fame.

Mariano Duncan was born in San Pedro de Macoris, Dominican Republic, on March 13, 1963. A six-foot, 160-pounder, the versatile right-hander could play in the infield or outfield. The Los Angeles Dodgers signed the 18-year-old free agent on January 7, 1982, and sent him to the minor leagues for seasoning. He made his major league debut at the age of 22, playing second base for the Dodgers against the Houston Astros on April 9, 1985. The Reds acquired Duncan on July 18, 1989. He immediately made an impact.

In 1990 Duncan had his best year at the plate, hitting above .300 for the first of two times in his major league career, while appearing in 125 games and playing second base, shortstop, and left field. He missed 15 games when he pulled a muscle in his rib cage while straining to reach first base on an infield hit against the Cubs on May 13. He was also suspended for one game and fined for throwing his batting helmet and touching umpire Mark Hirschbeck during a game against Pittsburgh. On July 4 he suffered strained neck muscles when the taxi he was riding en route to Montreal's Olympic Stadium was rear-ended by a bus. He was taken by ambulance to a hospital and fitted with a neck brace. He missed only three games before he was back in the lineup. Duncan led the National League in triples and hit .306, but had trouble against right-handed pitchers. He hit .410 against lefties, but only .227 against righties. The Reds granted him free agency on October 30, 1991. He signed with the Phillies and later played for the Reds again, the Yankees, and the Blue Jays. He played his last major league game for Toronto on September 17, 1997, but he was not through with baseball. He played in Japan in 1998. His final game as a professional player was with Calgary in the Pacific Coast League in 1999. He coached in the minor leagues from 2003–2005, for the Los Angeles Dodgers from 2006–2010, and in the minors since then. In 2014 he was hitting coach for the Chicago Cubs' Class A affiliate in Daytona.

Toward the end of spring training, Rick Mahler expressed concern over his role on the 1990 team. A Texan, Mahler had been drafted by the Atlanta Braves in 1975 as an amateur free agent. After four years in the minors, the righty made his major league debut with the Braves in 1979, pitching almost exclusively as a starter. Atlanta released him after the 1988 season and he signed with Cincinnati. He had been relegated to bullpen duty late in the 1989 season, and he didn't want it to happen again. "If I don't start here, I hope I get an opportunity to start somewhere else," the veteran said. "My role is as a starter. And I will ask for a trade.... I'd love to stay here because it's a great team with a chance to win everything. But I want to stay here as a starter. It's the only role I fit. If they feel the young guys are ready to step in, okay, I'm ready to move on. I'm sure there are clubs out there I can help."[32] He was not challenging the authority of general manager Quinn or field manager Piniella. "They've never seen me," he said. "They don't know what I can do."[33] He was merely asking for a chance. As it turned out, he made 16 starts and relieved 19 times during the 1990 season. He was released at the end of the season and divided 1991 between Atlanta and Montreal before retiring at the age of 38.

Around the first of April, another controversy erupted over Piniella's handling of the pitching staff. Ron Robinson became irate when he learned that Tom Browning would start the fourth game of the season in Atlanta. Claiming that pitching coach Stan Williams had promised him the start, Robinson exploded. "I confronted Stan and he confirmed it. I went from number four man in one day to not knowing if I even have a spot on the club."[34] Robinson insisted that he would not pitch in relief and said he wanted to be traded if he wasn't used as a starter. Why Williams had made such a promise is a mystery. Decisions about who starts a game are normally the province of the manager, not the pitching coach. At any rate, the Reds let it be known who was boss. Quinn said the pitcher should not put his personal program ahead of the interests of the team: "If he has a problem, let him work it out himself."[35] Piniella was more blunt: "First of all, no player tells us when or where they are going to play. I'm the one who makes decisions on who pitches. Pitchers are not going to tell me."[36] To emphasize his point, Piniella kept Robinson on the bench for the first 14 days of the season. He used him in relief in the 15th game. The Reds honored the disgruntled hurler's wish to be traded. They gave him a chance to showcase his talents in an exhibition game against their Nashville farm club on April 23, with scouts from three major league teams in attendance. "That's pressure," Robinson said. "My hands were sweating, and that never happens to me. I was thinking what would happen if I got hit hard by our Triple-A team. I haven't known scouts were in the stands specifically to watch me since high school."[37] The right-hander handled the pressure well, hurling three scoreless innings and striking out six. It was not until June 9, however, that a deal was worked out, with the Reds trading Robinson (with minor leaguer Bob Sebra) to the Milwaukee Brewers for Billy Bates and Glenn Braggs.

With only a short time available for spring training, new players had difficulty proving they belonged in the big leagues. Non-roster invitees Chris Brown and Neil Allen did not survive the cut. Although technically a rookie, Hal Morris was assured of a spot on the roster, leaving only one player without previous major league experience who made the team— Tim Layana.

On a non-baseball note, the Reds discovered that a retaining pool just outside their Plant City spring training facility was home not only to an alligator but also to a number of poisonous snakes. Pitcher Luis Vasquez captured eight water moccasins and clubbed them to death with a baseball bat. Another time, reliever Randy Myers dangled a snake from a squeegie and terrified his teammates by carrying it into the clubhouse.[38]

Alligators and snakes aside, Piniella did not find Plant City a very exciting place. The manager joked: "The gourmet shop's cheese of the week is Velveeta. The all-night diner closes at 4:30 in the afternoon."[39]

Pitcher Tim Birtsas, who had been traded by Oakland to Cincinnati in 1987, was another who was not enthralled by the Plant City training site: "I trained in Arizona when I was with Oakland, and it's different from Florida. In Arizona, they don't have four-foot roaches. I just don't like roommates that don't pay rent."[40]

Hot-Wire Start

Opening Day

Opening Day in baseball is a day like no other. Sportswriter George Vecsey summed it up: "There is no other sports event like Opening Day in baseball, in the sense of beating back the forces of darkness and the National Football League."[1] Actually, America's fascination with Opening Day goes back far beyond the time when there was a National Football League. Not only writers and fans, but players also shared the feeling that Opening Day was special. Hall of Fame pitcher Early Wynn was quoted as saying: "An opener is not like any other game. There's that little extra excitement, a faster beating of the heart. You have that anxiety to get off to a good start, for yourself and for the team."[2] Fellow Hall of Famer Joe DiMaggio said: "You always get a special kick on Opening Day, no matter how many you go through. You look forward to it like a birthday party when you're a kid. You think something wonderful is going to happen."[3]

If Opening Day was a special day throughout America, it was more than that in Cincinnati. Greg Rhodes quoted former Reds manager Sparky Anderson as saying: "It's a holiday—a baseball holiday! Ain't no other place in America got that!"[4]

For more than 100 years, Cincinnati had almost always opened the season at home. Only twice (1877 and 1966) had the Reds made their debut on the road, both times because rainouts cancelled the scheduled home opener. The tradition had become so firmly established that many fans believed the first game of the season had always been played in the Queen City before Opening Day in other cities. This is not quite true. Some seasons Cincinnati did open a day earlier than other clubs, perhaps to honor the long tradition of professional baseball in the baseball town. Some years the Reds shared the honor with Washington, which gave the President of the United States an opportunity to throw out the ceremonial first pitch of the new season. (In 1910 Cincinnati native William Howard Taft became the nation's first chief executive to participate in that ceremony.) In some other years several clubs opened the season on the same day. The 1990 schedule, constructed before the lockout, called for six Opening Day games on April 2, one in Cincinnati and the others in Baltimore, Chicago, Detroit, Los Angeles, and San Francisco. The lockout threw that schedule out the window. The revamped schedule had Cincinnati opening the 1990 season in the Houston Astrodome on April 9.

Would Cincinnati's famous Opening Day parade become a casualty of the lockout? The Reds had begun promoting Opening Day aggressively in the 1890s. Parades and other pre-game activities became a part of the opener each year. In the first parade there were three streetcars—one carrying the Reds, the second for the visiting team, and the third for a marching band. Soon fans took over the parades. Waving flags, singing, using noisemakers of various kinds, the fans paraded through town in decorated horse-drawn wagons. In order to accommodate overflow crowds, the Reds began putting up temporary seats in the outfield. By 1900, Opening Day had become, in the minds of the fans, a public holiday.

In 1920 the celebration took a giant step forward. Shopkeepers in the area around Findlay Market in Cincinnati's Over-the-Rhine district began sponsoring the event. The parade started featuring red convertibles, pickup trucks, high school marching bands, and politicians galore. When Marge Schott assumed control of the Reds, she used her connections with the Cincinnati Zoo (she was on the board of directors) to add elephants and other animals borrowed from the zoo to give the parade a circus atmosphere. One Opening Day an elephant delivered the ball to Sparky Anderson so he could throw out the first pitch.

What would the changed 1990 schedule do to this hallowed tradition? On March 26 *The Sporting News* carried a story in which parade, officials were quoted as canceling the event. In order to stage the parade they said they needed several weeks of planning, and the date of Cincinnati's home opener had not yet been announced. Marge Schott vowed to provide some sort of parade to replace the canceled one. "The parade is so much a part of Cincinnati and means so much to our fans that I'm going to do my best to see that there is an Opening Day parade in downtown Cincinnati. It's a primo thing here."[5]

By April 2 the Findlay area merchants resolved to try to reorganize the parade for April 17, which had been announced as the date of the Reds' first home game. They were successful. Jeff Gibbs, coordinator of the Findlay Market Parade, told a Cincinnati newspaper, "It's going to be the biggest one we've ever had."[6] He said they had lined up 130 entries, including high school bands, floats, fire engines, and lots of politicians.

The weatherman did not cooperate with parade organizers. April 17 dawned cool and foggy. A light rain fell in the early morning hours. That did not deter the participants. Their motto might have been: "You can rain on my parade. But you can't stop it." And the parade went on as planned despite .19 inches of rain and a chilly wind blowing from the west and northwest. Lockout or no lockout, rain or no rain, this baseball town was determined to have a festive parade on Opening Day. Tradition demanded it, and Queen City residents and visitors were eager to live up to the long-established customs of the day.

After sweeping the three-game opening set in Houston and a three-game sweep in Atlanta, the Reds were ready to treat their fans to some championship-caliber baseball. The hunt for a Reds October was well under way.

Major League Clubs and Divisions in 1990

National League East
Chicago Cubs
Montreal Expos
New York Mets
Philadelphia Phillies
Pittsburgh Pirates
St. Louis Cardinals

National League West
Atlanta Braves
Cincinnati Reds
Houston Astros
Los Angeles Dodgers
San Diego Padres
San Francisco Giants

American League East
Baltimore Orioles
Boston Red Sox
Cleveland Indians
Detroit Tigers
Milwaukee Brewers
New York Yankees
Toronto Blue Jays

American League West
California Angels
Chicago White Sox
Kansas City Royals
Minnesota Twins
Oakland Athletics
Seattle Mariners
Texas Rangers

April

In the first month of the 1990 season, pitching was the name of the game for the Cincinnati Reds. This should have come as no surprise. According to general manager Bob Quinn, Lou Piniella's reputation as an effective handler of pitchers was a major reason he was hired as skipper.[7] Piniella took the managerial reins of a club that was rich in pitching. "This club has good pitching," he said. "They have a wealth of good, young arms.

This is a good ball club I'm coming to. It's not like I'm going into a rebuilding process. This is a ball club that can win."[8] Pinella's observation was correct. The Reds did have a good young pitching staff, and they had enhanced it through trades during the offseason. Piniella hoped to carry ten pitchers on his staff—four in the rotation, three relievers, and three who might be used as spot starters or in long relief as the situation demanded. When it appeared that Danny Jackson would not be available during the first few weeks of the season, top contenders for the rotation were Jack Armstrong, Tom Browning, Rick Mahler, Jose Rijo, and Scott Scudder.

For only the third time in history, the Reds opened their season on the road. It was a night game on April 9 at Houston's Astrodome. Piniella had an easy time selecting his starting pitcher for the opener. Browning was clearly the ace of the Cincinnati staff, and he was primed to face off against Mike Scott, who had won 20 games for the Astros the previous year.

Born in Casper, Wyoming, on April 28, 1960, Browning is considered the Cowboy State's all-time best baseball player.[9] Drafted by the Reds out of Tennessee Wesleyan College in the ninth round of the 1982 amateur draft, Browning advanced rapidly through the Cincinnati farm system and made his major league debut on September 9, 1984.

Cincinnati's Opening Day pitcher in 1990, Tom Browning was considered the ace of the staff. As a rookie in 1985, he had become the first Reds rookie to win 20 games in a season since 1899. His perfect game against the Dodgers in 1988 remains the only perfect game ever pitched by a Cincinnati hurler. In 1990 Browning posted 15 regular season victories, plus one more each in the National League Championship Series and the World Series (National Baseball Hall of Fame Library).

In 1985 he was a 20-game winner for the Reds, the only Cincinnati rookie to gain that distinction since Noodles Hahn in 1899.[10] On September 9, 1988, Browning pitched a perfect game in defeating the Los Angeles Dodgers, 1–0, at Riverfront Stadium. It remains the only perfect major league game ever pitched by a Cincinnati hurler.

Despite their lofty credentials, neither Browning nor Scott made it through six innings. With the Reds trailing, 4–2, Browning was lifted for a pinch-hitter in the top of the fifth. The skipper made a fortuitous choice by sending outfielder Ken Griffey to the plate. The veteran delivered a sacrifice fly, driving in Joe Oliver from third base and cutting the deficit to one run. Tim Layana came in to pitch in the bottom of the frame and set the Astros down without a hit, although walking one, in his major league debut. Mariano Duncan tied the game, 4–4, by plating Paul O'Neill with a line drive single in the top of the sixth. Norm Charlton shut out the Astros from the sixth through the eighth innings. Rob Dibble did the same in the ninth. In the tenth Dibble gave up two hits, and Piniella brought in Randy Myers to put out the fire. At the end of the tenth inning, the score was still tied, 4–4. The relievers had come through for Sweet Lou. Barry Larkin broke the tie with a bases-loaded triple in the 11th inning and scored on a single by Eric Davis. Randy Myers picked up the win by shutting out Houston in the bottom of the inning for an 8–4 Reds triumph.

Browning had twice hit Glenn Davis by pitches during his stint on the mound, and Myers plunked the Houston first baseman in the 11th stanza. Davis thus tied a major league record by being hit by pitches three times in a game. Davis said that's not the kind of record you want to have. "All the pitches were breaking pitches, and I don't think they were throwing at me. At least I hope not. If it keeps up, it's something I might have to do something about."[11] When a reporter told Myers that the Astros weren't happy about Davis being hit three times, Myers boasted about the speed with which the Reds relievers could throw the ball and said if it comes down to a retaliation war, to just let him know. The reporter suggested that sounds pretty nasty. "Well, we're pretty nasty guys," Myers said.[12] Is that how the Nasty Boys appellation got started? Norm Charlton said it was.[13] But there are other explanations. Pitches that are especially difficult to hit are called filthy or nasty. The Nasty Boys had those pitches in their arsenal. Hal McCoy's version is probably the most accurate.[14] The sportswriter wrote that the nickname became attached to the Cincinnati relievers during spring training at Plant City when Myers was watching Rob Dibble mix 88-mph sliders with 98-mph fastballs. "Man, that's some nasty stuff," Myers reportedly said. So the trio adopted the name, Nasty Boys. However, the term was copyrighted by NBC for use in a television series about a Las Vegas police unit. So Myers' agent had to get permission from NBC for the Reds pitchers to use the name.

There was little doubt that bad blood now existed between Cincinnati and Houston. Cincinnati won the second game, 3–2, with Layana gaining his first major league win in relief of Rijo and Myers picking up his first save as a Red. Further unpleasantness erupted during this game. Astros lefthander Jim Deshaies hit Barry Larkin and narrowly missed Eric Davis. Reliever Charley Kerfeld barely missed hitting Davis in the ear. "Pitching inside is part of the game," Davis said. "But that ball Kerfeld threw was right at my head and that's a whole different world. When you throw at my head, you better be ready to fight because I'm not gonna take one on the head. That's my career. I'll fight before I let somebody mess with my career."[15] He added that a team would have to be crazy to mess with the Reds. "We got three guys in the bullpen, who are wild, throw 100, and are crazy enough not to care where their pitches go."[16]

Eric Davis was expressing the code of baseball. Pitching inside to intimidate batters is acceptable; headhunting is not. Great pitchers Bob Gibson, Don Drysdale, and Randy Johnson were notorious for throwing inside to keep the hitters off-balance and to capitalize on their fear of being hit. The fear is real and well-founded. According to sports analyst Tim Kurkjian, "There is nothing in sports as terrifying and dangerous as a baseball flying at your head at 95mph. When it hits you, those red seams bore into your skin like the teeth of a buzz saw, leaving an imprint of the ball for days, even weeks. If it hits you in the face, God help you."[17]

Most hitters will not admit to being afraid, because showing fear is inviting pitchers to throw inside and capitalize on the fear factor. Active players are reluctant to admit to being afraid, but former players, managers, and announcers readily talked about it to Kurkjian.[18] Joe Torre: "Fear of the ball is the deep dark secret in baseball that players won't talk about." Bobby Valentine: "For all humanoids, those who breathe, when someone throws a baseball from sixty feet, and throws it hard, the first thought is always, 'Do I duck or swing?'" Dusty Baker: "Fear of the ball is real." Larry Parrish: "It is there all the time, with every batter. Anyone who says he has never been afraid up there … is lying." Ken Harrelson: "I played nine years with fear. Everyone has it."

The fear was well founded. One player, Ray Chapman, was killed when hit by a pitch in 1920. Others, including Tony Conigliaro, Dickie

Thon, and Robby Thompson, had their careers ended or shortened by taking a ball in the face.

Tom Verducci wrote in *Sports Illustrated* about the difficulties a batter faces.

> A 90-mph fastball will get to home plate in 400 milliseconds, but the hitter needs 200 of those to see the ball, send the image to the brain, and process its speed, spin, and location. The swing itself takes 150 milliseconds—literally the blink of an eye. That leaves a scant 50 milliseconds to decide whether to swing [or duck]. To make matters worse, the batter must make his decision without actually being able to see the ball at the final instant. The eye can't follow an object moving that fast that close, so a hitter cannot track the pitch in its last five feet before it reaches the plate. Here is what that means: The batter loses sight of the baseball when the pitcher wants the pitch to break off its path.[19]

That explains why batters live in constant dread of being drilled in the head.

John Updike wrote that baseball looks easy until you step up to the plate "and see the fastball sailing inside an inch from your chin."[20] A good hitter can pick up the spin on the pitch and determine whether it is a fastball. He can tell whether the pitch is coming inside, but the pitch can swerve in the last tiny fraction of a second. If Verducci is correct, the batter cannot know whether the pitch will miss his chin by an inch, by three inches, or hit him smack in the face.

Pitchers who throw deliberately at a batter's head with the intent to do bodily harm are called headhunters, and they are pariahs. The Nasty Boys were nasty enough, but they were not headhunters. They wanted to intimidate hitters, not injure them. Astros pitchers were of the same ilk. Apparently the Astros felt they had attained sufficient revenge in game two of the series. The war of inside pitches did not escalate, and the Reds got out of town without any more hit batsmen on either side. Game three saw no untoward behavior on either side.

In the series finale Armstrong shut down the Astros on three hits in six innings, before turning the game over to Mahler, who preserved the shutout, 5–0, and gained credit for the save. Armstrong was the most pleasant surprise for the Reds early in the 1990 season. A native of New Jersey, born in Englewood on March 7, 1965, Armstrong had been drafted out of the University of Oklahoma in the first round by the Reds in 1987, but so far had failed to live up to his early promise. He made his major league debut for the Reds in 1988 and failed to attain a winning record either as a rookie or in his sophomore season. He was known more for his workout routine than for his performance on the mound. Armstrong would run up to eight miles a day, swim laps for 30 minutes, and then engage in weight training. After little success in his first two seasons, the "All-American Boy" unexpectedly won eight of his first nine decisions in the spring of 1990. By mid-season he had a record of 11 wins and three losses. He was named as the starting pitcher in the annual All-Star Game. It was the highlight of his career. He pitched two innings, gave up one hit, and shut down the powerful American League lineup. After that it was all downhill. Soon afterwards he developed arm trouble and won only one more game in 1990, finishing at 12–9. He never had another winning season in the majors. A torn rotator cuff led to his early exit from The Show at the age of 29.

Conventional wisdom held that the short spring training necessitated by the lockout would hurt pitchers more than hitters, as hurlers need more time to round into form. *The Sporting News* supported this view in an article written after the first three days of the season: "Comparisons of 1989 vs. 1990 suggest that hurlers clearly missed the conditioning they would have received during a normal spring training."[21] Three games is a small sample size on which to base a generalization. The 1990 Cincinnati Reds were certainly an exception to the rule, if indeed it was a rule. In their first three games of the season Cincinnati starters posted a 1.55 earned run average, while the relief corps chimed in with a 0.64 ERA. In April, the Reds' pitching staff won 13 games, lost three, and had an ERA of 3.23. The National League as a whole had a 3.79 ERA over the entire season, so the Reds' start looks good by comparison. Of course, the relievers deserved much of the credit for Cincinnati's great start. They had eight successful saves and no blown saves in April. During the first three games of the season, Randy Myers won one game and saved another. Grumbling about the Myers-Franco swap diminished accordingly.

After the three-game sweep in Houston, the Reds journeyed to Atlanta, for a scheduled four-game series, one of which was rained out. While in Georgia, it appeared that Scudder would not break into the Reds' starting rotation, so the right-hander was optioned to Nashville. "It is best for Scudder to pitch every five days," Piniella said. "If we need a pitcher, we can go down and get a good one."[22] Before the end of the season, Scudder was back with the parent club in time to participate in 21 games, including ten as a starter.

The Reds swept three games in Atlanta, bringing their streak in six wins in a row. The team returned from their highly successful road trip, ready to play their home opener at Riverfront Stadium on April 17. Originally scheduled as a night contest, the game was moved to 2:06 in the afternoon, timed to start just after completion of the Opening Day Parade, so that parade participants and observers would not have to wait hours for baseball activity to begin. The fans responded; 45,000 streamed into Riverfront Stadium for the game against the San Diego Padres. Cincinnati was a baseball town, and nothing could stop Cincinnatians from attending a baseball game on Opening Day—not the disappointing 1989 season, nor the lockout, nor opening on the road, nor the delayed Opening Day at home; not even the dreary weather (50 degrees, with overcast skies). The rain had stopped well before game time. Riverfront Stadium was well-drained. Although the artificial turf in the outfield was still wet, the playing surface posed no problems for the fielders.

The fans were rewarded with an exciting baseball game. The Reds scored two runs in the second inning. Todd Benzinger led off the frame with a base on balls; Joe Oliver followed with another walk, and Mariano Duncan knocked Benzinger in with a single for the first run of the ballgame. After two strikeouts, Billy Hatcher plated Oliver to give the Reds a 2–0 lead. Tom Browning and relievers Norm Charlton and Randy Myers made the two runs hold up. The Reds won, 2–1, their seventh victory without a defeat. Oliver had an outstanding defensive game for the Reds, showing that he was a catcher not to be run on. In the first inning he threw out the speedy Roberto Alomar on an attempted steal. In the fourth inning Oliver gunned down the future Hall of Famer for the second time. Over the season he threw out 35 percent of would-be basestealers, the second-highest percentage in the league. Although he hit only .231 in 121 games, his work behind the plate helped him earn his place as the club's number one catcher.

Joe Oliver was born in Memphis, Tennessee, on July 24, 1965. He attended high school in Orlando, Florida, where he starred as a catcher for the baseball team. He was drafted by the Cincinnati Reds in the second round of the 1983, amateur draft. The 17-year-old, right-handed catcher wasted no time in signing with the Reds. He started his professional career with the Billings Mustangs in the Pioneer League in late June and moved steadily up the chain. In mid-season 1989 he was called up from Nashville to join the parent club. Oliver made his major league debut at the age of 23 on July 15, 1989, in front of 34,997 fans at Riverfront Stadium in a Saturday game against the Montreal Expos. Batting sixth in the order, Oliver came up in the first inning and singled to right field off Mark Langston, for a hit in his first major league at-bat. He collected his first major league RBI with a sacrifice fly in the third inning. Oliver had solidified his place on the club.

The highlight of his season's hitting came in Game 2 of the World Series against the Oakland Athletics. Oliver drove in the winning run by lacing a single down the left field line in the tenth inning to score Billy Bates from second base. The hit helped propel the Reds to their four-game sweep.

Oliver's best season with the bat for the Reds came in 1992. In November 1994, he was released by the Reds. He signed as a free agent with the Milwaukee Brewers in March 1995. He played only one season for the Brewers and then was on the move again. In the seven years from 1995–2001, Oliver played for seven different major league clubs. His final major game came on October 6, 2001. He returned to Florida and became a high school baseball coach.

Riverfront Stadium, the scene of the action, had been built in 1970 to replace the venerable Crosley Field. The taxpayers of Cincinnati and Hamilton County helped finance the new stadium, mainly in a successful effort to lure Paul Brown and his National Football League club to the

In a successful effort to lure a professional football club to the Queen City, Riverfront Stadium was erected in 1970 to replace venerable Crosley Field. A multipurpose stadium, with artificial turf (and with all of the advantages and disadvantages of such a surface), it was home to the Reds for 30 years (National Baseball Hall of Fame Library).

city. As the name implies, Riverfront was on the Ohio River at Broadway and East Second Street, not far from a bridge connecting the Queen City to the Kentucky cities of Covington and Newport. In one direction fans could see the Cincinnati skyline, dominated by the Carew Tower. In another direction, across the Ohio River, rose the green hills of Kentucky. Riverfront was a multi-purpose stadium, as were many others being built in that era. Its announced seating capacity was 60,398 for football and 56,759 for baseball. The dimensions varied slightly over the years, but the distances were generally about 330 feet down the foul lines and 400 feet in center field.[23] It was considered to be a hitter-friendly ball park. The *Baseball Encyclopedia* awarded it the third highest hitters' park factor among the 12 stadia in the National League.[24]

The playing field was blessed or cursed, depending upon one's views, by having an AstroTurf surface. AstroTurf had been developed in Houston in 1966 because natural grass would not grow in a domed stadium. Riverfront was not domed, of course, so why AstroTurf there? Advocates said that balls would take truer bounces on artificial surfaces. Dave Concepcion took advantage of the surface to make his pegs to first base on the bounce, a practice that was soon copied by other middle infielders, even those playing on natural surfaces. Little thought was given to the damage accruing to the legs and knees of players, playing day after day on the hard surface. Lou Piniella was aware of the problem and was not enamored with artificial turf: "On turf, you have to rest people," he said. "You can't run 'em out there every day. You have to have people on the bench who can play. If you can get 145 games out of a guy in today's environment, you've gotten a full season.[25] (By that reckoning Piniella got a full season out of three players in 1990—Larkin, Sabo, and O'Neill.)

A circle in left-center commemorated Pete Rose's record-setting 4,192nd hit. It was erased in1989 after Rose was suspended permanently from baseball. (His hit is now memorialized in the Rose Garden between Great American Ball Park and the site of the former Riverfront Stadium.) In 1996 the arena's name was changed from Riverfront Stadium to Cinergy Field in a sponsorship deal with the Cinergy Corporation, formed by a merger of Cincinnati Gas and Electric and two other utility companies. Most fans, however, continued to refer to the stadium as Riverfront.

By the end of the 20th century, multi-purpose stadia had fallen out of favor. Riverfront Stadium hosted both the football Bengals and the baseball Reds until it was replaced by Paul Brown Stadium and the Great American Ball Park in 2000 and 2005, respectively.

Cincinnati won their first two home games of the 1990 season by defeating San Diego twice. In the second game on April 18, Danny Jackson made his first start of the season. He was hit hard, but the Reds had a great day at the plate. In the seventh inning, with Cincinnati leading, 9–7, Rob Dibble was brought in to protect the lead. The San Diego manager, Jack McKeon, complained about the slit sleeves in Dibble's uniform top. He claimed that the sleeves flapped when Dibble pitched, distracting the hitters. Umpire John McSherry ordered the pitcher to change the shirt. Dibble went to the dugout, borrowed a jersey from pitching coach Stan Williams, returned to the mound, finished the game, and picked up a save, as the Reds won their eighth game in a row. Dibble thought McKeon's protest was unwarranted. The pitcher said he slits his sleeves so they won't be too tight around his arms. "I've been doing it for two years in the big leagues, and nobody ever asked about it before," he said.[26]

In Jackson's next start, on April 29 against Montreal, he was hit on his left forearm by a line drive and was placed on the disabled list the next day with a severe bruise. He won only six games in 1990. The lefty had been Cincinnati's best pitcher in 1988, when he led the league with 23 wins. (No Reds pitcher won 20 in a season again until Johnny Cueto notched 20 wins in 2014.) He had been injured in 1989 and underwent off-season shoulder surgery. Although born in San Antonio, Texas, on January 5, 1962, Jackson played high school and junior college ball in Colorado. He was drafted out of the University of Oklahoma by the Kansas City Royals in the first round (first overall pick) of the January 1982 secondary draft. He made his major league debut for Kansas City on September 11, 1983, at the age of 23. Jackson had a losing record (37–49) in his years with the Royals, but the Reds saw potential in him. Cincinnati obtained him along with Angel Salazar in November 1987 for Ted Power and Kurt Stillwell. He immediately blossomed, but after 1988 Jackson never had another 20-win season. However, he remained in the majors until August 1997, winning a total of 112 major league games.

After the San Diego series, Atlanta came to town. The Reds won their ninth consecutive game by beating the Braves on April 21. That could have been the tenth in a row had not the weather gods thrown the Reds a curve ball. (The Reds had been leading by a fair margin when one of the earlier games was called because of rain before the fifth inning, thus washing out a potential Reds win.)

Excitement reigned in Reds country. Seemingly everybody knew that the Reds had one of the best-ever beginnings to a season. In all of the National League's long history, only four clubs had ever begun the season with a longer winning streak. Players talked about how they would celebrate if the winning streak continued. Some promised to shave their heads if they won ten in a row. Barry Larkin and Eric Davis both brought clippers to their lockers before the April 22 game. If the Reds won, they planned to shave each other's heads and anyone else's who wanted to join the festivities. Players joked about how ugly they would look with their crowning glory gone. But not Jose Rijo. He said, "I look good. I look sexy."[27] Some players said they would wait until the record got to 15–0 before losing their locks. Piniella joined the latter group, pledging to go bald if the club won 15 straight. The Reds already had the shortest hair of any club in the majors, thanks to owner Marge Schott's well-known aversion to long hair. Schott was adamant about dress and grooming.

Not all players agreed to go along with the head-shaving plan. Paul O'Neill, whose curly locks were his pride and joy, said nobody was going to shave him bald. Veteran Ken Griffey vowed that he would have to be tied down before anyone could shave his head. Pitcher Tom Browning said, "When I told my wife about this, she said, 'No way, I'll divorce you.'"[28] Outfielder Herm Winningham wondered how far the head shaving would have to go: "In my mind, it's the whole head, but a Mohawk is permissible, too.... If that happens, we won't be the prettiest team in the league. But we'll be the best."[29] One can only imagine how Schott would have reacted had one of her players showed up with a Mohawk.

The day that the Reds had a shot at the tenth in a row was a beautiful Sunday afternoon in the Queen City. It was sunny with the game-time temperature a pleasant 70 degrees. The largest crowd since Opening Day, nearly 30,000 fans, showed up to see Tom Browning face Tom Glavine. Alas, the head-shaving did not occur, and Cincinnati fans saw no Reds with a Mohawk until Jonny Gomes sported the style in 2012. Glavine made sure of that by pitching a masterpiece as the Braves downed Browning and the Reds, 3–1. It should come as no surprise that Glavine put an end to the Reds' streak. The crafty lefty had a 27–12 record against Cincinnati during his Hall of Fame career.

Browning lost the game, but had he saved his hair and perhaps his marriage? The lefty gave up three runs in six innings to qualify for what today's analysts foolishly call a quality start. (Three runs in six innings equates to an earned run average of 4.50. Clubs with a 4.50 ERA almost always lose more games than they win.) So the winning streak came to its inevitable end. Yes, the end was inevitable. Even Lou Piniella said, "I didn't think we'd go 162-and-oh. It was just a question of when we'd get beat."[30] Todd Benzinger had an opinion about the value of the streak: "What it did was let the other teams know we're a good team. We had the feeling this spring we were a good team, but you can't tell until you play games. Now we're confident. We know we're good, and the rest of the league knows when they play the Reds it won't be any easy game."[31]

During the nine-game winning streak, the Reds had prevailed by a combination of outstanding hitting, pitching, and fielding. As a team the Reds hit .334 during the stretch. Larkin at .564 and Mariano Duncan at .448 ranked one-two in National League batting averages. Larkin, Duncan, and Chris Sabo held down the top three spots in OPS rankings. It was a team effort. Six different players had game-winning hits in the nine victories. The pitching staff turned in a 2.60 earned run average, while striking out 76 and walking only 26 in the nine games. The relievers were even better than the starters, posting a 1.54 ERA. Fielders did their part, yielding only two unearned runs in the nine consecutive wins.

After the winning streak ended, the Reds traveled to Philadelphia. In the City of Brotherly Love, the Reds lost their second straight game. On April 24 they lost more than the ball game. The Reds, who had been devastated by injuries in 1989, suffered their first major injury of 1990, when Eric Davis sprained a knee ligament. Cincinnati was trailing, 2–0, in the second inning when Davis led off with a single, stole second, and took off for third. He beat the throw but slid awkwardly into the base. The sprained medial collateral ligament (MCL) led to the speedster being placed on the 15-day disabled list. He was expected to miss three or four weeks.

Just five days after the injury to Davis, Cincinnati suffered another blow. Danny Jackson had made his first start of the season on April 18 against San Diego. In his next start, on April 29 against Montreal, he was hit on his left forearm by a line drive and was placed on the disabled list the next day with a severe bruise. The injury came in the first inning, on Jackson's fourth pitch of the game. "I had no chance on it, no chance at all," said Jackson. "I couldn't move my hand and I thought I had broken my arm."[32] Before the injury, he thought he was beginning to regain the form that had made him Cincinnati's best pitcher in 1988, when he led the league with 23 wins. "I felt good, really good in the bullpen," he said. "The first three fastballs I threw in the game were really darting. I thought I'm going to have a really good day, then I get hit by the next pitch."[33]

Despite the loss of Davis and Jackson, the Reds won four of the next five games, ending April with a 13–3 mark. On the last day of the month, Jose Rijo earned his first victory of the season, defeating St. Louis, 6–2. He had started against Houston in the second game of the season on April 10 and pitched well, but received no decision when he was replaced in a double-switch with the score tied. His scheduled start against Atlanta on

April 20 was rained out. On April 24 he lost to the Phillies, 6–3. After his first win, Rijo was exhilarated. "If I'm healthy, nobody can stop me," he said. "Tonight I knew I was going to kick some tail. That was me; that was Jose. I'm back. When I'm healthy I can do anything I want."[34] In his exuberance, Rijo exaggerated somewhat, but he did have a fine season in 1990. In October he beat the Oakland Athletics twice and was named the Most Valuable Player as the Reds swept the World Series.

Rijo's 1990 success came after years of striving. Born in San Cristobal in the Dominican Republic on May 13, 1965, he was signed by the New York Yankees as a free agent in 1980 at the age of 15. Yes, that's right, at age 15! Prior to 1984 there was no minimum age below which Latin American players could not be signed to professional contracts. Rijo started his professional career in the Yankees' farm system at the age of 16 and made his major league debut on April 5, 1984, when he was 18 and the youngest player in the majors. He won only two games for the Yankees and was traded to Oakland at the end of the season. Rijo failed to enjoy much success in the Bay Area. His record for his first four years in the majors was 19 wins and 30 losses.

A native of the Dominican Republic, Jose Rijo was obtained by the Reds in a trade with Oakland in 1987. Despite battling injuries, he had an outstanding season for the Reds in 1990, winning 14 games. In the post-season he won three more games, going 1–0 against the Pirates in the NLCS and 2–0 with a 0.59 ERA against Oakland in the World Series, earning Most Valuable Player honors for the Fall Classic (National Baseball Hall of Fame Library).

Nevertheless, the Reds recognized his potential and sent Dave Parker to Oakland in exchange for Rijo and Tim Birtsas on December 8, 1987. Marge Schott had famously been accused of calling Parker and Eric Davis her "million dollar niggers."[35] Although the Reds owner denied the allegation, she admitted occasionally using the "n-word" in public. Parker was probably glad to get out of Cincinnati. Although Parker was by far the most prominent player involved in the trade, the deal worked out to Cincinnati's benefit. At 36, Parker's best years were behind him. In contrast, the 22-year-old Rijo appeared to have a bright future ahead of him. The righty came through for the Reds in a big way. After his great season in 1990 he had several more good years for the Reds, leading the league in winning percentage in 1991 and in strikeouts in 1993. He suffered an elbow injury in 1995. After several unsuccessful comeback attempts, he pitched his final major league game in 2002, having amassed 116 big league victories.

Rijo was married to Rosie Marichal, daughter of Hall of Fame pitcher Juan Marichal. When Rijo filed for divorce from Rosie in 1991, he feared it might jeopardize his relationship with his father-in-law, who had been a mentor to him. "I'm going to miss him," Rijo told the *New York Times*. "I miss him already. It's difficult, but I wish we could maintain our relationship. Even with my wife. I don't want to divorce my wife. I love my wife. But you gotta do what you gotta do."[36]

After his retirement from pitching, Rijo took a position as assistant to Jim Bowden, the general manager of the Washington Nationals. Bowden had worked in the Cincinnati front office when the pitcher was with the Reds and was pleased to have Rijo join him in Washington. However, Rijo was fired in 2009 after it was discovered that one of his scouting finds had lied about both his name and his age. Rijo was also operating a Dominican baseball academy, which was closed down after the fraud was unearthed. Unfortunately, some of his recent activities have been of questionable legality. In 2012 he was charged with money laundering for drug traffickers in the Dominican Republic.

After their unprecedented 9–0 start, the Reds fell back to Earth, going 4–3 the rest of the month. At the end of April the club had played only 16 games, fewest of any team in the league, but it was time to take stock. What was the outlook for the season? T. S. Eliot wrote that April is the cruelest month. After their injuries, Davis and Jackson might be inclined to agree with the poet, but to most of Reds fandom April was a time of joy and optimism. The optimism was tempered by knowledge of the club's recent past. Fans were aware that the 1989 Reds had been in pennant contention early in that season, before collapsing to finish fifth in their division. They remembered that the Reds had failed to live up to their potential, finishing second in four consecutive seasons from 1985–1988. Some agreed with Peter Pascarelli's assessment that in recent years Cincinnati had been baseball's most underachieving team.[37] A few even questioned whether this club had the character to win. But to repeat a well-worn cliché, hope springs eternal. Most fans looked forward to May with high expectations. Rijo's victory on April 30 enabled Cincinnati to end the month with a four and one-half game lead in the National League West and the best record in all of major league baseball. Sweet Lou had the Reds on a roll.

In one way, the National League schedule makers had a role in helping the Reds get off to such a great start. Cincinnati was to go the entire months of April and May without once facing the defending National League champion San Francisco Giants. The champs were a powerful club. Kevin Mitchell had led the league in both home runs and runs batted in the previous season and garnered the league's Most Valuable Player Award. Will Clark had been runner-up for the batting title, was second in hits, and led the circuit in runs scored. These sluggers and most of their teammates were back to defend the title. The Giants posed a terrific challenge to the Reds. Cincinnati fans looked forward with trepidation to June, when the Reds would face San Francisco for the first time. Their fear was well-placed. During the season the Reds would lose to the Giants 11 times in 18 games, the only club against whom the 1990 Reds had a losing record.

Rainouts had cost the Reds three games in April. Cincinnati played only 16 games during the month, contrasted to the 19 or 20 that most teams played. Early-season rainouts meant games had to be made up later, which indicated doubleheaders were in the offing. Doubleheaders during the heat of summer are not welcomed by the players or management. Dread of what the double dips might do to the pennant race were pervasive among those who looked ahead. Cincinnati fared even worse in the twin bills than anyone anticipated. Six doubleheaders yielded four wins and eight losses.

It was a good thing that the Reds had started off in such great fashion in April. It was essential to their pennant hopes to continue winning in the merry month of May.

Standings in National League
West After Games of April 30

Club	W	L	Pct.	GB
Cincinnati	13	3	.813	—
Los Angeles	11	10	.524	4½
San Diego	9	10	.474	5½
Houston	9	10	.474	5½
San Francisco	8	12	.400	7
Atlanta	4	13	.235	9

May

The surprising Cincinnati Reds entered the month of May with the best record in baseball at 13–3. How were they able to do it? Sportswriter Dave Nightingale asked, "Was the managerial genius of Lou Piniella, the new field boss, a major reason for the club's rocket-launch start in 1990?"[38] The scribe opined that Piniella had something to do with it, but it was tempting to give him too much credit. The players tended to think the new manager was responsible for a new team spirit.

During May the Reds continued winning, though not at April's unprecedented pace, of course. The Reds swept a four-game series at St. Louis, May 4–7, the first time the Cardinals had been swept in a four-game series at Busch Stadium in four years. By May 15, the 23–7 Reds had achieved the franchise's best 30-game start in the 20th century, bettering the 22–8 start of the nascent Big Red Machine in 1970. And they won despite injuries to key players. Eric Davis suffered a sprained medial ligament in his right knee on April 24, and Danny Jackson was placed on the 15-day disabled list after he was struck on the left forearm by a line drive. Mariano Duncan joined the disabled list on May 13 as he strained a muscle trying to beat out an infield hit in a game against the Cubs.

While the May 13 game was in progress, an airplane flew over Riverfront Stadium, carrying a streamer, with a message from Jose Rijo's wife on his 25th birthday: "Happy Birthday, Rijo. Rosie and Josie." The pitcher said, "That's class.... Now I'll have to think of something for her. Maybe I'll parade Marge Schott's elephant from the Cincinnati Zoo on the field for Rosie's birthday, if Marge will let me borrow it."[39]

A 16-inning marathon at Wrigley Field on the afternoon of May 22 was notable for the record-breaking performance of Cubs center fielder Andre Dawson, who became the first man in the long history of major league baseball to draw five intentional bases on balls in a game. Batting in the clean-up position against Tom Browning, Dawson came up in the bottom of the first inning with Mark Grace on base and drew an intentional walk. Dawson led off in the fourth inning. This time Browning induced him to ground out. The game was scoreless in the eighth inning when Dawson came to the plate with Ryne Sandberg on third base. Browning walked him for his second intentional pass of the game. Both starting pitchers did their jobs superbly, throwing shutout ball through nine innings.

The game was still a scoreless tie in the 11th inning when reliever Norm Charlton faced Dawson with Grace on first base. Charlton elected to pitch to Dawson, who responded by hitting a ground ball through the hole between shortstop and third base for his only hit of the game. The game continued scoreless into the 12th frame, with Tim Layana now pitching for the Reds. With two out and runners on first and second, Tim Birtsas entered the game, the fifth pitcher the Reds had used in the contest. Despite the fact that there was no open base (except third), the Reds elected to give Dawson another intentional pass. The move paid off, as Birtsas retired Lloyd McClendon and the game remained scoreless.

Chris Sabo broke the tie by leading off the top of the 13th with a home run. Randy Myers became the Reds' sixth hurler of the day and gave up a homer to the first man he faced, Luis Salazar. So the score was tied, 1–1, when Scott Scudder took the mound for the Reds in the 14th inning. Sandberg drew a walk, sandwiched between two outs. Up came Dawson again. Scudder uncorked a wild pitch, allowing Sandberg to advance to second. With first base open, Scudder gave Dawson his fourth intentional pass of the contest, enabling the Cubs outfielder to tie the major league record for the most intentional walks received in a game.

Scudder escaped further damage until the bottom of the 16th inning. The young pitcher started the frame by striking out Jerome Walton. Then he gave up an infield single to Sandberg. Grace reached on an error by the usually reliable Barry Larkin, with Sandberg going to third. With runners on first and third, Dawson came to the plate. Under the circumstances it made sense to walk him again, so Dawson became the first major leaguer in the history of baseball to receive five intentional bases on balls in a game. However, Dave Clark, who had replaced McClendon in the Cubs lineup, came through with a game-winning hit. The Reds fell, 2–1, for only their tenth loss of the young season.

Scott Scudder, who gave up the record-tying and record-breaking bases on balls, was born in Paris, Texas, in 1968. A right-handed pitching star in high school, he was drafted by the Cincinnati Reds in the first round (17th overall pick) of the 1986 amateur draft. After three years in the minors, he made his major league debut for the Reds on June 6, 1989. One week after the Dawson events, the Reds optioned him to Nashville, but called him back up later when Jose Rijo was injured. During July and August he won three of seven starts. The Houston Astros attempted to acquire him in the Bill Doran trade in early September, but the Reds refused to let him go, still considering him a potential front-line pitcher. However, Scudder never quite met the expectations the Reds held for him, winning only 21 games in a five-year big league career. They traded him to Cleveland after the 1991 season. He pitched his final major league game for the Indians on May 22, 1993, at age 25. He pitched two more seasons in the minors. Later he returned to his home town in Texas as a high school baseball coach. In 2010 Scudder served as a coach of Sweden's national baseball team, which participated in the European Baseball Championships.

A record of 17 wins and nine losses during May enabled the Reds to end the month with an eight-game lead over San Diego and Los Angeles. The defending National League champion San Francisco Giants were 14 games back, with a losing record. The great start in April and May gave the Reds the cushion they needed to survive the long, hot summer.

Standings in National League West After Games of May 31

Club	W	L	Pct.	GB
Cincinnati	30	12	.714	—
San Diego	24	22	.522	8
Los Angeles	25	23	.521	8
Houston	20	27	.426	12½
San Francisco	19	29	.396	14
Atlanta	17	27	.386	14

Only the Weather Is Hot

June

The Reds opened the month of June on a high note, winning three straight games from Los Angeles, pushing their record to 33–12 and a ten-game lead over the second-place San Diego Padres. Then things started going downhill rapidly. The club lost three straight to San Francisco and three out of four to Houston. When they lost a doubleheader, to Atlanta on June 12, it made eight losses in their last nine games. In only nine days their lead had been cut in half. In the second game of the doubleheader Rob Dibble was warned and fined for throwing a pitch over the head of Braves third baseman Jim Presley. Dibble was irate at the fine: "They were leaning over the plate and hitting our pitchers' sliders all over the place. I had to come inside. Now they're taking the pitchers' pitches away from them. They can fine me all they want; my job is to pitch inside."[1] Atlanta manager Russ Nixon responded, "The guy is nuts. Who the hell does he think he is?"[2]

The next day, Piniella held his first closed-door meeting as Reds manager and told the players not to panic. The skid ended, and the Reds won their next six in a row.

During the losing streak, on June 9 Bob Quinn pulled off another coup when he traded chronic complainer Ron Robinson and minor league pitcher Bob Sebra to the Milwaukee Brewers for Billy Bates and Glenn Braggs, both of whom made significant contributions to the Reds winning the world championship in 1990. Milwaukee was in desperate need of pitching, but as *The Sporting News* commented: "It seems that the talented Braggs ... should have been worth more than an erratic starter and a journeyman reliever."[3]

Braggs arrived with a mustache, which he kept for the first two games in violation of the club's policy against facial hair. He shaved it off prior to the Reds' victory over the Braves on June 13, a game in which the newly-acquired outfielder collected four hits. Hitting coach Tony Perez jokingly told Braggs that he hit better without the mustache because he was now able to keep his head up, whereas the weight of the mustache had pulled his head down.[4]

The so-called erratic starter, Ron Robinson, was born in Exeter, California, on March 24, 1962. The 18-year-old right-handed pitcher was drafted by the Cincinnati Reds in the first round of the 1980 amateur draft, the 19th pick overall. After spending four seasons in the Reds' farm system, he made his major league debut on August 14, 1984, at the age of 22. He returned to the minors in 1985, but was called back up to Cincinnati in mid–May and worked both as a starter and reliever. In 1986 he worked solely as a reliever, but he became a swingman again in 1987. From 1988 on, he was almost exclusively a starter. The high point of his career came on May 2, 1988, when he came within one strike of throwing a perfect game against the Montreal Expos. With two outs in the ninth inning and two strikes on pinch-hitter Wallace Johnson, Robinson threw a curveball that the hitter lined to left field for a clean single. "I think if I get that curveball down, I could have gotten it," Robinson said, "but I got the curve up, and it was a base hit.... That's baseball. That's what makes the game exciting."[5]

Robinson became disgruntled with the Reds early in the 1990 season. When Piniella announced that Robinson would not start in the series against Atlanta in early April, the hurler lost his cool. He said he would not pitch in relief and demanded to be traded if he wasn't used as a starter. Piniella immediately set him straight on who made decisions on who pitches and when. After Robinson simmered down, he blew up again and stormed out of a meeting with pitching coach Stan Williams on May 29, irate because the coach told him his next pitching turn would be skipped. "I ain't one bit happy about it," the hurler said.[6] Less than two weeks later, Robinson was shipped to Milwaukee.

The trade cost Robinson a chance for a World Series ring. "I wish I had been there (for the Series)," he said. "I felt I wasn't treated right there and it was time to move on.... I got frustrated sitting on the bench in Cincinnati.... Lou Piniella didn't know who I was. He didn't know anything about me. He told us in spring training everybody was the No. 1 pitcher.... But then he went back on his word."[7] Robinson had his most successful stint in the majors with Milwaukee in the remainder of 1990, posting a 12–5 mark. In 1991 he suffered an elbow injury that cost him most of the season. He attempted a comeback in 1992, but could not make it. He appeared in his last major league game on July 2, 1992, at the age of 30.

In return for Robinson and minor league pitcher Bob Sebra, the Reds acquired Glenn Braggs and Billy Bates. Braggs hit .299 for the Reds in the remainder of the 1990 season. He was born in San Bernardino, California, on October 17, 1962. He was drafted out of San Bernardino High School by the New York Yankees in the sixth round of the 1980 amateur draft, but turned down the Yankees in order to play baseball at the University of Hawaii at Manoa from 1981–1983. He was drafted by the Milwaukee Brewers in the second round of the 1983 amateur draft at the age of 20. In four minor league seasons in the Brewers' farm system, he played for clubs in four different states or provinces—Kentucky, California, Texas, and British Columbia. The right-handed outfielder averaged .331 over the four seasons, earning a promotion to the big leagues. He made his major league debut with the Brewers on July 18, 1986.

In the 1990 National League Championship Series against the Pittsburgh Pirates, he made a game-saving catch in the ninth inning of Game 6. In the World Series against the Oakland Athletics, Braggs was hitless, but drove in the tying runs in Games 2 and 4. In the eighth inning of Game 2, Braggs pinch-hit for Hal Morris and hit a grounder that enabled Billy Hatcher to score from third base. In Game 4 he again hit an eighth-inning groundout enabling a runner, Barry Larkin, to score from third. Braggs played two more seasons with the Reds, but never in as many as 100 games in a year. He played his final major league game on September 10, 1992, at the age of 29. He then played four seasons in Japan for the Yokohama Bay Stars. After retiring from baseball, Braggs became a real estate agent in the Los Angeles area.

Billy Bates was born in Houston on December 7, 1963. As an 18-year-old high school star he was drafted by the Philadelphia Phillies in the eighth round of the 1982 amateur draft, but wisely opted for college instead of signing with the Phils. The diminutive (5'7") second baseman led the Texas Longhorns to the College World Series championship in his freshman year and helped Texas to runner-up finishes the next two seasons. He made the all-tournament team all three years and set a College World Series career record by scoring 21 runs.

In 1985 Bates was selected by the Milwaukee Brewers in the fourth round of the amateur draft. After four seasons in the Milwaukee farm system, he made his major league debut on August 17, 1989, at the age of 25. He was never able to fulfill in the majors the promise that he had shown in high school and college. On June 9, 1990, the Brewers sent him along with Glenn Braggs to Cincinnati in exchange for Ron Robinson and Bob Sebra. Bob Quinn said he made the trade because although "we felt comfortable with our pitching staff, we didn't feel comfortable with the right-handed batters off the bench."[8] (Braggs batted right-handed; Bates hit from the left side.) The Reds sent Bates down to their Class AAA Nashville Sounds, but fortunately called him up in time to make him eligible for post-season play. He played his first game for the Reds on September 11, appeared in eight games, mainly as a pinch-runner, and collected no hits in the regular season.

Bates's main claim to fame in Cincinnati was the cheetah race. Marge Schott was a leading supporter of the Cincinnati Zoo, so when the Zoo wanted to stage a race between a human and a cheetah as a promotion, Schott agreed to host the event at Riverfront Stadium. As the fastest man on the team, Bates was selected to participate. "I got stuck with it, being the new guy. All I knew I was going to go as fast as I could. I saw the cheetah and the big teeth and I was scared to death."[9] The race was supposed to be from the outfield to home plate. Bates was given a five-second head start and never looked back. Halfway through the race his hat flew off. Thinking the hat might be food, the cheetah chased it. By the time his handlers got him back on course, Bates had crossed the plate, defeating the fastest mammal on the planet.

After the season, Bates, thinking he had no chance to make the post-season roster, was preparing to drive home to Houston when he learned that second baseman Bill Doran was out with a back injury. Bates took his spot on the roster. The unsung rookie played a key role in his team's World Series win.[10] Bates did not play second base for the Reds in the Series. That role was filled by Mariano Duncan. Bates had only one plate appearance, but it was crucial. In Game 2 the score was tied, 4–4, in the bottom of the tenth. With one out, Piniella sent Bates in to pinch-hit for Rob Dibble. Coach Tony Perez instructed the young man, "Put the ball in play and run like hell."[11] Bates did precisely as he was instructed. He hit the ball weakly to third base and beat out an infield single. Consecutive singles by Chris Sabo and Joe Oliver allowed Bates to score the game-winning run.

George Vecsey wrote in the *New York Times*: "Piniella sent Bates up to pinch-hit in the 10th. The little man promptly chopped a single off the concrete-hard turf and soon scored the winning run. In this old river town, Billy Bates was now a man for the ages, like Cookie Lavagetto, who hit that double off Bill Bevens, and Al Gionfriddo, who made that catch off DiMaggio, both in the 1947 Series for Brooklyn. Neither Lavagetto nor Gionfriddo ever played in the majors again. Nobody mentioned that to Billy Bates on Wednesday night."[12] After those heroics, did Bates go on to major league stardom? No. Almost as though Vecsey were prescient, Bates never played another game in the big leagues. He played in Nashville in 1991, but was not re-signed. The Cubs picked him up, and he played his final season of professional ball for the Iowa Cubs in 1992. At the age of 28, his baseball career was over. He returned to Houston and worked as an equipment supplier in the oil industry.

After getting off to such a hot start, the Reds cooled down considerably in June, going 16–14 for the month. They ended June with a 9½-game lead over resurgent San Francisco, as both San Diego and Los Angeles posted losing records for the month.

Standings in National League West After Games of June 30

Club	W	L	Pct.	GB
Cincinnati	46	26	.639	—
San Francisco	38	37	.507	9½
Los Angeles	36	38	.486	11
San Diego	35	37	.486	11
Houston	32	43	.427	15½
Atlanta	30	42	.417	16

The All-Star Game

According to the rules in force at the time, starting position players for the 1990 All-Star Game were determined by a vote of the fans. All pitchers and reserves were selected by the managers of the defending league champions.

Fans voted one member of the Cincinnati Reds into the National League's starting lineup—third baseman Chris Sabo.

Chris Sabo was born in Detroit in 1962. A star baseball and hockey player at Detroit Central Catholic High School, he was drafted by the Montreal Expos in the 30th round of the 1980 amateur draft, but elected not to sign with the Expos. He opted instead to play baseball at the University of Michigan. In 1983 he led the Wolverines to the College World Series, where they won two games before being eliminated by the eventual champion Texas Longhorns. Sabo was named to the All-Tournament team, as was the Texas leadoff hitter and second baseman, Bill Bates, who later became a teammate of Sabo's on the 1990 Reds. Another of Sabo's future Cincinnati teammates—Barry Larkin—was with him on the 1983 University of Michigan squad. After the 1983 season, Sabo was drafted in the second round by the Reds, started his professional career with Cedar Rapids, and moved quickly through the Cincinnati farm system.

Sabo made his major league debut on April 4, 1988, and immediately became a star. He was named to the National League All-Star team and was honored as the National League Rookie of the Year. Sabo wore wraparound goggles that became his trademark. He thought the goggles protected him in headfirst slides better than contacts or regular glasses would. Pete Rose nicknamed him Spuds because he thought the goggles made the third baseman resemble Spuds MacKenzie, the bull terrier star of a Bud Light advertising campaign. Sabo slumped somewhat in 1989, but came back strong in 1990. He credited a new stance, emphasizing leg drive, which was suggested to him by Piniella during spring training. "It gives me better balance," the right-handed hitter said. "If I hit it square, it goes farther than it used to go."[13] The new stance apparently worked. Sabo had never hit more than 12 home runs in any of his seven previous seasons as a professional. In 1990 he hit 25 homers.

Sabo had perhaps his best season in 1991, making the All-Star team for the second straight year and the third time overall. An opposing manager, Bobby

The early career of Chris Sabo resembled that of his teammate, Barry Larkin. Both were born in Cincinnati, played at the University of Michigan, and joined their hometown Reds in the late 1980s. Sabo was named National League Rookie of the Year in 1988. Both Sabo and Larkin were named to the 1990 All-Star team, Sabo as a starter and Larkin as a reserve. In 1991 Sabo made the All-Star team for the third time in four years. However, he suffered an injury in 1992 from which he never fully recovered, depriving him of any chance to join Larkin in Cooperstown (National Baseball Hall of Fame Library).

Cox of the Atlanta Braves, waxed enthusiastic about Sabo. "He hates the opposing team. He just wants to win, and he plays with a vengeance. I love the guy. He would have fit right in with the Gas House Gang."[14]

Injuries suffered in 1992 hampered his play, and Sabo never again reached the heights he had attained from 1988 to 1991. The Reds granted him free agency after the 1993 season. The next few years he played a few games for Baltimore, the White Sox, and St. Louis. The Reds brought him back in 1996. He played his final major league game on September 2 at the age of 34.

After retiring from baseball, Sabo became a serious amateur golfer, playing in various tournaments. In 2013 he told interviewer Solomon Crenshaw: "It's the only thing in which I can still compete athletically at some kind of level."[15] At the time Sabo was an assistant golf coach at the University of Cincinnati.

As manager of the defending National League champion San Francisco Giants, it was the duty and privilege of Roger Craig to select the reserves and the pitchers for the 1990 All-Star Game. He chose one reserve from the Reds—shortstop Barry Larkin. Furthermore, he named Jack Armstrong as the starting pitcher and added Cincinnati relievers Rob Dibble and Randy Myers to the squad, giving the Reds five representatives on the team, more than any other club.

Barry Larkin was born in Cincinnati in 1964. A star in both baseball and football at Moeller High School, he was drafted by the Reds in the second round of the 1982 amateur draft, but did not sign. An all-state

Barry Larkin, a native son of Cincinnati, was the club's Most Valuable Player during the 1990 regular season and the National League MVP in 1995. During his career, all of which was played with his hometown club, Larkin was named to the All-Star team 12 times. He won three Gold Gloves and nine Silver Slugger Awards. The popular shortstop was elected to the National Baseball Hall of Fame in 2012 (National Baseball Hall of Fame Library).

defensive back, he went to the University of Michigan to play football. After being redshirted his freshman year, he decided to give up football and play baseball only. According to Larkin, football coach Bo Schembechler was furious with him. The coach reportedly told him, "Larkin, this is the University of Michigan! No one comes to the University of Michigan and plays stinkin' baseball. You get out of this office, and you come back tomorrow when you come to your senses."[16]

Larkin stuck to his guns and played baseball. It appears to have been an appropriate choice. As a freshman Larkin hit .352 and stole 13 bases in 16 attempts. He and his then and future teammate, Chris Sabo, took the Wolverines to the College World Series in 1983. Although overshadowed by the exploits of Sabo, the young infielder acquitted himself well. In one game he hit a triple, in another he hit two doubles, and in a game against Stanford he scored three runs. In his sophomore year he was named the Big Ten Player of the Year and selected to the United States team to play a "demonstration" tournament in the 1984 Olympics. His baseball reputation grew to the point where the Reds selected him in the first round, the fourth overall pick, in the 1985 amateur draft. He quickly proved that he was worthy of a first-round selection. The Reds sent him to Vermont for the remainder of the 1985 season and promoted him to Denver in 1986, where his play earned him advancement to the parent club. He made his major league debut on August 13, 1986.

The youthful shortstop quickly reached stardom with his hometown Reds. He was named to the All-Star team in 1988, the first of 12 times he made the midsummer classic squad. Over the years he won three Gold Glove Awards and nine Silver Slugger Awards. He missed 65 games due to injuries in 1989, contributing to Cincinnati's disappointing season. He came back strong in 1990, leading the club with 156 games played and playing a major role in the successful hunt for a Reds October. In 1995 he was named the National League's Most Valuable Player. He spent his entire 19-year major league playing career with Cincinnati, playing his final game on October 3, 2004, at the age of 40.

Since the end of his playing career, he has remained active in baseball, serving variously as a special assistant in the Washington Nationals organization, as a television baseball analyst, coaching the United States team in the 2009 World Baseball Classic (WBC), and managing the Brazilian team in the 2012 WBC. He was elected to the National Baseball Hall of Fame in 2012.

Larkin came from an athletic family. His two brothers and his son all played professional sports. One brother, Byron, was a high school all-

American football safety at Moeller and a college all-American basketball player at Xavier University, before embarking on a professional career overseas. Another brother, Stephen, spent most of his professional career in minor league baseball, but played one major league game. That lone game was one for the record books. It was the last game of the season on September 27, 1998. Stephen played first base for the Reds, Barry was at shortstop, and the other two infield positions were filled by the Boone brothers, Bret at second and Aaron at third. It is the only game in the history of baseball where two sets of brothers were on the field for the same team at the same time. Barry's son, Shane, was a basketball star at the University of Miami. In 2014 he was playing for the Dallas Mavericks in the National Basketball Association.

The 1990 All-Star Game got under way at Chicago's Wrigley Field on July 11, with Cincinnati's Jack Armstrong on the mound for the National League. Some people were surprised that Craig selected Armstrong as his starting pitcher, ahead of the more heralded Ramon Martinez or Frank Viola. However, Armstrong clearly deserved the start. He had a record of 11 wins and three losses. After winning eight of nine decisions in April and May, the young right-hander had encountered a brief snag, losing consecutive games on June 5 and 10. Known for a rigorous running and weight-lifting regimen between starts, Armstrong had eased up temporarily. He blamed his change in routine for the losses. "Now I'm cranking it back up," he said. "Back to boot camp.... People see how hard I'm working and they're afraid I'm going to get tired, so they tell me to back off. Most people don't realize the capabilities of the human body. I get mentally focused by getting physically exhausted."[17] Whatever the reason, Armstrong got back on track, winning three straight decisions. He was eager, able, and deserving to start the All-Star Game.

In an effort to get every able-bodied player into the game, neither manager allowed a pitcher to go more than two innings. Armstrong and the other hurlers on both squads shut down the opposition through the first six innings. With the score 0–0 in the top of the seventh, San Francisco pitcher Jeff Brantley (a future Red) gave up consecutive singles to the first two batters in the frame. Craig summoned Rob Dibble from the bullpen. The Cincinnati hurler promptly gave up a two-run double to Julio Franco, and the American Leaguers took a 2–0 lead. Although Dibble escaped further damage and subsequent National League pitchers (including Cincinnati's Randy Myers) held the American League in check the rest of the way, the two runs were all the junior circuit needed for the win. Although Franco's blow off Dibble was the winning hit, Brantley was responsible for putting the two runners on base and was saddled with the loss. Bret Saberhagen, who pitched scoreless ball through the fifth and sixth innings, was the pitcher of record at the time of Franco's hit and was credited with the win.

Cincinnati's two position players in the game were both hitless as the National League garnered only two hits in the game. Sabo played the first five innings before giving way to Tim Wallach. Larkin entered the game in the third inning as a pinch-runner for Tony Gwynn and replaced Ozzie Smith at shortstop in the next frame. In turn he was benched in favor of Shawon Dunston in the sixth stanza, as Craig continued shuffling his lineup in an attempt to give all his men some playing time. Only two players on the National League squad did not get into the game. Catcher Benito Santiago was disabled by an injury suffered in mid–June. In the ninth inning, pitcher Neal Heaton was warming up in the bullpen, ready to enter the game if the contest went into extra innings. It did not happen. Lenny Dykstra led off the ninth with a single, but Dennis Eckersley retired the next three batters in a row to pick up a save and deprive Heaton of an opportunity for an All-Star Game appearance.

July

As morning dawned on the first day of July, Cincinnati had a comfortable lead in the National League West—9½ games over San Francisco and 11 games over both Los Angeles and San Diego. The Reds started the month by winning four of the seven games prior to the All-Star break, with the victories being credited to Browning, Armstrong, Jackson, and Mahler. With not quite one-half of the season completed, the Reds had a record of 50 wins and 29 losses for a percentage of .633. They maintained an eight-game lead over the defending National League champion San Francisco Giants and had increased the margin over the Dodgers and Padres to more than a dozen games.

During the break, the Reds called Chris Hammond up from Nashville, where the lefty had a spectacular 10–1 record with a 2.26 earned run average. Piniella said, "Early in the spring Hammond was not overly impressive. But we took him to Kissimmee (presumably for an exhibition game against the Houston Astros) late last spring, and I really liked what I saw. I mentioned to the staff then that next year Hammond merited a long look. Well, his time has come sooner. He had some control problems last year, but he has dominated the American Association this season."[18]

Hammond was born January 21, 1966, in Atlanta. He was drafted by Cincinnati in the sixth round of the January 1986 draft out of Gulf Coast Community College. He was in his fifth season in the Reds' farm system when he received his chance to perform in the big leagues. He made his major league debut on July 16, 1990. He was unable to post a victory in three starts for the Reds that season and finished the year at Nashville, where he won five more games without a defeat and lowered his ERA to 2.17. Hammond pitched for the Reds in 1991 and 1992 and was then traded to the Florida Marlins for Gary Scott and Hector Carrasco. His best year with the Marlins came in 1995, when he was 9–6 as a starter. However, the next year the Marlins converted him to a reliever. From 1996–2006 he pitched for seven major league clubs and five minor league outfits, mostly as a middle reliever. In 2006 he was back in Cincinnati and made his final major league appearance on June 29 at the age of 40.

Chris and his wife Lynne founded the Chris Hammond Youth Foundation in the small town of Wedowee, Alabama. The purpose of the foundation was to raise funds for the construction and maintenance of recreational and athletic facilities to serve youngsters in rural areas of Alabama. The Internal Revenue Service has revoked the foundation's nonprofit status for its failure to file mandated forms. In 2014 the foundation was using a celebrity golf tournament as its main funding source.

After the break, the Reds went on a roll. They won three of five from the Mets, swept the Expos in three straight, and split a four-game set with the Phillies. Browning's win over the Padres on July 23 pushed Cincinnati's lead over the second-place Giants to 11 games, their biggest margin of the season. To this point it was smooth sailing, but suddenly the seas turned choppy. The Reds lost the next three games in San Diego, were swept in four games by San Francisco, and lost to Los Angeles on July 30 for their eighth consecutive loss, their longest losing streak of the season.

On July 26 the Reds optioned Tim Birtsas to the Nashville Sounds of the Class AAA American Association and called up Keith Brown from the Sounds. Keith Brown was born on Valentine's Day, February 14, 1964, in Flagstaff, Arizona. He played high school baseball in Shasta Lake, California, and college ball at California State College, Sacramento. He was drafted by the Cincinnati Reds in the 21st round of the 1986 amateur draft. He spent most of two seasons in the Cincinnati farm system before making his big league debut on August 25, 1988, at the age of 24. The right-hander spent the next several years shuffling back and forth between Cincinnati and the minors. During the Reds' championship season of 1990, he appeared in eight big league games, but had no decisions or saves and had a minimal impact on the pennant race. His last major league appearance came on July 11, 1992.

In 1993 Brown was diagnosed with non-Hodgkin's lymphoma. He persevered through treatment and personal problems (bankruptcy and a divorce). A Nashville newspaper said Brown had been knocked down more times that the headpin in a bowling alley.[19] In 1995 he attempted a comeback with the Florida Marlins' Class AAA team in Charlotte, but gave it up after four games. His most successful professional experience had been with the Nashville Sounds, and he has made Nashville his home since the 1980s. For many years he has been an instructor at the Nashville Baseball Training Academy. "I'm a pitcher," he said. "Who better to tell you how to hit? I can see by your stance and swing how to strike you out! And as a pitcher, I know what it takes to control the game."[20]

The Reds won 13 of the first 20 games they played during July. By July 23, it appeared that the hunt for a Reds October would surely come to a successful conclusion. But suddenly things went downhill with an eight-game losing streak to West Coast teams. Rijo stopped the skid by beating the Dodgers, 5–2, on the last day of the month. The losing streak was largely responsible for Cincinnati having its first losing month of the season, going only 14–15. In the last few days of July, their lead in the National League West was cut in half, falling to five and one-half games over San Francisco. The pennant race was not yet over.

Standings in National League West After Games of July 31

Club	W	L	Pct.	GB
Cincinnati	60	41	.594	—
San Francisco	55	47	.539	5½
Los Angeles	52	49	.515	8
San Diego	45	56	.446	15
Houston	43	61	.413	18½
Atlanta	40	61	.396	20

A Question of Survival

August

The Reds ended a disastrous West Coast road trip with a 6–3 win by Scott Scudder over San Diego on the first day of August. It was only their third victory in the 11-game trek, during which their once seemingly safe lead in the National League West was trimmed in half. After the win on August 1, the Reds dropped three in a row to the Padres at home. On August 4, the lead was reduced to 3½ games, the smallest it had been all summer. "It's like that old Revolutionary War saying, 'Don't fire until you see the whites of their eyes,'" Piniella said. "Well, we're seeing the whites, and it's time to start firing."[1] Armstrong suggested, "It's time to see what we're made of."[2]

Piniella benched Benzinger and Braggs, who had been platooning at first base and left field, respectively, and decided to go full-time with Morris and O'Neill at those positions. Benzinger had started the season as the Reds' regular first baseman and was hitting .285 when he injured his wrist on June 29. Upon his return he was unable to regain his hitting stroke, and his batting average fell precipitously. Braggs had been acquired in June and hit nearly .300, but showed little power and was considered to be a defensive liability. The move did not yield immediate results, however, as the Reds continued losing. On August 8 the beleaguered manager called a team meeting. He lamented, "I wish I was a Vince Lombardi and could go in there and say all the proper things [to get the team back on track.]"[3] Pitcher Norm Charlton told his skipper not to worry. "We're not in trouble. We've played as bad as we can, and the other teams are playing about as well as they can. As soon as we start playing well, you're going to see the lead jump to where it was and it'll be all over."[4]

On August 10 the onrushing San Francisco Giants arrived at Riverfront, ready for an important four-game series with the Reds. The defending National League champions had won ten of their last 15 games, cutting their deficit in half, from nine games to four and one-half. The slumping Reds had lost 13 of their last 17 games. Their National League lead was in jeopardy. Marge Schott showed the team a home movie to motivate them for the series. The tape featured Marge's sister, Winnie, a paraplegic, who competed in various sports. Winnie's message was never to give up in hard times. The owner also gave Piniella a wad of Schottzie's hair to rub on his chest as a good-luck charm.

The Reds called upon Charlton to right the ship. Although Charlton was best known as a member of the Nasty Boys relieving crew, he had been moved into the starting rotation in mid–July. Injuries to Jackson and Rijo prompted Piniella to give Charlton his first start since 1988 on July 15. Starting Charlton strengthened the rotation, but weakened the relief corps, where he had been the primary set-up man for Dibble and Myers. "With Rijo out and the fact we're in a pennant race, we want to run experienced pitchers out there," Piniella said. "Norm is very capable. He has outstanding stuff and this has been in the back of my mind for a long time."[5]

In his new role, Charlton had won two and lost two before the San Francisco series started. Against the Giants, he pitched brilliantly, defeating them on a three-hit shutout, 7–0, and getting the Reds back on track. His performance generated a controversy. After the game, San Francisco manager Roger Craig accused Charlton of throwing spitballs. The pitcher indignantly replied, "They checked me five or six times. I haven't been checked that much in my career."[6]

Norm Charlton was born on January 6, 1963, in Fort Polk, Louisiana. The left-hander pitched at Madison High School in San Antonio and for Rice University, where he had a triple major in political science, religion, and physical education. He was selected by the Montreal Expos' in the first round (28th overall pick) of the 1984 amateur draft. While he was still in the Expos farm system, he was traded with Tim Barker to the Cincinnati Reds for Wayne Krenchicki on March 31, 1988. Charlton made his major league debut for the Reds on August 19, 1988, as a starting pitcher. The following season he was converted into a reliever. In 1990 and 1991 he was an occasional starter, but after 1991 he was exclusively a reliever for the remainder of his major league career, sometimes as a set-up man, sometimes as a closer.

On November 17, 1992, Charlton was traded to the Seattle Mariners for Kevin Mitchell, rejoining his former manager Lou Piniella, who was now field boss of the Mariners. "We hate to give up a hitter like Kevin

Mitchell," Piniella said. "But when you have a chance to get a closer like Charlton, you have to do it."[7] Charlton pitched off and on for Seattle in parts of five seasons, and toiled occasionally for Philadelphia, Baltimore, Atlanta and Tampa Bay. His last major league appearance was for the Mariners on October 7, 2001. Charlton spent one season (2008) as the Mariners' bullpen coach, but most of his retirement years have been spent hunting and fishing. He lives in Rockport, Texas, and is a fishing guide. He has earned a captain's license, which allows him to run charter trips into Aransas Bay.[8]

On August 11, 1990, the Giants beat Jose Rijo, 4–2, to even up the series. In the third game, Craig persuaded umpires to call a ball when reliever Rob Dibble wiped perspiration from his mouth and went directly to the ball. After the game, won by the Reds, 6–4, Piniella said: "We're going to come out and beat them tomorrow. It's that plain and simple. No Humm-Baby. No nothing."[9] Craig reacted by saying, "When guys make statements like he made, that's a sign of insecurity.... That's high school stuff what Lou said."[10] The war of words was on. Piniella exploded: "Take it like a man, Roger. Take it like a man. When we lost four straight in San Francisco, I took it like a man.... What else is he gonna say after he gets his butt whipped?"[11]

On August 13, the Reds downed San Francisco, 6–5, to win the series three games to one and increase their lead to six and one-half games. They won two from St. Louis and then stumbled in Pittsburgh, losing four straight to the Pirates. On August 20 they lost to the Cubs for their fifth straight loss. Piniella was frustrated with the losses and upset that the umpires had called the Cubs game because of rain in the ninth inning with the Reds trailing, 3–1. That the arbiters waited until 1 a.m. before calling the game did not mollify the manager. He was still fuming the next day when a close call at first base went against the Reds. Piniella argued vehemently with umpire Dutch Rennert, who ejected the irate skipper. Piniella picked up the first base bag and heaved it toward second base. He retrieved it and threw it down the right field line, earning a $500 fine from National League president Bill White. The Reds went on to win the game, 8–1, sparked by the pitching of Rick Mahler and four doubles by Billy Hatcher, which tied a major league record for the most two-baggers in a game.

Whether the fiery skipper's antics had anything to do with it or not is debatable, but the Reds started winning again—two in a row over the Cubs, three out of four from Pittsburgh, a two-game split with St. Louis, and three out of four from the Cubs. Cincinnati ended August and started September on an upbeat note, with nine wins in a 12-game stretch.

The deadline for being on the roster in time to be eligible for post-season play was Friday night, August 31. Pennant contenders scrambled to strengthen their teams, while non-contenders traded veterans for prospects. One of the most lopsided deals in the history of baseball occurred the day before the deadline when the Houston Astros sent the veteran Larry Andersen to Boston in exchange for a minor league third baseman named Jeff Bagwell. The other trade Houston made that day did not work out quite so well for them. They sent second baseman Bill Doran to the Reds for three minor leaguers to be named later (catcher Terry McGriff and pitchers Butch Henry and Keith Kaiser). Houston had coveted Scott Scudder and Chris Hammond, but the Reds were unwilling to give up either of those young hurlers, thinking they might develop into reliable starters.

Some have suggested that the Astros traded Doran in order to free up second base for Craig Biggio. Not so. A catcher, Biggio did not become a second baseman until 1992. Doran was succeeded at the keystone sack by the unheralded Dave Rohde. The reason the Astros traded Doran was to avoid losing him to free agency in the off-season. Meanwhile, some Cincinnati fans questioned why the Reds would acquire Doran when incumbent second baseman Mariano Duncan was having a career year. Duncan was hitting over .300 and leading the league in triples. However, Piniella was concerned about Duncan's ability to hit right-handed pitching. At the time of the trade, Duncan was hitting .463 against left-handers and only .212 against right-handers. A switch-hitter, Doran would have no such problems. "I like his offense," the manager said. "He can steal a base, he puts the ball in play, using all fields, and he knows how to work a pitcher for a walk. And we didn't get him just for September. He figures in our future, too."[12]

The trade brought Doran back to his home town. He was born in the Queen City on May 28, 1958. He attended Mount Healthy High School and played baseball at nearby Miami University. He was selected by Houston in the sixth round of the 1979 draft. He spent nearly four years in the Astros' minor league system before making his major league debut on September 6, 1982, at the age of 24. He quickly established himself as a favorite of the Houston fans. He had his best year in 1987, hitting .283 with 16 home runs, and leading the league with a .992 fielding percentage. After his return to Cincinnati in September 1990, he got off to a torrid start. In his first nine games he hit .593, with five doubles, a homer, three stolen bases, seven runs scored, and three runs batted in. He was looking forward to helping his home town team win the World Series. But it was not to be. He played 17 games for the Reds before coming down with a herniated disk in his back. On September 29, as the Reds clinched the pennant, Doran was checking into a hospital to have back surgery. There was to be no World Series for Bill Doran in 1990. "I missed the whole thing," he lamented. "I didn't feel like I belonged."[13]

Free agent Doran signed with the Reds in December 1990, and played in his home town during the 1991 and 1992 seasons, but, beset by injuries, he never regained his old form. The Milwaukee Brewers purchased his contract in January 1993. He played 28 games for the Brew Crew before retiring on July 8, 1993, at the age of 35. Since his retirement Doran has served in various capacities for the Reds. He served as a coach for the Kansas City Royals from 2005–2007 and as their interim manager in 2006, before returning to Cincinnati as the minor league infield and baserunning coordinator.

With a record of 15–14 for the month, the Reds played barely over .500 ball in August, but ended the month with the same 5½ game lead they had at its beginning, although over a different contender. San Francisco fell back in the standings, but Los Angeles emerged as a challenger, with an 18–12 mark, to gain on the Reds.

Standings in National League West After Games of August 31

Club	W	L	Pct.	GB
Cincinnati	75	55	.577	—
Los Angeles	70	61	.534	5½
San Francisco	67	64	.511	8½
San Diego	60	69	.465	14½
Houston	59	72	.450	16½
Atlanta	51	80	.389	24½

September

On September 1, a major league team's roster expands from the 25-man active roster to the entire 40-man roster. On or about this date, the Reds made several roster moves. Catcher Terry McGriff, first baseman Terry Lee, and pitcher Tim Birtsas were recalled from Nashville, and pitcher Rosario Rodriguez was brought up from Chattanooga. Chris Hammond was optioned to Nashville. Jack Armstrong was placed on the 15-day disabled list.

At last long-time minor leaguer Terry Lee had made it to the big-time.

Lee was born in San Francisco on March 13, 1962. He was signed by the Cincinnati Reds out of Boise State University as an undrafted free agent on July 30, 1982. He played outfield and first base in Eugene, Oregon, in 1982, moved to Cedar Rapids in 1983, and played for Vermont, Denver, Greensboro, Chattanooga, and Nashville before making his major league debut for the Reds on September 3, 1990, at the age of 28. He participated in 12 games for the Reds in 1990 and three games in 1991, playing his last major league game on August 21, 1991. On the Reds' 40-man roster in the autumn of 1991, Lee refused assignment to the minors and became a free agent, hoping to sign with another major league club. He never made in back to the majors, playing five more seasons in the minors, including one year in Mexico and three years in Canada. His last professional baseball was played for Winnipeg in 1997. After 14 seasons in the minors and two very brief visits to the majors, Lee retired to his home town of San Francisco.

Unlike Lee, Terry McGriff had previous trials with the Reds, having debuted with the big league club in 1987. McGriff came from a baseball family. His father had been a catcher at Southern University and two relatives—Fred McGriff and Charles Johnson—were major league stars. Terry McGriff was born September 23, 1963, in Fort Pierce, Florida. He knew from age five that he wanted to be a major league catcher. At the age of 17, he was drafted out of Westwood High School in Fort Pierce by the Cincinnati Reds in the eighth round of the 1981 amateur draft. He had starred in both baseball and football in high school, but he chose baseball because he thought he was too thin to go far in the pigskin game.[14] At the time he weighed 170 pounds, but he eventually added 25 pounds to his 6'2" frame. The Reds sent him to Billings in the Pioneer Rookie League, and he advanced slowly up the ladder—Eugene, Tampa, Vermont, Denver, and Nashville—before making his major debut on July 11, 1987.

When he reached the Reds, he found six new suits in his locker, gifts from his boyhood idol, Johnny Bench. The Hall of Famer sought out the rookie and gave him advice about the job and responsibilities of a major league catcher. McGriff said of making the majors, "It was an honor. It was really a dream come true. I just wish it could have lasted a little longer."[15] His major league career was short in number of games played—126 spread over six years. In 1990 he appeared in two games for the Reds and failed in make a hit in four times at bat. On September 7 he was sent to Houston as part of the deal that had brought Bill Doran to Cincinnati. Later he played a few games for Houston, Florida, and St. Louis. His last major league appearance came for the Cardinals on August 7, 1994.

McGriff never achieved the major league success that he had anticipated. He blamed it on his role as a backup catcher. He told an interviewer, "You can never know your full potential until you play pretty much every day. That's what upsets me; they said I never reached my potential. Well, I don't know anyone who will ever reach their potential when you're backing up.... I don't know one Hall of Famer who started as a backup."[16]

McGriff played in the International League in 1995 and 1996 and in the Mexican League in 1997. He then played four years with the Bluefish, an independent club in Bridgeport, Connecticut. From 2003 through at least 2011, he coached the Bluefish. In 2014 he worked for Dream Makers Baseball in Lutz, Florida, giving individual lessons in catching at $40 for a half-hour and $65 for a full hour.[17]

Rosario Rodriguez was born in Los Mochis, Sinaloa, Mexico, on July 8, 1969. The Reds signed the 17-year-old hurler as a free agent on March 16, 1987. They compensated Nuevo Laredo of the Mexican League, which also claimed the youngster.[18] He pitched a perfect inning in relief in his major league debut against Pittsburgh on September 1, 1989. He won one game and lost one in his first big league season. At the age of 20, he was the youngest player in the National League that season.

Rodriguez was the beneficiary of a violation of the Reds' dress code by Eric Davis. When Davis boarded a flight without wearing a jacket, manager Tommy Helms told him, "I'm fining you. And I'm going to tell you what the fine is. You know the kid we just brought up from the minors, Rosario Rodriguez? He can use a good sports coat. So you buy him one, and it had better be a good one."[19] Davis bought not just a sport coat, but a suit for the non-English-speaking rookie.

After his September call-up in 1990, Rodriguez appeared in nine games for the Reds, but had no wins, losses, or saves. In December the Pittsburgh Pirates acquired him off waivers from the Reds. In 1991 he duplicated his rookie record with one win and one loss, but spent most of the season with Buffalo, the Pirates' American Association farm club. He rejoined the parent club in time to pitch in the National League Championship Series against Atlanta. His final major league experience was not a pleasant one, as he gave up three runs in the one inning he pitched. His major league career was over at the age of 22. He returned to the land of his birth and played for several teams in the Mexican League from 1993–2005.

Another pitcher—Gino Minutelli—had a brief stint with the Reds in September 1990. Minutelli was born in Wilmington, Delaware, on May 23, 1964. He played baseball at Sweetwater High School in National City, California. His first experience in Organized Baseball was with the Tri-

Cities Triplets in the Northwest League in 1985.[20] After Cincinnati acquired him, they assigned Minutelli to their Cedar Rapids club, where he made the Midwest All-Star team, based on his 9–1 start. He finished the season at 15–5, but never again equaled those numbers. The young lefty had a good year in 1990, going 14–7 with Chattanooga and Nashville, earning a September call-up to the big leagues.

Minutelli made his major league debut on September 18, 1990, and it was a rough start. He entered the game against San Francisco in the ninth inning, faced three men, never got an out, and left with the bases loaded. He walked the first batter he faced, Brett Butler; hit the second, Kevin Bass, with a pitch; allowed both runners to advance on a wild pitch; and walked Will Clark to fill the sacks. At this point, he was relieved by Keith Brown. Brown got Kevin Mitchell to ground out and Matt Williams to hit into a double play, but Butler had scored on Mitchell's grounder and the run was charged to Minutelli. Over the rest of the 1990 season, Minutelli made one more appearance and fared much better the second time out, retiring all three batters he faced.

In 1991 Minutelli divided the season between the minors and Cincinnati, losing both of his decisions with the Reds. He spent the entire 1992 season with Nashville and was granted free agency at the end of the season. He signed with San Francisco and played mostly for the Giants' Class AAA club in Phoenix, but got into only nine games for the Giants, losing his only decision. He made his final major league appearance on September 9, 1993, finishing with a career record of no wins and three losses in the big leagues. He pitched in the minors in 1994. The Major League Baseball Players Association went on strike on August 12, 1994, forcing cancellation of the remainder of the 1994 season. Owners were determined to play a schedule in 1995, using replacement players if necessary. Clubs searched for players willing to cross the imaginary picket line. In February 1995, the Atlanta Braves signed Minutelli, but he never actually played in a game for them. The Braves sent him to their Class AAA affiliate in Richmond, where he appeared in five games with no win-loss record before retiring. At last report he was back in California, living in his former home town of National City.

The Reds did not fare well in the early and middle parts of September 1990. Three consecutive losses brought their record for the month to 8–11 on September 20. Meanwhile, the Los Angeles Dodgers were winning and cutting into the Cincinnati lead. The Reds' loss on September 20 was particularly galling. Reliever Randy Myers carried a 2–1 lead into the bottom of the ninth inning at Houston. With two outs and the bases loaded, pinch-hitter Chet Nichols hit a line drive to left-center to pin a 3–2 loss on the Reds, reducing their lead in the National League West to 3½-games over the Dodgers. It was one of the low points of the season. A successful outcome to the hunt for a Reds October was starting to look doubtful. Back in July the Reds' lead over San Francisco had been reduced to the same 3½-game margin, but they had beaten the challenge. Could they do it again? Yes. Behind the stellar pitching of Jose Rijo and an explosive offense, the Reds defeated San Diego, 10–1, on September 21, starting a four-game sweep of the Padres. Danger was averted.

In September Eric Davis revealed to fans what his life was like with the Reds. "After a night game, I sleep until 11:30 or noon. Then I'll get up and play with my daughters. Then I'll watch my soap operas and head to the ball park around 3, 3:30. Then I'll have treatment on my knee with ice, ultrasound, whirlpool and then exercise before getting a rubdown massage. Then I'll get taped on my ankles and wrists, take batting practice and infield, and it's time for the game."[21] Davis had his first cortisone shot in an effort to alleviate the pain in his right knee. "I don't like to take drugs of any kind, and I avoid them," the outfielder said. "But this was necessary to get me through the season. It still hurts, but I try not to think about it. I just try to go out and play hard. I know the pain is going to be there. I've given up a little speed, but I try to make up for it with hustle and desire, and I try to run the bases with some smarts."[22]

The Reds clinched the 1990 NL West title on September 29, when San Francisco eliminated Los Angles by defeating the Dodgers, 4–3. Meanwhile, back in Cincinnati the Reds' game against San Diego was delayed by rain. During the delay, players were able to watch the Dodgers loss on TV in their clubhouse. When the Dodgers' elimination became official, the Reds exchanged victory hugs, donned championship T-shirts and caps, and went to the field, where they bowed to the water-soaked crowd. Several players celebrated with head-first dives on the wet tarp. Cincinnati became the first team since the introduction of the 162-game schedule to lead wire-to-wire. "We started in first place and we're still in first place," Dibble said. "All year long people said we can't do it.... Well, we did it."[23] When the rain let up, the Reds lost to San Diego, 3–1. No matter; they had become champions of the West.

The last day of September was also the last day in the major league playing career of Alex Trevino, a long-time backup catcher and utility player. Born August 26, 1957, in Monterrey, Mexico, he entered professional baseball at the age of 15 with Ciudad Victoria of the Mexican Central League on May 16, 1973. One year later he was purchased by the New

York Mets. He played five years in the minors and made his major league debut for the Mets in September 1978. In 1982 the Mets traded Trevino to Cincinnati. Soon he was on the move again—to Atlanta, San Francisco, Los Angeles, Houston, and the Mets again, before returning to Cincinnati on September 7, 1990. He appeared in only seven games for the Reds in 1990 before being released. Trevino then played several years in the minors and the Mexican League. In 2005 he became a broadcaster for the Houston Astros.

Cincinnati had a losing record again in September, going 14–15 for the month. However, they lost only one-half game in the standings as the Dodgers broke even for the month and the San Francisco charge fell short.

Standings in National League
West After Games of September 30

Club	W	L	Pct	GB
Cincinnati	89	70	.560	—
Los Angeles	84	75	.528	5
San Francisco	84	75	.528	5
San Diego	74	85	.465	15
Houston	74	85	.465	15
Atlanta	63	96	.396	26

October

With the National League West flag already clinched, the Reds had only a three-game series with Houston in the first three days of October left to finish the regular season. The third day of October marked not only the end of the regular season, but also the end of the major league career of Tim Birtsas and the big league debut of Glenn Sutko. Born in Pontiac, Michigan, in 1960, Birtsas was a left-handed pitcher and a varsity basketball player in high school. In 1979 he enrolled at Michigan State University on a baseball scholarship, one year after fellow Pontiac native Kirk Gibson won all–American honors in both baseball and football for the Spartans.

Birtsas was selected by the New York Yankees in the second round of the 1982 amateur draft. After two years with the Yankee's farm club in Fort Lauderdale, he was traded to the Oakland Athletics in December 1984. He made his major league debut for the A's on May 3, 1985, winning ten games in his first big league season, a number that he never approached again. After the 1987 season he was traded, along with Jose Rijo, to the Cincinnati Reds for Dave Parker. At 6'7" and 240 pounds, he was the biggest man on the Reds' roster, but contributed little to the Reds' championship season. He made his final major league appearance on October 3, at the age of 30, and was released soon thereafter. In five major league seasons Birtsas had collected only one hit. That one hit was a home run off Mets pitcher Sid Fernandez on July 2, 1989. He was not the only player ever to homer for his only big league hit, but it surely was the high point of his career.

In 1991 Birtsas pitched for the Tokyo Yakult Swallows in Japan. He pitched in Italy in 1992 before retiring with hip problems. In 1993 Birtsas returned to Michigan and started a real estate development and investment company called RBI Construction management, in partnership with his Pontiac neighbor and fellow Michigan State alumnus, Kirk Gibson. By 2009 Birtsas was simultaneously executive vice president of RBI and vice president for business management of the Oakland County (Michigan) Cruisers, an independent baseball club. He planned to build a stadium in Ypsilanti to house the club in 2010, but was unable to secure sufficient funding for the project. In 2012 the club moved to London, Ontario.

On the final day of the 1990 season, Glenn Sutko made his major league debut. Sutko was born in Atlanta on May 9, 1968, and was drafted by Cincinnati out of Spartanburg Methodist College in the 45th round of the 1987 amateur draft. After three years in the Reds' minor league system, the young catcher was called up at the tail end of the 1990 season. He made his first big league appearance in the sixth inning of the October 3 game, in relief of Joe Oliver. He had his first at-bat in the eighth inning, striking out swinging. He returned to the minors, but got one more chance at the majors. In July 1991, both Reds catchers were briefly on the shelf. Jeff Reed was out with a rib injury, and Joe Oliver had a bout of the flu. Sutko appeared in ten games, hit .100, and was sent back to the minors. He spent a total of eight seasons in the bushes before returning to the Atlanta area, where he developed a very successful youth baseball program. In 2012 he was arrested on charges of disregarding a traffic signal and driving under the influence of alcohol. In that instance he wasn't a very good role model as the mentor of young ball players.

Cincinnati won two of the three regular season games played in October and finished five games ahead of the second-place Los Angeles Dodgers to become the champions of the West. How did they do it? *The Sporting News* claimed that some things defy explanation. "How could the Reds, a fifth-place club in 1989 and strangers to new Manager Lou Piniella, hope to finish first in the National League West?" asked a *TSN* columnist. "There are no answers here," he wrote. "Some things are not meant to be logical."[24]

In retrospect, it seems that the Reds won through a total team effort all the way from ownership down to the bench players. Reviled though she was, Marge Schott made some wise decisions in hiring Bob Quinn and Lou Piniella. Quinn's trades and Piniella's leadership set the tone for the season, but games are won by players on the field, and the players came through. Infielders, outfielders, catchers, bench players, starting pitchers, and relievers all did their part in the successful hunt for a Reds October.

National League West Final Standings 1990

Club	W	L	Pct.	GB
Cincinnati	91	71	.562	—
Los Angeles	86	76	.531	5
San Francisco	85	77	.525	6
San Diego	75	87	.463	16
Houston	75	87	.463	16
Atlanta	65	97	.401	26

October Surprise

League Championship Series

The National League Championship Series opened in Riverfront Stadium on Thursday night, October 4, with the Cincinnati Reds, champions of the West, hosting the Pittsburgh Pirates, champions of the East. Jose Rijo, fully recovered from his mid-season ills, was on the mound for the Reds, opposed by Bob Walk. The Reds scored first, plating three runs in the bottom of the first inning on a walk to Larkin, a single by Morris, and consecutive doubles by Davis and O'Neill. But Cincinnati did not score again. Pittsburgh scored a run in the second inning and tied the game in the top of the fourth, when Sid Bream homered with Barry Bonds on base via a walk. The Pirates took the lead in the seventh, when Gary Redus got a pinch-hit single off Norm Charlton and Andy Van Slyke knocked him in with a double. The Reds threatened in the bottom of the ninth inning. Benzinger led off with a single, Eric Davis followed with a walk, and Oester hit into a fielder's choice, leaving runners on first and second. Bates came in to pinch-run for Oester, but was thrown out as the trailer on an attempted double steal. Sabo struck out swinging, and the Reds lost Game 1, 4–3.

In Game 2, Pittsburgh manager Jim Leyland sent his ace, 22-game-winner and eventual Cy Young Award recipient Doug Drabek, to the mound. Drabek responded by pitching a five-hitter, but it wasn't good enough, as the Pirates lost, 2–1. "That was the turning point," Leyland said. "We had a shot at Browning in the first inning. He wasn't the Browning he usually is, and we let it get away."[1] Redus and Jay Bell led off the game with consecutive singles, but Browning pitched out of trouble and held the Pirates to only one run, on a homer by Jose Lind in the fifth inning. Cincinnati scored in the first inning when Larkin walked, stole second, went to third on a single by Winningham, and scored on O'Neill's single. After Lind tied the game, Cincinnati again took the lead when Winningham reached on a fielder's choice, stole second, and scored on O'Neill's double. Dibble and Myers pitched three innings of hitless relief, with Myers picking up the save.

After two days off, the clubs traveled to Pittsburgh for Game 3. Danny Jackson started for Cincinnati against Zane Smith, and the Reds hit the Pittsburgh hurler hard, pounding out a 6–3 win. The big blows were home runs by Hatcher and Duncan. All three of the Nasty Boys were involved, giving up one run in 3⅓ innings. Myers collected his second save of the series.

Game 4 was a rematch of the Game 1 starters. Pittsburgh grabbed a first-inning lead, 1–0. Cincinnati went in front, 2–1, in the fourth when a solo home run by O'Neill was followed by singles by Davis and Morris and a sacrifice fly by Sabo. Pittsburgh tied the game in the bottom of the frame. Going into the seventh inning, the score remained, 2–2. The Reds took the led for good when Morris singled and came home on Sabo's two-run shot, to make it 4–2. Each club added one run, but the Reds had a 5–3 victory. Rijo got the win. Myers and Dibble each pitched one inning in relief, with Dibble earning the save.

In Game 5 Pittsburgh started Drabek and the Reds countered with Browning. Neither pitcher got off to a good start. Larkin led off with a double and scored on Winningham's sac fly to give the Reds a short-lived 1–0 lead. Bell was hit by a pitch and scored on Van Slyke's triple to tie the game. Van Slyke scored on a groundout to put the Pirates up, 2–1. Both pitchers settled down, each giving up only one run the rest of the way. Pittsburgh won the game, 3–2, and the series was still alive.

The NLCS returned to Riverfront Stadium for Game 6 on Friday night, October 12, with the Reds leading the series, three games to two. Cincinnati needed one more win to clinch the pennant and qualify for the World Series. Pittsburgh needed a win to stave off elimination and force a Game Seven.

Pittsburgh manager Jim Leyland surprised fans by starting Ted Power on the mound. It was a rare start for Power, a former Red and primarily a relief pitcher. The Reds countered with Danny Jackson. The Reds took a 1–0 lead in the bottom of the first inning, as Barry Larkin led off with a single, stole second, advanced to third on an error, and scored on a groundout by Eric Davis. Jackson held the Pirates hitless through the first four innings. In the fifth, Barry Bonds walked and scored on a double by Carmelo Martinez, the only hit the Pirates collected all night. The Reds took a 2–1 lead in the bottom of the seventh. With Zane Smith pitching for Pittsburgh, Oester led off the frame with a single, went to third on a hit by Hatcher, and scored on a line-drive single by Luis Quinones, pinch-hitting for O'Neill. In the ninth inning, the Pirates threatened to take the lead. With one out Bonds drew a base on balls. Martinez, who had doubled earlier, hit a long drive to deep right field for a potential two-run homer, but Braggs raced back and made a spectacular against-the-fence catch for the second out of the inning. Reliever Randy Myers then struck out Don Slaught to end the game. The Cincinnati Reds were National League champions and headed for the World Series.

Two unlikely heroes had helped the Reds win Game 6—Luis Quinones with his pinch-hit that gave the Reds the lead, and Glenn Braggs with his spectacular catch that preserved the lead.

Luis Quinones was born in Ponce, Puerto Rico, on April 28, 1962. On his 18th birthday he was signed as an amateur free agent by the San Diego Padres. The Padres failed to place him on their 40-man roster, and he was taken by Oakland in the Rule 5 draft on December 6, 1982. The switch-hitting utility man made his major league debut for the A's on May 27, 1983, at the age of 21. He participated in only 19 major league games that season before being sent down to the minors. Over his career he was shuttled back and forth between the majors and the minors, playing for 5 different big league clubs and 16 minor league outfits in a long career. He came to Cincinnati on April 1, 1988, in a trade with the Chicago Cubs for Bill Landrum. He spent parts of four seasons with the Reds, playing in 97 games in both 1989 and 1991. In the Reds' pennant-winning season of 1990, he played in 83 games, logging time at all four infield positions.

The highlight of his major league career was his RBI pinch-hit single in the sixth game of the 1990 National League Championship Series, which drove in the winning run as the Reds eliminated the Pittsburgh Pirates. He did not play in the World Series. After the 1991 season, he was released by the Reds and signed as a free agent with the Minnesota Twins. He played in only three games for Minnesota, with his final major league appearance coming on April 11, 1992, at the age of 29. The Twins sent him to Portland of the Pacific Coast League for the remainder of the 1992 season, then released him in October. From 1993–1999 he played for various minor league or independent squads. Recently he has served as a hitting coach in the Detroit Tigers' organization

The hitting star of the 1990 NLCS was a native Ohioan, Paul O'Neill. Born in Columbus on February 25, 1963, he was the son of a former minor league pitcher. At the age of five, O'Neill started playing baseball with his four older brothers in the family's backyard. He played in elementary and middle school and on a Little League team coached by his father. At

Brookhaven High School, he participated in baseball, basketball, and football. Despite offers of college scholarships in both basketball and baseball, he decided to play professional baseball. He was selected by the Cincinnati Reds' in the fourth round of the 1981 amateur draft. After five minor league seasons, he made his major league debut on September 3, 1985, at the age of 22. O'Neill shuttled back and forth between Cincinnati and the minors until becoming the Reds full-time right-fielder in 1988. One of the highlights of his 1990 season came on July 29 against the Giants in Candlestick Park. With two out in the ninth inning, he hit a single to break up Scott Garrelts' no-hit bid. In the NLCS he hit. 471, with four doubles, a home run, and four runs batted in. He had a 1.324 OPS.

O'Neill became a fan favorite in the Queen City and was devastated when he was traded (along with minor leaguer Joe DeBerry) to the New York Yankees for Roberto Kelly in November 1992. He had been a Reds fan since childhood and did want to leave Cincinnati. However, he thrived in the Bronx, winning the American League batting championship in 1994 and averaging over 100 runs batted in per season the next six years. He played his final game at the age of 38 on October 7, 2001, the game in which Arizona won the World Series by defeating the Yankees on Luis Gonzalez's hit off Mariano Rivera. During his 17-year career with the Reds and Yankees, he played in the All-Star Game five times and was a member of an equal number of world championship teams.

After retiring, O'Neill returned to his native Ohio, settling in Montgomery, a Cincinnati suburb. During the baseball season he works as a color commentator and analyst for the Yankees' television network. In October 2013 he expressed interest in becoming manager of the Cincinnati Reds before the position was assigned to Bryan Price.

Despite the Game 6 heroics of Quinones and Braggs and the hitting of O'Neill, the real stars of the 1990 NLCS were clearly the Nasty Boys. Dibble and Myers accounted for saves in every game the champions won and were named co-winners of the Most Valuable Player Award. Including Charlton, the trio appeared in four games each and permitted a total of six hits and one earned run in 15⅔ innings, an ERA of 0.57. *The Sporting News* reported: "Dibble, who wears the crazed glare of a man possessed, rang up 10 strikeouts in his five hitless innings. Charlton and Myers were only slightly more hittable."[2]

Rob Dibble was born in Bridgeport, Connecticut, on January 24, 1964. At Southington High School, he briefly considered a career in hockey. "I was a goon," Dibble said. "I tripped guys. I interfered with guys to keep them occupied. I kind of enjoyed that role as a disrupter. That was my mentality. Take a guy out of his game plan and ruin his day."[3]

Instead of pursuing his hockey dreams, Dibble played baseball briefly at Florida Southern College. He enrolled in September 1982 and was gone by December, unable to handle college academics. Florida Southern baseball coach Chuck Anderson said, "School and baseball did not go hand and hand with Rob. Fortunately, Rob is one of the few who made it anyway.... Without a doubt Dibble would have been one of the best college pitchers ever. I wish I could have had him longer so I could have refined his mechanics. He is still a wild-armed thrower."[4]

Dibble was drafted by the St. Louis Cardinals in the 11th round of the 1982 amateur draft, but did not sign. One year later the Cincinnati Reds took him in the first round (the 20th overall pick). After two years as a minor league starting pitcher, Dibble was converted into a reliever at Cedar Rapids in 1985. He made his major league debut on June 29, 1988, at the age of 24. He never started a game during

Rob Dibble, along with fellow Nasty Boys Randy Myers and Norm Charlton, headed up a formidable relief corps for the Reds in 1990. In the NCLS the trio combined for 15⅔ innings in which they gave up only one earned run. Dibble and Myers were named co–MVPs of the series. Throughout his career Dibble was involved in controversy because of his competitive nature and inability to control his temper.

his major-league career, always working out of the bullpen, sometimes as a set-up man and frequently as a closer, the role that he much preferred. He complained vociferously about the Reds' management not using him often enough as the closer.

Throughout his career with the Reds, Dibble was involved in controversy, perhaps because of his competitive nature or perhaps because he did not control his temper. Some have questioned whether the term "nasty" as in Nasty Boys might apply not only to his pitches but also to his personality and intentions.

In 1989 Dibble was fined and or suspended three times, first for throwing at Willie Randolph of the Dodgers. On July 9 he hit Tim Teufel of the Mets in the back with a pitch, precipitating a bench-clearing brawl. Dibble and Teufel were both ejected, along with the Mets' Juan Samuel and the Reds' Norm Charlton, for engaging in the action. Dibble was fined $400 and suspended for three days. Later in the same season he was fined and suspended for five days for heaving a bat belonging to Terry Pendleton against the screen behind home plate at Riverfront Stadium.

In 1990 Dibble was warned and fined for throwing a pitch over the head of Atlanta third baseman Jim Presley on June 12. "They were leaning over the plate," Dibble said. "I had to come inside. Now they're taking the pitchers' pitches away from them. They can fine me all they want; my job is to pitch inside."[5] Braves manager Russ Nixon was not mollified: "The guy is nuts. Who the hell does he think he is?"[6] Before a game on July 20, Dibble dumped a bucket of ice water on the head of *Cincinnati Enquirer* sportswriter Mike Paolercio in retaliation for some erroneous quotes the scribe had attributed to him.

In 1991 Dibble was fined $1,000 and suspended for three days for throwing a pitch behind Houston's Eric Yelding on April 11, after Astros reliever Curt Schilling had knocked in a run in his first major league at-bat. Yelding threw his helmet, hitting Dibble in the left shoulder, and tried to tackle him, sparking a brief, bench-clearing affair. Dibble later apologized to Yelding, confessing that he was at fault. "I admit that I lose my temper too easily," Dibble said. "But I'm not as crazy as I used to be.... Hey, everybody loses it once in a while. I'm not going to say I'm one of the nicer pitchers in the league, but I have this reputation of being a head hunter.... That's ridiculous."[7]

On April 28 Dibble lost his temper again. Even though he got the save in a 4–3 victory over the Cubs, he was irate about giving up five hits and two runs in the two innings he pitched. After the final out, he hurled a ball into the center field stands at Riverfront Stadium, hitting a first grade teacher, Meg Porter, with the heave. Fortunately, the teacher was not seriously injured, although she did receive medical treatment. For this incident, Dibble was hit with a four-day suspension and an undisclosed fine.

Dibble's reputation suffered another blow in late July when he fielded a bunt by Chicago's Doug Dascenzo and threw it at Dascenzo as he was running down the first base line. Dibble insisted the ball slipped, but not everyone believed him.

In 1992 the hot-tempered pitcher nearly made it through the season without controversy, but on September 17 he got into a dispute with his equally hot-tempered manager. Piniella had used Steve Foster instead of Dibble to close a recent game. The skipper told reporters it was because Dibble was unavailable due to soreness in his shoulder. According to *The Sporting News,* Dibble responded by saying "Lou's full of ____."[8] Sweet Lou lost his cool, and a shoving match ensued, quickly broken up by players and coaches. No fines or suspensions were levied for this unseemly encounter.

Dibble was granted free agency by the Reds after the 1994 season. He played for the White Sox and the Brewers in 1995, playing his final major league game for Milwaukee on September 30, 1995, at the age of 31. In 1998 he joined ESPN as a baseball analyst. Ten years later he moved to the FOX Network. In 2009 he became the color voice of the Washington Nationals on MASN. He was fired in 2010 after some controversial remarks on the air. Since then he has been mostly on talk radio, although he coached baseball at Calabasas, California, High School for ten games in 2013 before being fired. At last report he was broadcasting Los Angeles Angels games on radio for Compass Media.

1990 World Series

The 1990 World Series started on October 16, with the Reds hosting the powerful Oakland Athletics. Led by future Hall of Famer Rickey Henderson and sluggers Jose Canseco and Mark McGwire, the A's were a fearsome aggregation. Their pitching staff featured Dave Stewart and Cy Young Award winner Bob Welch as leaders of the rotation and future Hall of Famer Dennis Eckersley in the bullpen. Oakland had won three straight American League pennants, swept the San Francisco Giants in the 1989 World Series and eliminated the Boston Red Sox in four straight in the 1990 American League Championship Series. Red Sox manager Joe Morgan said, "Oakland isn't a dynasty yet, but it's as good a team as I've seen in years. Aw, hell, they're the best in the world."[9]

Joseph Wallace wrote that the Reds seemed destined to fall easily to the powerful A's. He opined that it was a shock when they defeated the Pirates in the playoffs, but no one gave them much of a chance against Oakland and the "Bash Brothers" (Canseco and McGwire).[10]

Paul Schulman, a media buyer, lamented that CBS would lose millions due to the perceived lopsidedness of the World Series, unless the Reds should make an unexpected run and challenge the A's. "It would help if the National League wins the first game, and people would think the A's might not win so easily," Schulman said. "What would really help would be for Commissioner Fay Vincent to issue a special ruling whereby the A's could have only two outs per inning, while the other team still gets three. In that case the Series might go five or six game."[11]

One baseball man who thought the Reds had a chance was the other Joe Morgan, one of the stars of Cincinnati's last World Series champions, the 1976 Big Red Machine. He wrote, "It's fashionable these days to talk about how dominating the Oakland A's appear to be heading into the World Series against Cincinnati. The A's are good, make no mistake about that. But ... it's easy to see how the Reds match up surprisingly well, and I expect them to make this very interesting."[12]

It didn't take very long to show that either the A's were overrated, the Reds were underrated, or anything can happen in a short series. In Game 1, Jose Rijo faced Dave Stewart, who had won six straight post-season decisions. Rijo set down the side in order in the top of the first inning. In the bottom of the frame, with Hatcher on base via a walk, Davis unloaded a two-run homer on the first pitch he saw. The myth of Stewart's invincibility was shattered. Rijo pitched seven scoreless innings, and Dibble and Myers shut out the A's in the eighth and ninth, while Cincinnati got to Stewart and his relievers for five more runs. The Reds posted an easy victory, 7–0.

No one could have been more deserving than Davis of the plaudits he received for his exploits in Game 1. He had endured a season of pain and frustration ever since he severely strained his right knee while stealing third base in Philadelphia on April 24.

Eric Davis was born in Los Angeles on May 29, 1962. He was drafted out of Fremont High School by the Cincinnati Reds in the eighth round of the 1980 amateur draft a few days after his 18th birthday. Originally a shortstop, he was converted into an outfielder while in the Reds' minor league system. He made his major league debut on May 19, 1984. In 1986 he stole 80 bases. The next year he clubbed 37 home runs. With his hitting, baserunning, and outstanding fielding, he became one of the game's most exciting stars, drawing comparisons to Willie Mays. "The Say Hey Kid" said, "It's an honor to be compared to Eric Davis."[13]

Beset by injuries throughout his career, Davis never appeared in more than 135 games in a season. The 1990 injuries were perhaps the most serious, causing him to miss 35 games, and when he did play he was in intense pain. He wore an electrical stimulation device that was designed to

This photograph shows Eric Davis batting in Game 2 of the 1990 World Series. The catcher is Oakland's Ron Hassey. With his hitting, baserunning, and outstanding fielding, Davis could have had a Hall of Fame career, but for a series of injuries. In 1990 he endured a season of pain and frustration to become one of the stars of the World Series. His home run in the first inning of Game 1 got the Reds off to a winning start. In the next two games he continued hitting. While diving for a ball in first inning of Game 4 he suffered a lacerated kidney, which required surgery. Much to the disgust of his teammates, the Reds' owner and general manager refused to send a charter plane to bring him back to Cincinnati (National Baseball Hall of Fame Library).

improve the circulation in his knee. He then slipped a support brace over the knee that left a bulge clearly visible under his uniform pants. After each game he put heavy ice bags on both knees.

Cincinnati fans, sometimes viewed as among the best in baseball, were not sympathetic to Davis. His every failure was met with a loud chorus of boos at Riverfront Stadium. Callers on radio talk shows unfairly accused him of malingering. His teammates continued to support him. "Having Eric in the lineup is important to this team," Larkin said. "Even with a knee that drives him crazy, he can hit with power and run. We need him in there."[14] Mariano Duncan chimed in, "When you think of the Cincinnati Reds, you think of Eric Davis, and we wouldn't be where we are without him. Those people who boo, they don't know what he goes through just to get in the lineup every day."[15] Dibble opined that it was sick to hear people in Cincinnati boo Davis.

After his heroics in Game 1 of the 1990 World Series, Davis collected two hits and two RBI in the next two games. While diving for a ball in the first inning of Game 4, he suffered a lacerated kidney, which required surgery. Writing in *The Sporting News*, Mark Whicker expressed his views: "Let's hope Eric Davis silenced those who criticized his hunger. With a bruised kidney he still insisted on finishing the first inning of Game 4. Davis is simply not physically equipped to play the way he insists: shoulder-first into walls, chest-first into turf. But he does it anyway."[16]

The refusal of Marge Schott and Bob Quinn to treat Davis with the dignity and respect he deserved by providing a charter plane after this injury left a huge blemish on their reputations.

After the 1991 season, the Reds traded Davis, along with Kip Gross, to the Los Angeles Dodgers for Tim Belcher and John Wetteland. In turn, the Dodgers traded him to Detroit in 1993. Injuries forced him to retire after the 1994 season, but he attempted to come back with the Reds in 1996. Injuries again cut down on his playing time. In 1997 he signed with Baltimore as a free agent. Although diagnosed with colon cancer in May, he was able to return to the team and hit a game-winning home run in Game 5 of the American League Championship Series. His exploits earned him the Roberto Clemente Award. In 1998 Davis had one of his best years, hitting .327 with 28 home runs. It was his last good year. The injury jinx plagued him again. He played his final major league game for the San Francisco Giants on October 7, 2001, at the age of 39.

Davis retired to his hometown of Los Angeles and became a business entrepreneur for a few years. In 2006 he returned to the Reds as an instructor during spring training. In 2014 he served as a special assistant to the general manager.

A fitting tribute to Davis was paid by Hal McCoy, who covered the Cincinnati Reds for the *Dayton Daily News* for more than 40 years, starting in 1973. McCoy told a blogger: "My favorite player of all-time is Eric Davis. He could hit home runs, he could steal bases. He was a great defensive player, and most of all, he was a great person."[17]

Game 2 of the 1990 World Series pitted Danny Jackson of the Reds against the A's 27-game-winner, Bob Welch. The A's took an early lead. Henderson led off the game with a single, stole second, went to third on a sacrifice bunt, and scored on a groundout by Canseco. The Reds scored twice in the bottom of the first, starting with consecutive doubles by Larkin and Hatcher. After Hatcher advanced to third on a long fly to deep center field by O'Neill, he scored on a groundout by Davis, giving the Reds a 2–1 lead. Jackson couldn't hold the lead. In the top of the third, Canseco homered, McGwire singled, and Henderson and Willie Randolph both walked. Ron Hassey's sacrifice fly scored McGuire, and Mike Gallego knocked Jackson out of the box with a line-drive hit to center field, giving Oakland a 4–2 lead. The Reds cut the deficit to one run in the fourth on a double by Oliver and a single by Oester. The score remained 4–3 until the bottom of the eighth inning. Hatcher led off with a triple. Braggs, pinch-hitting for Morris, knocked Hatcher in with a groundout and the score was tied, 4–4. Relievers Rick Honeycutt and Rob Dibble held the opposition scoreless in the ninth and the top of the tenth. In the bottom of that extra inning, the A's best reliever, Dennis Eckersley, entered the game and gave up a single to Billy Bates, pinch-hitting for Dibble. Consecutive singles by Sabo and Oliver plated Bates with the winning run. Cincinnati led the Series, two games to nil.

After an off-day for travel, the Series moved to the Oakland-Alameda County Stadium for Game 3. Browning was on the mound for the Reds, facing Mike Moore. Sabo hit a home run in the second inning, giving the Reds a short-lived 1–0 lead. Harold Baines put the A's on top in the bottom of the frame with a two-run homer. The Reds put the game out of reach in the top of the third, scoring seven runs. The inning featured Sabo's second home run of the game, but Davis, Morris, Oliver, Duncan, and Larkin also batted in runs. Henderson led off the bottom of the third with a home run, making the score 8–3. Neither Browning nor the relievers for either club gave up any more runs. The 8–3 win gave the surprising Reds a 3–0 lead in the Series.

Game 4 again featured the starters from the opener, Rijo and Stewart. The A's jumped out to a 1–0 lead in the first inning when Carney Lansford knocked in Willie McGee, who had singled. Those were the only two hits Oakland collected in the entire game. Stewart was brilliant also, pitching shutout ball through seven innings. In the top of the eighth, Larkin led off with a single and advanced on a bunt that Winningham beat out for a hit. O'Neill attempted a sacrifice bunt, and was safe when Stewart made an errant throw. With the bases loaded, Larkin scored the tying run on a groundout by Braggs. Morris put the Reds in front, 2–1, with a sacrifice fly that plated Winningham. Rijo struck out Dave Henderson for the first out in the bottom of the ninth. Then Piniella called in Myers to finish the job. The Reds won the game, 2–1. They had taken the World Series four games to none.

As many had predicted, the 1990 World Series had produced a sweep, but it was the underdog Cincinnati Reds, not the heavily favored Oakland Athletics, who wielded the broom. There were heroes aplenty for the Reds.

Billy Hatcher set a record for a four-game series by hitting .750 (9-for-12), breaking the mark set way back in 1928 by somebody named Babe Ruth. Chris Sabo hit two home runs and matched Eric Davis with five runs batted in. The Nasty Boys (Charlton, Dibble, and Myers) combined for 8⅔ innings without giving up a single earned run. In four games they had one win, one save, and an earned run average of 0.00. The Most Valuable Player Award was given deservedly to Jose Rijo, for his two sparkling pitching performances, which netted the Reds two victories. Rijo's record was 2–0, with an ERA of 0.59.

Special mention should be made of Herm Winningham, who was 2-for-3 in Game 4 and scored the winning run of the Series. Winningham had played in only 84 games during the regular season and was not counted among the team's stars. But he blossomed in the post-season, playing an important role in Cincinnati's win over Pittsburgh in the National League Championship Series and hitting .500 in the World Series. Herm Winningham was born in Orangeburg, South Carolina, on December 1, 1961. He played baseball at Wilkinson High School in his home town and was drafted by the Pittsburgh Pirates in the 1979 amateur draft, but chose not to sign. The young outfielder played at Georgia Perimeter College and attracted the attention of several major league clubs, who tried to sign him. In secondary phases of drafts he turned down Milwaukee in January 1980, and Montreal that June. He signed with the New York Mets, who drafted him in the first round of the January 1981 secondary draft.

After starting in their farm system, Winningham made his major league debut for the Mets on September 1, 1984, at the age of 22. In December he was traded to Montreal. The Expos' vice president of player development, Jim Fanning, who had scouted him at Georgia Perimeter, was thrilled to get him, saying, "He has a chance of becoming a very fine, all-star type of player. He has speed, excellent range, and he's a line drive hitter."[18] Unfortunately, Winningham did not live up to the hype. In July 1988 the Expos traded him to Cincinnati, where he was usually a platoon player until he was granted free agency after the 1991 season. In 1992 Winningham played for the Boston Red Sox, making his final major league appearance on October 3, at the age of 30. He played in the minors in 1993 before retiring as an active player. In 2013 he was coaching at Wilkinson High School in Orangeburg, where he had played high school ball three decades earlier.

Although most commentators were surprised by Cincinnati's success, Lou Piniella professed that he saw it coming. "Last spring, when I took over the club, I saw I had a lot of talent, a team with speed, power, arms, defense, and youth," the manager said. "All I told my guys was this: 'You've played together for four or five years and you're young and talented, but you haven't won anything. This year it's your turn; it's your time.'"[19]

The Cincinnati Reds had won their first World Series in 14 years. The 1990 club did not have a colorful nickname like the Big Red Machine of the 1970s. What should they be called? "I'll tell you what you can call us," said Barry Larkin. "You can call us World Champions."[20]

Epilogue

The 1990 world's championship season was not the harbinger of a new dynasty for the Cincinnati Reds. It was more like the closing of a success story. Since 1990 the Reds have not played in a World Series, much less won one. From 1991–2014 is a stretch of 24 consecutive seasons without a world title, one of the longest such periods for Cincinnati since the first modern World Series was played in 1903.

Despite their sweep of the Oakland Athletics in the 1990 Series, the Reds were not favored to repeat in 1991. Clouds were on the horizon. Behind the scenes during the 1990 season, there had been a great deal of grumbling about salaries, arguments over playing time, and unhappiness with the way Piniella handled some of his players.[1] During the off-season, dissension became public. Rob Dibble, for example, was an angry young man. He vented about Schott and Schottzie, about Piniella, and about the Queen City and even some of his teammates.[2] Eric Davis was understandably upset by the seeming indifference to his injuries displayed by Quinn and Schott. Some of his teammates joined in the view that Davis was treated unfairly. Maury Allen wrote that Cincinnati could self-destruct.[3] Perhaps self-destruct is too harsh a term, but the Reds finished the 1991 season with a losing record, next-to-last in the National League West, 20 games behind the division champions.

Although the Reds rebounded somewhat in 1992, the architects of the 1990 success were gone at the end of the season. Bob Quinn was fired in early October, for reasons never made public. Lou Piniella declined a contract extension, citing a lack of communication from Schott and some misunderstandings as the reasons.[4] Under pressure from the commissioner's office, Schott gave up control of the club in 1998. Since 1992 the Reds have played under the guidance of four different general managers and ten (yes, ten!) field managers. Since Schott's heyday, the fortunes of the franchise have ebbed and flowed under two prominent Cincinnati businessmen as principal owners, first Carl H. Lindner Jr., then Robert Castellini.

If Quinn deserves credit for building the championship club of 1990 (and we hold that he does), he also shares blame for the decline in subsequent years. Some of the club's woes were due to unavoidable injuries; Quinn cannot be faulted for those. But he also made some bad trades and inappropriate personnel decisions that hurt the club. However, his successors made even worse mistakes. Within five years all of the top players on the 1990 club, except Hal Morris, Jose Rijo, and Barry Larkin, were gone from the Queen City, with the Reds getting little in return for most of them. The result was 14 losing seasons in the 23 years from 1991 through 2013, a record of 1,824–1,836 for a percentage of .498.

In 1994 Cincinnati was deprived of a chance for a league title and a possible World Series championship by a strike, which ended the season on August 12. Although the Reds were leading the NL Central when play was halted, Major League Baseball declined to designate any division winners. For the first time since 1904, no World Series was played. In the abbreviated season, Kevin Mitchell set Cincinnati club records for slugging average and on-base plus slugging with marks of .681 and 1.110, respectively. It was Mitchell's second season with the Reds since his acquisition from Seattle in a trade for Nasty Boy Norm Charlton. It was also his last full season on the banks of the Ohio, as he elected to play in Japan in 1995.

Animated by the sparkling play of MVP Barry Larkin, the Reds won the National League Central in 1995 and swept the Los Angeles Dodgers in the Division Series, but lost the NLCS to Atlanta in four straight. That was their last year under manager Davey Johnson, who was fired after the season by Schott. Two strong and stubborn personalities were bound to clash, but it was alleged that Johnson's departure was hastened by Schott's objection to his living with his fiancee prior to marriage.[5]

After 1995 it was another 15 years until the Reds copped another division title. In 2010 Joey Votto powered Cincinnati, managed by Dusty Baker, to first place in the NL Central, only to lose the Division Series to the Philadelphia Phillies in three straight. The Reds came back two years later with the same star and the same manager to win 97 games, the most victories the club had posted since the days of the Big Red Machine, way back in 1976. The 2012 club lost the NLDS to the San Francisco Giants, three games to two. In 2013 the Reds won 90 games, but lost a tie-breaker with the Pittsburgh Pirates for a wild card spot. After the season Baker was let go, despite being the third-winningest manager in franchise history. His 740 wins on the banks of the Ohio were outpaced only by Bill McKechnie with 744 and Sparky Anderson with 863.

Going into 2014, residents of the baseball town were cautiously optimistic about the future of their Reds. They had a new and untested manager in Bryan Price and a proven general manager in Walt Jocketty, who had achieved much success in building the St. Louis Cardinals into perennial contenders.

Former MVP and four-time all-star Joey Votto was back, as was Brandon Phillips, a three-time All Star and worthy possessor of four Gold Gloves. Jay Bruce, a two-time All-Star and winner of two Silver Slugger Awards, was returning, as was sensational reliever Aroldis Chapman, another two-time All-Star. Johnny Cueto and Mat Latos headed a formidable pitching staff, which included promising starters such as Homer Bailey and Mike Leake and several quality relievers. Queen City fans had good reason to hope. However, injuries to several key players, most notably Votto, derailed the Reds express. The cry in the baseball town became, "Wait till next year!"

Appendices

A. Results Game by Game

Game	Date	Opponent	Result	Record	Starter	Decision	Save
1	4–09	Houston	W 8–4	1–0	Browning	Myers	
2	4–10	Houston	W 3–2	2–0	Rijo	Layana	Myers
3	4–11	Houston	W 5–0	3–0	Armstrong	Armstrong	Mahler
4	4–13	Atlanta	W 5–2	4–0	Browning	Browning	Myers
5	4–15	Atlanta	W 13–6	5–0	Mahler	Birtsas	
6	4–16	Atlanta	W 5–3	6–0	Armstrong	Armstrong	Dibble
7	4–17	San Diego	W 2–1	7–0	Browning	Browning	Myers
8	4–18	San Diego	W 11–7	8–0	Jackson	Layana	Dibble
9	4–21	Atlanta	W 8–1	9–0	Armstrong	Armstrong	
10	4–22	Atlanta	L 1–3	9–1	Browning	Browning	
11	4–24	Philadelphia	L 3–6	9–2	Rijo	Rijo	
12	4–25	Philadelphia	W 12–7	10–2	Mahler	Mahler	
13	4–27	Montreal	W 3–2	11–2	Browning	Dibble	
14	4–28	Montreal	W 6–4	12–2	Armstrong	Armstrong	Myers
15	4–29	Montreal	L 3–6	12–3	Jackson	Robinson	
16	4–30	St. Louis	W 6–2	13–3	Rijo	Rijo	Dibble
17	5–01	Philadelphia	L 2–4	13–4	Mahler	Birtsas	
18	5–02	New York	L 0–5	13–5	Browning	Browning	
19	5–03	New York	W 5–0	14–5	Armstrong	Armstrong	Myers
20	5–04	St. Louis	W 8–3	15–5	Robinson	Robinson	Dibble
21	5–05	St. Louis	W 4–2	16–5	Rijo	Rijo	Myers
22	5–06	St. Louis	W 5–1	17–5	Scudder	Scudder	Charlton
23	5–07	St. Louis	W 3–0	18–5	Browning	Browning	
24	5–09	Pittsburgh	L 2–6	18–6	Armstrong	Armstrong	
25	5–10	Pittsburgh	W 10–4	19–6	Rijo	Charlton	
26	5–11	Chicago	W 7–5	20–6	Scudder	Charlton	Dibble
27	5–12	Chicago	L 2–4	20–7	Browning	Browning	
28	5–13	Chicago	W 13–9	21–7	Robinson	Dibble	
29	5–14	Pittsburgh	W 5–3	22–7	Armstrong	Armstrong	Myers
30	5–15	Pittsburgh	W 5–4	23–7	Rijo	Layana	
31	5–17	St. Louis	L 0–3	23–8	Browning	Browning	
32	5–18	St. Louis	W 1–0	24–8	Robinson	Charlton	
33	5–19	St. Louis	W 4–0	25–8	Armstrong	Armstrong	
34	5–20	St. Louis	L 2–6	25–9	Jackson	Jackson	

Game	Date	Opponent	Result	Record	Starter	Decision	Save
35	5–21	Chicago	W 4–3	26–9	Rijo	Rijo	Myers
36	5–22	Chicago	L 1–2	26–10	Browning	Scudder	
37	5–24	Montreal	W 2–1	27–10	Robinson	Robinson	
38	5–25	Montreal	W 5–0	28–10	Armstrong	Armstrong	
39	5–26	Montreal	W 5–3	29–10	Jackson	Dibble	Myers
40	5–27	Montreal	L 3–5	29–11	Rijo	Birtsas	
41	5–29	New York	W 2–1	30–11	Browning	Browning	Myers
42	5–31	Los Angeles	L 1–2	30–12	Armstrong	Charlton	
43	6–01	Los Angeles	W 5–2	31–12	Jackson	Jackson	Dibble
44	6–02	Los Angeles	W 8–3	32–12	Rijo	Charlton	
45	6–03	Los Angeles	W 2–0	33–12	Browning	Browning	Myers
46	6–04	San Francisco	L 1–10	33–13	Robinson	Robinson	
47	6–05	San Francisco	L 1–6	33–14	Armstrong	Armstrong	
48	6–06	San Francisco	L 2–3	33–15	Jackson	Dibble	
49	6–07	Houston	W 6–1	34–15	Rijo	Rijo	
50	6–08	Houston	L 1–3	34–16	Browning	Myers	
51	6–09	Houston	L 1–4	34–17	Mahler	Mahler	
52	6–10	Houston	L 2–4	34–18	Armstrong	Armstrong	
53	6–12	Atlanta	L 3–8	34–19	Jackson	Jackson	
54	6–12	Atlanta	L 2–3	34–20	Rijo	Rijo	
55	6–13	Atlanta	W 13–4	35–20	Browning	Browning	
56	6–14	Atlanta	W 4–3	36–20	Mahler	Dibble	
57	6–15	Houston	W 6–3	37–20	Armstrong	Armstrong	Myers
58	6–16	Houston	W 6–2	38–20	Jackson	Jackson	Dibble
59	6–17	Houston	W 7–1	39–20	Rijo	Rijo	
60	6–19	Atlanta	W 4–2	40–20	Browning	Charlton	Myers
61	6–19	Atlanta	L 0–3	40–21	Mahler	Mahler	
62	6–20	Atlanta	W 9–8	41–21	Armstrong	Myers	
63	6–21	Atlanta	L 3–4	41–22	Jackson	Dibble	
64	6–22	Los Angeles	L 6–7	41–23	Rijo	Myers	
65	6–23	Los Angeles	W 11–6	42–23	Browning	Browning	Layana
66	6–24	Los Angeles	W 10–6	43–23	Mahler	Mahler	Charlton
67	6–25	San Francisco	W 5–2	44–23	Armstrong	Armstrong	Myers
68	6–26	San Francisco	W 3–2	45–23	Jackson	Myers	
69	6–27	San Francisco	L 3–8	45–24	Browning	Browning	
70	6–28	New York	L 4–5	45–25	Rijo	Rijo	
71	6–29	New York	L 2–4	45–26	Mahler	Mahler	
72	6–30	New York	W 7–4	46–26	Armstrong	Charlton	Myers
73	7–01	New York	L 2–3	46–27	Jackson	Charlton	
74	7–03	Montreal	W 2–0	47–27	Browning	Browning	Myers
75	7–04	Montreal	L 3–5	47–28	Scudder	Scudder	
76	7–05	Philadelphia	W 9–2	48–28	Armstrong	Armstrong	
77	7–06	Philadelphia	W 4–1	49–28	Jackson	Jackson	Myers
78	7–07	Philadelphia	W 5–0	50–28	Mahler	Mahler	
79	7–08	Philadelphia	L 3–4	50–29	Browning	Charlton	
80	7–12	New York	L 3–10	50–30	Mahler	Charlton	
81	7–12	New York	W 3–2	51–30	Jackson	Jackson	Myers
82	7–13	New York	W 4–2	52–30	Browning	Browning	Myers
83	7–14	New York	L 3–6	52–31	Armstrong	Armstrong	
84	7–15	New York	W 2–1	53–31	Charlton	Charlton	Myers
85	7–16	Montreal	W 8–3	54–31	Hammond	Layana	

Game	Date	Opponent	Result	Record	Starter	Decision	Save
86	7–17	Montreal	W 6–2	55–31	Scudder	Scudder	
87	7–18	Montreal	W 8–7	56–31	Browning	Mahler	
88	7–19	Philadelphia	L 2–5	56–32	Armstrong	Armstrong	
89	7–20	Philadelphia	W 5–1	57–32	Charlton	Charlton	Dibble
90	7–21	Philadelphia	W 6–1	58–32	Rijo	Rijo	Mahler
91	7–22	Philadelphia	L 2–6	58–33	Scudder	Scudder	
92	7–23	San Diego	W 9–2	59–33	Browning	Browning	
93	7–24	San Diego	L 0–10	59–34	Armstrong	Armstrong	
94	7–25	San Diego	L 1–2	59–35	Charlton	Charlton	
95	7–25	San Diego	L 4–10	59–36	Mahler	Mahler	
96	7–26	San Francisco	L 3–4	59–37	Rijo	Rijo	
97	7–27	San Francisco	L 3–4	59–38	Scudder	Scudder	
98	7–28	San Francisco	L 2–3	59–39	Browning	Myers	
99	7–29	San Francisco	L 0–4	59–40	Armstrong	Armstrong	
100	7–30	Los Angeles	L 1–4	59–41	Charlton	Charlton	
101	7–31	Los Angeles	W 5–2	60–41	Rijo	Rijo	Myers
102	8–01	San Diego	W 6–3	61–41	Scudder	Scudder	
103	8–02	San Diego	L 5–8	61–42	Browning	Browning	
104	8–03	San Diego	L 2–3	61–43	Armstrong	Dibble	
105	8–04	San Diego	L 3–7	61–44	Charlton	Mahler	
106	8–05	San Diego	W 6–2	62–44	Rijo	Rijo	
107	8–07	Los Angeles	W 1–0	63–44	Browning	Browning	Myers
108	8–08	Los Angeles	L 2–4	63–45	Scudder	Scudder	
109	8–09	Los Angeles	L 3–10	63–46	Armstrong	Armstrong	
110	8–10	San Francisco	W 7–0	64–46	Charlton	Charlton	
111	8–11	San Francisco	L 2–4	64–47	Rijo	Rijo	
112	8–12	San Francisco	W 6–4	65–47	Browning	Browning	Myers
113	8–13	San Francisco	W 6–5	66–47	Scudder	Layana	Myers
114	8–14	St. Louis	W 9–4	67–47	Armstrong	Armstrong	Mahler
115	8–15	St. Louis	W 3–1	68–47	Charlton	Dibble	Layana
116	8–17	Pittsburgh	L 1–7	68–48	Rijo	Rijo	
117	8–17	Pittsburgh	L 3–4	68–49	Browning	Layana	
118	8–18	Pittsburgh	L 1–3	68–50	Hammond	Hammond	
119	8–19	Pittsburgh	L 3–6	68–51	Armstrong	Armstrong	
120	8–20	Chicago	L 1–3	68–52	Charlton	Charlton	
121	8–21	Chicago	W 8–1	69–52	Mahler	Mahler	
122	8–22	Chicago	W 4–1	70–52	Rijo	Rijo	
123	8–23	Pittsburgh	L 3–9	70–53	Hammond	Hammond	
124	8–24	Pittsburgh	W 4–3	71–53	Armstrong	Dibble	Myers
125	8–25	Pittsburgh	W 6–1	72–53	Charlton	Charlton	
126	8–26	Pittsburgh	W 6–2	73–53	Mahler	Mahler	Dibble
127	8–28	St. Louis	W 2–1	74–53	Rijo	Rijo	Myers
128	8–29	St. Louis	L 1–9	74–54	Browning	Browning	
129	8–30	Chicago	W 6–5	75–54	Jackson	Jackson	Myers
130	8–31	Chicago	L 3–4	75–55	Charlton	Myers	
131	9–01	Chicago	W 8–1	76–55	Mahler	Mahler	
132	9–02	Chicago	W 6–2	77–55	Rijo	Rijo	
133	9–03	Atlanta	L 6–8	77–56	Browning	Layana	
134	9–04	Atlanta	L 4–7	77–57	Jackson	Jackson	
135	9–05	San Francisco	W 5–3	78–57	Charlton	Charlton	Dibble
136	9–06	San Francisco	L 2–6	78–58	Mahler	Mahler	

Game	Date	Opponent	Result	Record	Starter	Decision	Save
137	9–07	Los Angeles	L 1–3	78–59	Rijo	Rijo	
138	9–08	Los Angeles	W 8–4	79–59	Browning	Browning	Myers
139	9–09	Los Angeles	L 4–6	79–60	Jackson	Jackson	
140	9–11	Houston	W 5–3	80–60	Charlton	Charlton	Myers
141	9–12	Houston	L 1–3	80–61	Rijo	Layana	
142	9–13	Houston	W 7–5	81–61	Mahler	Dibble	
143	9–14	Los Angeles	L 4–10	81–62	Browning	Browning	
144	9–15	Los Angeles	L 0–3	81–63	Jackson	Jackson	
145	9–16	Los Angeles	W 9–5	82–63	Charlton	Scudder	
146	9–17	San Francisco	W 4–0	83–63	Rijo	Rijo	
147	9–18	San Francisco	L 3–5	83–64	Browning	Browning	
148	9–19	Houston	L 2–5	83–65	Jackson	Jackson	
149	9–20	Houston	L 2–3	83–66	Charlton	Myers	
150	9–21	San Diego	W 10–1	84–66	Rijo	Rijo	
151	9–22	San Diego	W 6–4	85–66	Scudder	Dibble	Myers
152	9–22	San Diego	W 9–5	86–66	Browning	Browning	Mahler
153	9–23	San Diego	W 9–2	87–66	Jackson	Jackson	
154	9–25	Atlanta	L 0–10	87–67	Charlton	Charlton	
155	9–26	Atlanta	W 5–2	88–67	Rijo	Rijo	
156	9–27	Atlanta	W 4–2	89–67	Browning	Browning	Dibble
157	9–28	San Diego	L 1–2	89–68	Jackson	Myers	
158	9–29	San Diego	L 1–3	89–69	Charlton	Charlton	
159	9–30	San Diego	L 0–3	89–70	Rijo	Rijo	
160	10–01	Houston	W 4–3	90–70	Browning	Myers	
161	10–02	Houston	W 3–2	91–70	Armstrong	Scudder	Myers
162	10–03	Houston	L 2–3	91–71	Jackson	Birtsas	

• •

B. Players and Management

Players

Player	Age	Ht.	Wt.	Throw	Bat	Place of Birth
Jack Armstrong	25	6'5"	215	R	R	Englewood, New Jersey
Billy Bates	26	5'7"	155	R	L	Houston, Texas
Todd Benzinger	27	6'1"	190	R	Both	Dayton, Kentucky
Tim Birtsas	29	6'7"	240	L	L	Pontiac, Michigan
Glenn Braggs	27	6'3"	210	R	R	San Bernardino, California
Keith Brown	26	6'4"	215	R	Both	Flagstaff, Arizona
Tom Browning	29	6'1"	190	L	L	Casper, Wyoming
Norm Charlton	27	6'3"	205	L	Both	Fort Polk, Louisiana
Eric Davis	27	6'3"	185	R	R	Los Angeles, California
Rob Dibble	26	6'4"	230	R	L	Bridgeport, Connecticut
Bill Doran	31	5'11"	175	R	Both	Cincinnati, Ohio
Mariano Duncan	27	6'	185	R	R	San Pedro de Macoris, Dom. Rep.
Ken Griffey	39	6'	200	L	L	Donora, Pennsylvania
Kip Gross	25	6'2"	195	R	R	Scottsbluff, Nebraska
Chris Hammond	24	6'1"	195	L	L	Atlanta, Georgia

Player	Age	Ht.	Wt.	Throw	Bat	Place of Birth
Billy Hatcher	29	5'9"	175	R	R	Williams, Arizona
Danny Jackson	28	6'	205	L	R	San Antonio, Texas
Barry Larkin	25	6'	190	R	R	Cincinnati, Ohio
Tim Layana	26	6'2"	195	R	R	Inglewood, California
Terry Lee	28	6'5"	15	R	R	San Francisco, California
Rick Mahler	36	6'1"	202	R	R	Austin, Texas
Terry McGriff	26	6'2"	195	R	R	Fort Pierce, Florida
Gino Minutelli	25	6'	180	L	L	Washington, District of Columbia
Hal Morris	25	6'4"	215	L	L	Fort Rucker, Alabama
Randy Myers	27	6'1"	215	L	L	Vancouver, Washington
Paul Noce	30	5'10"	175	R	R	San Francisco, California
Ron Oester	33	6'2"	190	R	Both	Cincinnati, Ohio
Joe Oliver	24	6'3"	210	R	R	Memphis, Tennessee
Paul O'Neill	27	6'4"	215	L	L	Columbus, Ohio
Luis Quinones	27	5'11"	175	R	Both	Ponce, Puerto Rico
Jeff Reed	27	6'2"	190	R	L	Joliet, Illinois
Jose Rijo	24	6'2"	200	R	R	San Cristobal, Puerto Rico
Ron Robinson	28	6'4"	235	R	R	Exeter, California
Rosario Rodriguez	20	6'	185	L	R	Los Mochis, Mexico
Rolando Roomes	28	6'3"	180	R	R	Kingston, Jamaica
Chris Sabo	28	6'	185	R	R	Detroit, Michigan
Scott Scudder	22	6'2"	185	R	R	Paris, Texas
Glenn Sutko	21	6'3"	225	R	R	Atlanta, Georgia
Alex Trevino	32	5'11"	170	R	R	Monterrey, Mexico
Herm Winningham	28	5'11"	185	R	L	Orangeburg, South Carolina

Management

Owner—Marge Schott
GM—Bob Quinn
Field Manager—Lou Pinella
Coaches—Jackie Moore, Tony Perez, Sam Perlozzo, Larry Rothschild, Stan Williams

Broadcasters

Johnny Bench   Gordy Coleman
Marty Brennaman   Steve LaMar
Joe Nuxhall

• •

C. Reds Broadcasters

In 1990 fans were able to enjoy play-by-play accounts of the games and color commentary on the hunt for a Reds October by means of radio, network television, or cable television

The Reds Radio Network was one of the largest in professional sports, with affiliates in seven states—Ohio, Indiana, Kentucky, West Virginia, Tennessee, North Carolina, and Florida. Every regular season game was broadcast on flagship station WLW and the network. By 1990 color commentator Joe Nuxhall and play-by-play man Marty Brennaman had been together for 18 years on the Reds Radio Network, and their collaboration would continue for many more years.

Nuxhall had been a Reds broadcaster since 1968. Prior to that he had gained fame as the youngest player in major league history. Born in Hamilton, Ohio, July 30, 1928, he starred in baseball, basketball, and football in high school and played baseball for a semipro team managed by his father. With player shortages due to World War II, the Reds called him up for one game in 1944. On June 10, he pitched ⅔ of an inning at the age of 15. He returned to high school the next year and did not make another big league appearance until 1952, when he started a long pitching career. He played his last game on October 2, 1966, and became a broadcaster soon thereafter. With his folksy charm and affable personality, he became one of the most beloved sports figures in the history of the Queen City, known for closing his broadcasts with: "This is the ol' left-hander rounding third and heading for home," He was inducted into the Reds Hall of Fame in 1968. A bronze-cast sculpture of the pitcher was erected in Crosley Terrace, outside the Great American Ball Park, in 2003. Nuxhall retired in 2004, but continued making guest appearances occasionally. Despite multiple health problems he was active in many community charitable activities, increasing his popularity among Cincinnati fans. He died November 15, 2007.

The other half of the "Marty and Joe Show," Marty Brennaman was born in Portsmouth, Virginia, on July 28, 1942. After graduating from the University of North Carolina, he entered a career in broadcasting, first with small stations in North Carolina, then in Norfolk, Virginia, where he announced the games of the Virginia Squires in the American Basketball Association. (Later he was briefly a television voice of the University of Kentucky basketball team.) In 1971 he started announcing baseball games for the Tidewater Tides of the International League. He was named Sportscaster of the Year four times in Virginia. After coming to Cincinnati, he won the Ohio award twelve times. Although known mainly for his radio work, he also did play-by-play for several innings per game on the Reds Television network, swapping booths with Steve LaMar. In 2000 he was awarded the Ford C. Frick Award by the National Baseball Hall of Fame. Despite his numerous awards Brennaman is not universally admired. His outspoken manner and sometimes contentious behavior can antagonize players and fans alike. In 2012 he won some new friends by allowing his head to be shaved in public in return for fans contributing $20,000 to the

Reds Community Fund. In 2014 he was still broadcasting Reds games at the age of 72.

In 1990 Reds games were available on two television networks. The Reds Television Network had 25 affiliates, in six Midwestern or Southeastern states. Sports Channel Cincinnati reached 32 markets in Ohio, Indiana, Kentucky, and Tennessee. (This channel was replaced by Fox Sports Ohio in 1998.) Veteran sportscasters Steve LaMar and Marty Brennaman handled play-by-play on the telecasts while ex–Reds players Gordy Coleman and Johnny Bench provided analysis.

LaMar started broadcasting major league baseball games for the New York Mets in 1982. From 1985 through 1988 he announced Cleveland Indians games on radio and television. He worked in Cincinnati from 1990 to 1992. No biographies of him are currently available. Coleman joined the Reds broadcast team in 1990, the same year as LaMar. Gordy Coleman was born July 5, 1934, in Rockville, Maryland. He attended Duke University on a football scholarship, but turned to professional baseball after his freshman year, signing with the Cleveland Indians at the age of 18. He was traded to Cincinnati in 1960 and played for the Reds until 1967. He worked in public relations for the Reds for many years. He was color commentator on TV telecasts from 1990 to 1994. He died of a heart attack on arch 12, 1994, at the age of 59.

Bench was one of the greatest Reds players of all time. He was born in Oklahoma City on December 7, 1947. Drafted by Cincinnati in the second round of the 1965 amateur draft, he spent his entire 17-year major league career with the Reds. He was the National League Rookie of the Year in 1968, a two-time National League MVP, and was selected for the All-Star Game 14 times. Bench was elected to the Hall of Fame in 1989. A statue of the catcher was erected outside Great American Ball Park in 2011. After retiring as a player he appeared on baseball telecasts, not only in Cincinnati, but also nationally. In 2014 he was working as a special assistant to the general manager of the Reds.

• •

D. Statistics

Position Players with 100 or More Games Played

Player	G	AB	R	H	HR	RBI	SB	BA	OBP	SLG	OPS
Todd Benzinger	118	376	35	95	5	46	3	.253	.291	.340	.631
Eric Davis	127	453	84	118	24	86	21	.260	.347	.486	.833

Player	G	AB	R	H	HR	RBI	SB	BA	OBP	SLG	OPS
Mariano Duncan	125	435	67	133	10	55	13	.306	.345	.476	.821
Billy Hatcher	139	504	68	139	5	25	30	.276	.327	.381	.708
Barry Larkin	158	614	85	185	7	67	30	.301	.358	.396	.753
Hal Morris	107	309	50	105	7	36	9	.340	.381	.498	.880
Joe Oliver	121	364	34	84	8	52	1	.231	.304	.360	.664
Paul O'Neill	145	503	59	136	16	78	13	.270	.339	.421	.761
Chris Sabo	148	567	95	153	25	71	25	.270	.343	.476	.819

Position Players with Fewer Than 100 Games Played

Player	G	AB	R	H	HR	RBI	SB	BA	OBP	SLG	OPS
Billy Bates	8	5	2	0	0	0	2	.000	.000	.000	.000
Glenn Braggs	72	201	22	60	6	28	3	.299	.385	.443	.828
Bill Doran	17	59	10	22	1	5	5	.373	.448	.559	1.007
Ken Griffey	46	63	6	13	1	8	2	.206	.235	.286	.521
Terry Lee	12	19	1	3	0	4	0	.211	.273	.263	.536
Terry McGriff	2	4	0	0	0	0	0	.000	.000	.000	.000
Paul Noce	1	1	0	1	0	0	0	1.000	1.000	1.000	2.000
Ron Oester	64	154	10	46	0	13	1	.299	.339	.377	.716
Luis Quinones	83	145	10	35	2	17	1	.241	.301	.331	.632
Jeff Reed	72	175	12	44	3	16	0	.251	.340	.360	.700
Rolando Roomes	30	61	5	13	2	7	0	.213	.213	.311	.525
Glenn Sutko	1	1	0	0	0	0	0	.000	.000	.000	.000
Alex Trevino	7	7	0	3	0	1	0	.429	.500	.571	1.071
Herm Winningham	84	160	20	41	3	17	6	.256	.314	.425	.739

Pitchers

Player	G	AB	R	H	HR	RBI	SB	BA	OBP	SLG	OPS
Jack Armstrong	29	47	2	5	0	3	0	.106	.143	.106	.249
Tim Birtsas	29	4	0	0	0	0	0	.000	.000	.000	.000
Keith Brown	8	0	0	0	0	0	0	—	—	—	—
Tom Browning	38	75	6	7	0	4	0	.093	.117	.120	.237
Norm Charlton	57	37	4	5	0	0	0	.135	.238	.135	.373
Rob Dibble	68	7	0	0	0	0	0	.000	.000	.000	.000
Kip Gross	5	0	0	0	0	0	0	—	—	—	—
Chris Hammond	3	3	0	0	0	0	0	.000	.000	.000	.000
Danny Jackson	23	37	1	2	0	0	0	.054	.054	.108	.162
Tim Layana	55	5	0	0	0	0	0	.000	.000	.000	.000
Rick Mahler	35	35	1	4	0	2	0	.114	.135	.143	.278
Gino Minutelli	2	0	0	0	0	0	0	—	—	—	—
Randy Myers	66	4	0	1	0	1	0	.250	.250	.250	.500
Jose Rijo	29	62	3	10	0	2	1	.161	.188	.177	.365
Ron Robinson	6	11	0	1	0	1	0	.091	.091	.091	.182
Rosario Rodriguez	9	0	0	0	0	0	0	—	—	—	—
Scott Scudder	21	18	1	1	0	0	0	.056	.150	.056	.206
Team Total	**162**	**5525**	**693**	**1466**	**125**	**644**	**166**	**.265**	**.325**	**.399**	**.724**

Pitching

Starting Pitchers—Regular Rotation

Pitcher	W	L	Pct.	ERA	G	GS	CG	SHO	Saves	SO	WHIP
Jack Armstrong	12	9	.574	3.42	29	27	2	1	0	110	1.265
Tom Browning	15	9	.625	3.80	35	35	2	1	0	99	1.261
Danny Jackson	6	6	.500	3.61	22	21	0	0	0	76	1.355
Jose Rijo	14	8	.636	2.70	29	29	7	1	0	152	1.162

Starter/Relievers

Pitcher	W	L	Pct.	ERA	G	GS	CG	SHO	Saves	SO	WHIP
Norm Charlton	12	9	.571	2.74	56	16	1	1	2	117	1.302
Rick Mahler	7	6	.538	4.28	35	16	2	1	4	68	1.298
Scott Scudder	5	5	.500	4.90	21	10	0	0	0	42	1.451

Occasional Starters

Pitcher	W	L	Pct.	ERA	G	GS	CG	SHO	Saves	SO	WHIP
Chris Hammond	0	2	.000	6.35	3	3	0	0	0	4	2.206
Ron Robinson	2	2	.500	4.88	6	5	0	0	0	14	1.596

Relief Pitchers

Pitcher	W	L	Pct.	ERA	G	GS	CG	SHO	Saves	SO	WHIP
Tim Birtsas	1	3	.250	3.86	29	0	0	0	0	41	1.812
Keith Brown	0	0	—	4.76	8	0	0	0	0	8	1.324
Rob Dibble	8	3	.727	1.74	68	0	0	0	11	136	0.980
Kip Gross	0	0	—	4.26	5	0	0	0	0	3	1.263
Tim Layana	5	3	.625	3.49	55	0	0	0	2	53	1.438
Gino Minutelli	0	0	—	9.00	2	0	0	0	0	0	2.000
Randy Myers	4	6	.400	2.08	66	0	0	0	31	98	1.119
Rosario Rodriguez	0	0	—	6.10	9	0	0	0	0	8	1.645
Team Total	**91**	**71**	**.562**	**3.39**	**162**	**162**	**14**	**12**	**50**	**1029**	**1.292**

Blown Saves: Charlton 1; Dibble 6; Myers 6

Fielding

1B	G	TC	PO	A	E	DP	Pct.
Todd Benzinger	95	765	707	52	6	58	.992
Hal Morris	80	645	589	53	3	50	.995
Others	16	80	72	7	1	3	.988
Total	162	1490	1368	112	10	111	.993

2B	G	TC	PO	A	E	DP	Pct.
Mariano Duncan	115	547	245	287	15	51	.973
Ron Oester	50	171	80	88	3	14	.982
Others	26	122	50	69	3	18	.975
Total	162	840	375	444	21	83	.975

SS	G	TC	PO	A	E	DP	Pct.
Barry Larkin	156	740	254	469	17	86	.977
Others	21	59	24	29	6	7	.898
Total	162	799	278	498	23	93	.971

3B	G	TC	PO	A	E	DP	Pct.
Chris Sabo	146	355	70	273	12	17	.966
Others	29	63	12	47	4	0	.843
Total	162	418	82	320	16	17	.962

C	G	TC	PO	A	E	DP	Pct.
Joe Oliver	118	751	686	59	6	8	.992
Jeff Reed	70	389	358	26	5	1	.987
Others	4	18	16	2	0	1	1.000
Total	162	1158	1060	87	11	10	.991

OF	G	TC	PO	A	E	DP	Pct.
Eric Davis	122	270	257	11	2	1	.993
Billy Hatcher	131	319	308	10	1	2	.997
Paul O'Neill	141	285	271	12	2	0	.993
Glenn Braggs	60	124	110	10	4	3	.968
Herm Winningham	64	92	89	3	0	0	1.000
Others	41	83	81	1	1	0	.988
Total	162	1173	1116	47	10	6	.991

P	G	TC	PO	A	E	DP	Pct.
Total pitchers	162	283	90	182	11	8	.961
Cincinnati Reds	**162**	**6161**	**4369**	**1690**	**102**	**126**	**.983**

• •

E. Dismantling the 1990 Champions

Cincinnati slowly lost members of the 1990 championship team during the following years, culminating in Barry Larkin's retirement in 2004. The following section shows how each player left the team. The first chart lists the players in alphabetical order; the second lists the roster moves in chronological order.

Player	Date	Action
Jack Armstrong	11-15-1991	traded with Joe Turek and Scott Scudder to Cleveland for Greg Swindell
Billy Bates	3-29-1991	reassigned to Reds' minor league system
Todd Benzinger	7-11-1991	traded to Kansas City for Carmelo Martinez
Tim Birtsas	12-11-1990	released
Glenn Braggs	10-26-1992	granted free agency
Keith Brown	10-16-1992	granted free agency
Tom Browning	10-11-1994	granted free agency
Norm Charlton	11-17-1992	traded to Seattle for Kevin Mitchell
Eric Davis	11-27-1991	traded with Kip Gross to Los Angeles for Tim Belcher and John Wetteland
Rob Dibble	10-11-1994	granted free agency
Bill Doran	1-13-1993	sold to Milwaukee
Mariano Duncan	10-30-1991	granted free agency
Ken Griffey	8-24-1990	released

Player	Date	Action
Kip Gross	11-27-1991	traded with Eric Davis to Los Angeles for Tim Belcher and John Wetteland
Chris Hammond	3-27-1993	traded to Florida for Gary Scott and Hector Carrasco
Billy Hatcher	7-9-1992	traded to Boston for Tom Bolton
Danny Jackson	11-5-1990	granted free agency
Barry Larkin	10-29-2004	granted free agency
Tim Layana	3-31-1992	released
Terry Lee	11-20-1991	released
Rick Mahler	11-5-1990	granted free agency
Terry McGriff	9-7-1990	traded with Keith Kaiser and Butch Henry to Houston for Bill Doran
Gino Minutelli	9-22-1992	granted free agency
Hal Morris	10-29-1997	granted free agency
Randy Myers	12-8-1991	traded to San Diego for Bip Roberts and Craig Pueschner
Paul Noce	10-3-1990	granted free agency
Ron Oester	11-5-1990	granted free agency
Joe Oliver	11-3-1994	released
Paul O'Neill	11-3-1992	traded with Joe DeBerry to New York Yankees for Roberto Kelly
Luis Quinones	11-20-1991	released
Jeff Reed	10-27-1992	granted free agency
Jose Rijo	10-15-2003	granted free agency
Ron Robinson	6-9-1990	traded with Bob Sebra to Milwaukee for Billy Bates and Glenn Braggs
Rosario Rodriguez	12-20-1990	waived to Pittsburgh
Rolando Roomes	6-18-1990	waived to Montreal
Chris Sabo	10-25-1993	granted free agency
Scott Scudder	11-15-1991	traded with Jack Armstrong and Joe Turek to Cleveland for Greg Swindell
Glenn Sutko	after 17-17-1991	reassigned to Reds minor league system
Alex Trevino	12-2-1990	granted free agency
Herm Winningham	11-5-1991	granted free agency

Date	Player/Action
6-9-1990	Ron Robinson traded with Bob Sebra to Milwaukee for Billy Bates and Glenn Braggs
6-18-1990	Rolando Roomes waived to Montreal
8-24-1990	Ken Griffey released
9-7-1990	Terry McGriff traded with Keith Kaiser and Butch Henry to Houston for Bill Doran
10-3-1990	Paul Noce granted free agency
11-5-1990	Danny Jackson granted free agency
11-5-1990	Rick Mahler granted free agency
11-5-1990	Ron Oester granted free agency
12-2-1990	Alex Trevino granted free agency
12-11-1990	Tim Birtsas released
12-20-1990	Rosario Rodriquez waived to Pittsburgh
3-29-1991	Billy Bates reassigned to Reds minor league camp

Date	Player/Action
7-11-1991	Todd Benzinger traded to Kansas City for Carmelo Martinez
c7-17-1991	Glenn Sutko reassigned to Reds' minor league system
10-30-1991	Mariano Duncan granted free agency
11-5-1991	Herm Winningham granted free agency
11-15-1991	Jack Armstrong traded with Joe Turek and Scott Scudder to Cleveland for Greg Swindell
11-20-1991	Terry Lee released
11-20-1991	Luis Quinones released
11-27-1991	Eric Davis traded with Kip Gross to Los Angeles for Tim Belcher and John Wetteland
12-8-1991	Randy Myers traded to San Diego for Bip Roberts and Craig Pueschner
3-31-1992	Tim Layana released
7-9-1992	Billy Hatcher traded to Boston for Tom Bolton
9-22-1992	Gino Minutelli granted free agency
10-16-1992	Keith Brown granted free agency
10-26-1992	Glenn Braggs granted free agency
10-27-1992	Jeff Reed granted free agency
11-3-1992	Paul O'Neill traded with Joe DeBerry to New York Yankees for Roberto Kelly
11-17-1992	Norm Charlton traded to Seattle for Kevin Mitchell
1-13-1993	Bill Doran sold to Milwaukee
3-27-1993	Chris Hammond traded to Florida for Gary Scott and Hector Carrasco
10-25-1993	Chris Sabo granted free agency
10-11-1994	Tom Browning granted free agency
10-11-1994	Rob Dibble granted free agency
11-3-1994	Joe Oliver released
10-29-1997	Hal Morris granted free agency
10-15-2003	Jose Rijo granted free agency
10-29-2004	Barry Larkin granted free agency

• •

F. The 1990 Reds Rated

The Faber System of rating baseball players was developed by researcher Charles F. Faber several decades before the term sabermetrics became popular. In the system, for each batter a yearly point total is compiled by adding the number of runs scored or runs batted in (whichever is higher) to the mean of the batting average and the on-base percentage. To equalize among deadball and lively ball eras, the player's points are subtracted from the league mean to obtain each year's rating. For fielders, the accuracy with which a player executes plays and the amount of ground he covers (the range factor) are the two factors making up the rating. The range factor is differentiated among positions. For middle infielders and third basemen, assists and putouts are counted equally. For catchers, first basemen, and outfielders, an adjustment is made with assists receiving ten times the weight of putouts. Traditional statistics credit the catcher with a put-out whenever the pitcher strikes out a batter; this actually has little to do with the catcher's fielding ability. On the other hand, it takes considerable skill to throw out base runners, and the Faber System rewards catchers accordingly. Similarly, putouts by first basemen and outfielders are frequently the result of routine plays, whereas assists usually call for a more athletic performance. As with the batting ratings, fielding ratings are computed by comparing each player's totals to the league average, in order to compensate for differences in baseball over the years. As scoring runs and preventing the opposition from scoring are equally important, a player's total value is computed by adding his batting and fielding points. Catchers play an additional role; that is, in handling the pitching staff. No objective measure has yet been devised to assess this attribute, so the Faber System uses a surrogate figure derived from the team's winning percentage and the number of games caught by each backstop.

Building upon the weighted rating system devised by Ted Oliver in the 1940s,[1] the Faber System rates pitchers by considering their wins, winning percentage, and weighted rating. Many modern researchers use a variation of the weighted system, called wins above team, whether or not they are aware of Oliver's pioneering efforts. Relief pitching was not a big deal when Oliver wrote his seminal book. By 1990 it was well on the way to being indispensable. The Faber System computes a reliever's rating by adding his saves and excess or deficit in relief wins over losses to one-half the points yielded by the formula for starting pitchers. The precise formulae utilized in computing ratings for hitters, fielders, and pitchers of both ilks are explicated in Faber's *Baseball Ratings.*[2]

Position Players

Player	Position	Hitting	Fielding	Total
Todd Benzinger	1b	-59	-9	-68
Eric Davis	of	32	22	54
Mariano Duncan	2b	21	-42	-21
Billy Hatcher	of	-7	30	23
Barry Larkin	ss	40	64	104
Hal Morris	1b	36	-4	32
Joe Oliver	c	-59	30	8*
Paul O'Neill	of	17	14	31
Chris Sabo	3b	45	14	59

*includes bonus of 37 points

Pitchers

Pitcher	W	L	Pct.	WR	Saves	Points
Jack Armstrong	12	9	.571	225	0	42
Tom Browning	15	9	.625	1776	0	55
Norm Charlton	12	9	.571	225	2	42
Rob Dibble	8	3	.727	1947	11	60
Rick Mahler	7	6	.539	-338	4	19
Randy Myers	4	6	.400	-1720	31	37
Jose Rijo	14	8	.636	1914	0	56

Chapter Notes

Preface

1. Luke Salisbury, *The Answer Is Baseball* (New York: Vintage Books, 1989), 12.
2. *Ibid.*, 205.
3. Jacques Barzun, *God's Country and Mine: A Declaration of Love with a Few Harsh Words* (New York: Little, Brown, 1954).
4. Gerald Early, cited in Geoffrey C. Ward and Ken Burns, *Baseball: An Illustrated History* (New York: Alfred A. Knopf, 2010), 463.

Introduction

1. John Thorn, *Baseball in the Garden of Eden: The Secret History of the Early Game* (New York: Simon & Shuster, 2011), 142.
2. Thorn, 146.
3. Greg Rhodes, "The Atlantic Storm," in Bill Felber, ed. *Inventing Baseball: The 100 Greatest Games of the Nineteenth Century* (Phoenix: Society for American Baseball Research, 2013), 72.
4. Cited by John Liepa, "The Cincinnati Red Stockings and Cal Mcvey, Iowa's First Professional Baseball Player," *Iowa Heritage* (Spring 2006), 15.
5. Greg Rhodes and John Erardi, *The First Boys of Summer* (Cincinnati: Road West Publishing, 1994), cited by Liepa, 16.
6. Philip J. Lowry, *Green Cathedrals* (New York: Walker & Co., 2006), 62.
7. Paul Browne, "A Glorious Victory," in Felber, 178.
8. James A. Riley, *The Biographical Encyclopedia of the Negro Baseball Leagues* (New York: Carroll & Graf, 2002), 764.
9. Jules Tygiel, "Black Ball," in Thorn, 661.
10. Leslie A. Heaphy, *The Negro Leagues, 1869–1960* (Jefferson, NC: McFarland, 2003), 24.
11. Charles F. Faber, "J. L. Wilkinson," www.sabr.org, May 18, 2012.

12. Dick Clark and Larry Lester, eds., *The Negro Leagues Book* (Cleveland: Society for American Baseball Research, 1994).
13. *Ibid.*, 31.
14. Henry V. Lucas, quoted by Baseball-Almanac.com.
15. www.baseball-reference.com.
16. Lowry, 63.
17. *Ibid.*, 65.
18. Charles F. Faber, "Winners of a Tarnished Crown: The 1919 Cincinnati Reds," Paper delivered at a meeting of the Pee Wee Reese Chapter of the Society for American Baseball Research, Louisville, KY, June 12, 1994.
19. *The Sporting News*, October 2, 1919.
20. Faber, *Baseball Ratings*, 113.
21. Tom Meany, *Baseball's Greatest Teams* (New York: A. S. Barnes, 1949), 154.
22. *Ibid.*, 81.
23. Charles F. Faber, and Richard B. Faber, *Spitballers: The Last Legal Hurlers of the Wet One* (Jefferson, NC: McFarland, 2006), 28.
24. *The Sporting News*, October 16, 1919.
25. Susan Dellinger, "A Shadow in the Night ... The Graying of the White: Edd Roush and the 1919 World Series," in Mark Stang and Dick Miller, eds., *Baseball in the Buckeye State* (Cleveland: Society for American Baseball Research, 2004), 21. All quotes attributed to Moran and Eller are from Dellinger's account.
26. "Sidney Weil: Owner of the Cincinnati Reds, 1929–1933," in Stang and Miller, 29.
27. *Ibid.*
28. *The Sporting News*, February 8, 1934.
29. www.crosley-field.com.
30. *Ibid.*
31. *Ibid.*
32. *Ibid.*
33. Pete Palmer and Gary Gillette, eds., *The Baseball Encyclopedia* (New York: Barnes & Noble, 2004, 1481.
34. Kates.
35. Arthur Daley, quoted by Dwayne Isrig.

"Bill Dewitt," in Charles F. Faber, ed., *The 1934 St. Louis Cardinals: The World Champion Gas House Gang* (Phoenix: Society for American Baseball Research, 2014).

36. *Chicago Tribune*, December 6, 1966.

37. *Cincinnati Enquirer*, October 10, 1969.

38. *The Sporting News*, October 14, 1972.

39. Frederick Ivor-Campbell and David Pietrusza, "Postseason Play," in John Thorn, et al, eds., *Total Baseball*, 8th ed. (Wilmington, DE: Sports Media Publishing, 2004), 404.

40. Paul Dickson, *The Paul Dickson Baseball Dictionary* (New York: W. W. Norton, 1989), 192.

41. Joe Morgan, and David Fellman, *Joe Morgan: A Life in Baseball* (New York: W. W. Norton, 1993), 160.

42. Joe Posnanski, *The Machine* (New York: HarperCollins, 2009), 27.

43. *Ibid.*

44. *Ibid.*, 25.

45. *Ibid.*, 64.

46. *Ibid.*, 90.

47. *Ibid.*, 222.

48. *The Sporting News*, October 18, 1975.

49. Posnanski, 223.

50. Joseph Wallace, *World Series: An Opinionated Chronicle of 100 Years* (New York: Harry N. Abrams, 2003), 170.

51. Bill James, *The Bill James Historical Baseball Abstract* (New York: Villard, 1988), 255.

52. John Thorn, et al, eds., *Total Baseball* (Wilmington, DE: Sport Media Publishing, 2004), 246.

53. Posnanski, 245.

54. Wallace, 172.

55. *Ibid.*, 170.

56. *Boston Globe*, October 22, 1975.

57. www.cincinnati.reds.com, May 19, 2011.

58. *Ibid.*

59. Wallace, 172.

60. *Ibid.*, 173.

61. *Ibid.*, 168.

62. *New York Daily News*, October 22, 1976.

63. *Ibid.*, March 6, 1977.

64. www.cincinnati.reds.mlb.com.

Chapter 1

1. Bill Felber, ed., *Inventing Baseball: The 100 Greatest Games of the Nineteenth Century* (Phoenix, Arizona: Society for American Baseball Research, 2013).

2. John Thorn, "Introduction," in Felber, xiv.

3. www.baseball-almanac.com lists Cincinnati as the birthplace of at least 179 major league baseball players.

4. Charles F. Faber, *Baseball Ratings: The All-Time Best Players at Each Position, 1876 to the Present*, 3rd ed (Jefferson, NC: McFarland, 2008), 169.

5. *Ibid.*, 176.

6. www.cmws.org.

7. Lonnie Walker, "America's Best Amateur Team: The Midland Redskins," in Mark Stang and Dick Miller, eds., *Baseball in the Buckeye State* (Cleveland: Society for American Baseball Research, 2004), 66.

8. *Ibid.*, 68.

9. *Washington Post*, July 25, 1997.

10. Paul Daugherty, *Fair Game* (Wilmington, OH: Orange Frazer Press, 1999), 97.

11. Bill Werber and C. Paul Rogers III, *Memories of a BallPlayer: Bill Werber and Baseball in the 1930s* (Cleveland: Society for American Baseball Research, 2001), 86–87.

12. Paul DeBono, "A Common Thread: Black Baseball in Redland." in Mark Stang and Dick Miller, eds., *Baseball in the Buckeye State* (Cleveland: Society for American Baseball Research, 2004), 57.

13. Charles F. Faber, "Baseball Town," unpublished lyrics (Lexington, KY, 2013.).

14. Kevin Ralegh, www.artssci.uc.edu, April 30, 2011.

15. The 13 counties include two counties in Indiana—Dearborn and Ohio; six counties in Kentucky—Boone, Campbell, Gallatin, Grant, Kenton, and Pendleton; and five in Ohio—Brown, Butler, Clermont, Hamilton, and Warren.

16. The 1810 census reported the city population as 96.8 percent white; 3.2 percent black. The 1990 data were 60.5 percent white, 37.9 percent black, 0.2 percent American Indian, 1.1 percent Asian or Pacific Islander, 0.3 percent other, and 0.7 percent two or more races. About one percent of the population self-identified as Hispanic.

17. "Two Centuries on the Ohio River," www.gocincy.com.

18. Upton Sinclair, *The Jungle* (New York: Doubleday, 1906).

19. www.cincinnativiews.net/taverns. All data about breweries, saloons, and beer consumption are taken from this source.

20. William A. Cook, *August A. Herrmann: A Baseball Biography* (Jefferson, NC: McFarland, 2008).

21. *Cincinnati Post*, June 23, 1905.

22. Stephen Hess, *America's Political Dynasties*, 306.

Chapter 2

1. *The Sporting News*, March 6, 1989.

2. *Ibid.*, April 1, 1989.

3. *Ibid.*

4. *Ibid.*, April 3, 1989.

5. David Nemec, et al, *The Baseball Chronicle* (Lincolnwood, IL: Publications International, Ltd., 2008), 555.

6. *The Sporting News*, March 19, 1990.

7. *Athlon's Baseball '90* (Nashville: Athlon Sports Communications, 1990), 160.

8. *New York Times*, August 3, 1989.

9. *Ibid.*, May 7, 1990.

10. *Ibid.*

11. *Ibid.*

12. *Ibid.*

13. *Ibid.*, October 16, 1989.

14. www.baseball-reference.com.

15. Rick Riley, "Heaven Help Marge Schott," *Sports Illustrated*, May 20, 1996.

16. Warren Corbett, "Marge Schott," SABR BioProject. www.sabr.org.

17. Jim Sandoval and Bill Nowlin, eds., *Can He Play? A Look at Baseball Scouts and Their Profession* (Phoenix: Society for American Baseball Research, 2011), 117.

18. *Ibid.*, 1.

19. *Lexington Herald-Leader*, January 14, 2014.

20. Daugherty, 97.

21. Cited by Jim McLennan, "Marge Schott by Both Sides," www.snakepit.com, May 9, 2011.

22. *Ibid.*

23. Rick Riley.

24. *Ibid.*

25. Werber and Rogers, 93.

26. Erardi and Luckhaupt, 231.

27. *Ibid.*

28. McLennan.

29. *Philadelphia Inquirer*, February 4, 1993.

30. www.wikipedia.org.

31. *The Sporting News*, October 23, 1989.

32. *Los Angeles Times*, October 14, 1989.

33. Erardi and Luckhaupt, 19.

34. *The Sporting News*, October 16, 1989.

35. *The Sporting News*, November 13, 1989.

36. Erardi and Luckhaupt, 19–20.

37. Mike Shatzkin, ed., *The Ballplayers* (New York: Arbor House, 1990), 409.

38. Erardi and Luckhaupt, 25.

39. *The Sporting News*, November 20, 1989.

40. *Ibid.*

41. *The Sporting News*, April 9, 1990.

42. *Ibid.*

43. *The Sporting News*, November 13, 1989.

44. Paul Daugherty, *Fair Game* (Wilmington, OH: Orange Frazer Press, 1999), 119.

45. *Ibid.*

46. Erardi and Luckhaupt, 73.

47. *The Sporting News*, May 7, 1990.

48. *Ibid.*

49. *Ibid.*

50. *The Sporting News*, November 20, 1989. Gullett accepted a position as pitching coach

for the Reds' Double-A affiliate in Chattanooga, but was sidelined by triple-bypass surgery in June 1990.

51. *The Sporting News*, January 29, 1990.

52. *The Sporting News*, January 15, 1990.

53. Rory Costello, "Rolando Roomes," SABR BioProject, October 3, 2011.

54. *Dayton Daily News*, June 15, 1990.

55. www.caribvoice.org, November 13, 2007.

56. Ken Kaiser and David Fisher, *Planet of the Umps* (New York: St. Martin's, 2003), 40.

57. *Ibid.*, 131–132.

58. *The Sporting News*, May 7, 1990.

59. Erardi and Luckhaupt, 31.

60. *The Sporting News*, January 1, 1990.

61. Erardi and Luckhaupt, 32. Quotes by other players are from pages 33–34 in this source.

62. *The Sporting News*, February 19, 1990.

63. Erardi and Luckhaupt, 60.

64. Erardi and Luckhaupt, 131; *The Sporting News*, May 28, 1990.

65. www.baseballhistorianblogspot.com, June 12, 2011.

66. *The Sporting News*, January 1, 1990.

67. *Ibid.*

68. *Ibid.*

69. *Ibid.*, April 16, 1990.

70. *Ibid.*

71. *Ibid.*

Chapter 3

1. Baltimore Federal Baseball Club v. National League (259 U.S. 200).

2. Flood v. Kuhn (407 U.S. 258).

3. *The Sporting News*, March 25,1990.

4. *The Sporting News*, March 19, 1990.

5. *The Sporting News*, March 5, 1990.

6. *Ibid.*

7. Erardi and Luckhaupt, 45.

8. William Shakespeare, *Romeo and Juliet*, Act 3, Scene 1. President Franklin D. Roosevelt famously used the phrase in commenting on labor-management strife in June 1937. FDR was an outstanding orator, but John L. Lewis bested the president in his response. In a speech on September 3, 1937, the legendary labor leader said: "It ill behooves one who has supped at labor's table and who has been sheltered in labor's house to curse with equal fervor and fine impartiality both labor and its adversaries when they are locked in deadly embrace."

9. Barzun, 159–60.

10. Barzun, quoted by Douglas McDaniel in "Jacques Barzun, Baseball's Best Cultural Critic, Turns His Back on the Game," www.bleacherreport.com, July 6, 2009.

11. *Ibid.*
12. Palmer and Gillette, 1581.
13. *The Sporting News*, April 2, 1990.
14. Maury Allen, "National League," *Street and Smith's Baseball* (March 1991), 68.
15. Hal McCoy, cited by Mike Lynch, "1990 Baseball Predictions: How Did They Turn Out?" www.seamheads.com, June 18, 2010.
16. *The Sporting News*, May 7, 1990.
17. *The Sporting News*, May 14, 1990.
18. Erardi and Luckhaupt, 52.
19. *The Sporting News*, April 16, 1990.
20. Bill Stern, *Bill Stern's Favorite Baseball Stories* (Garden City, NY: Doubleday, 1949), 40–41.
21. George Will, *Men at Work* (New York: Macmillan, 1990), 75.
22. *The Sporting News*, March 26, 1990.
23. *Athlon's Baseball*, 163.
24. Associated Press account in various newspapers, April 9, 1990.
25. *Ibid.*
26. *Ibid.*
27. *The Sporting News*, May 7, 1990.
28. *Ibid.*
29. *Ibid.*
30. *Ibid.*, April 9, 1990.
31. *Ibid.*, November 27, 1976.
32. *Ibid.*
33. *Ibid.*
34. *Ibid.*, April 16, 1990.
35. *Ibid.*
36. *Ibid.*
37. *Ibid.*, May 7, 1990.
38. *Ibid.*, April 16, 1990.
39. *Ibid.*, April 1, 1991.
40. *Ibid.*, April 3, 1989.

Chapter 4

1. George Vecsey, *A Year in the Sun* (New York: Crown, 1989), 133.
2. www.baseball-almanac.com.
3. *Ibid.*
4. Greg Rhodes, "History of Opening Day," www.findlaymarketparade.com.
5. *The Sporting News*, March 26, 1990.
6. *Cincinnati Enquirer*, April 16, 1990.
7. *The Sporting News*, November 13, 1989.
8. *Ibid.*
9. Chris Jensen, *Baseball State by State* (Jefferson, NC: McFarland, 2012), 324.
10. Lyle Spatz, ed., *The SABR Baseball List & Record Book* (New York: Scribner, 2007), 356.
11. *The Sporting News*. April 23, 1990.
12. Erardi and Luckhaupt, 23.
13. *Ibid.*
14. *The Sporting News*, May 29, 1990.

15. *Ibid.*, April 23, 1990.
16. *Ibid.*
17. Tim Kurkjian, *Is This a Great Game, or What?* (New York: St. Martin's, 2007), 97.
18. *Ibid.*, 97–100.
19. Tom Verducci, "The Swing," *Sports Illustrated* (August 28, 2013), 28.
20. John Updike, *Endpoint* (New York: Knopf, 2009.) Reprinted in *The Writer's Almanac*, June 25. 2013.
21. *The Sporting News*, April 23, 1990.
22. *Ibid.*, April 16, 1990.
23. Lowry, 67.
24. Pete Palmer, and Gary Gillette, eds., *The Baseball Encyclopedia* (New York: Barnes and Noble, 2004), 1580.
25. *The Sporting News*, January 15, 1990.
26. *The Sporting News*, April 30, 1990.
27. Erardi and Luckhaupt, 86.
28. *The Sporting News*, May 7, 1990.
29. *Ibid.*
30. Erardi and Luckhaupt, 87.
31. *The Sporting News*, May 7, 1990.
32. *The Sporting News*, May 14, 1990.
33. *Ibid.*
34. *Ibid.*
35. *Cincinnati Enquirer*, October 10, 1998.
36. *New York Times*, March 13, 1991.
37. *Ibid.*, October 30, 1989.
38. *Ibid.*, May 7, 1990.
39. *Ibid.*, May 28, 1990.

Chapter 5

1. *Ibid.*, June 25, 1990.
2. *Ibid.*
3. *Ibid.*
4. *Ibid.*
5. *Los Angeles Times*, May 3, 1988.
6. *The Sporting News*, June 11, 1990.
7. *Los Angeles Times*, March 10, 1991.
8. *Harlan* (Kentucky) *Daily Enterprise*, June 10, 1990.
9. www.cincinnati.com, July 24, 2010.
10. Larry Stone, "Once in a Lifetime," *Baseball Digest* (September/October, 2013), 27, 29.
11. *Cincinnati Enquirer*, July 24, 2010.
12. *New York Times*, October 20, 1990.
13. *The Sporting News*, June 11, 1990.
14. *Ibid.*, July 15, 1991.
15. www.al.com, October 7, 2013.
16. http://news.cincinnati.com, July 16, 2012.
17. *The Sporting News*, July 9, 1990.
18. *The Sporting News*, July 23, 1990.
19. www.nashvillecitypaper.com, June 25, 2004.
20. www.zoominfo.com, March 12, 2006.

Chapter 6

1. *The Sporting News*, August 13, 1990.
2. *Ibid.*
3. *Ibid.*, August 20, 1990.
4. *Ibid.*
5. *Ibid.*, July 16, 1990.
6. *Ibid.*, August 27, 1990.
7. *Ibid.*, November 30, 1992.
8. www.caller.com, November 4, 2012.
9. *The Sporting News*, August 27, 1990.
10. *Ibid.*
11. *Ibid.*
12. *The Sporting News*, September 24, 1990.
13. www.houston.astros.mlb.com, May 5, 2002.
14. www.astrosdaily.com, December 28, 2001.
15. www.greatest21days.com, May 5, 2011.
16. www.astrosdaily.com, December 28, 2001.
17. www.dreammakersbaseball.com.
18. *The Sporting News*, September 18, 1989.
19. *Ibid.*, October 16, 1989.
20. The tri-cities are Kennewick, Pasco, and Richland in Washington State. Although Cincinnati signed him as an amateur free agent on May 19, Minutelli was not really an amateur, as he was playing for the unaffiliated Tri-Cities club. The Reds rectified the situation by purchasing his contract from the independent club that fall. *The Sporting News*, June 16, 1986.
21. *Ibid.*, September 24, 1990.
22. *Ibid.*, October 1, 1990.
23. *Ibid.*, October 8, 1990.
24. *Ibid.*, October 15, 1990.

Chapter 7

1. *The Sporting News*, October 22, 1990.
2. *Ibid.*
3. *Ibid.*, October 29, 1990.
4. *Ibid.*, March 5, 1990.
5. *Ibid.*, June 25, 1990.
6. *Ibid.*
7. *Ibid.*, April 29, 1991.
8. *Ibid.*, September 28, 1992.
9. Rick Swaine, *Baseball's Comeback Players* (Jefferson, NC: McFarland, 2014), 34.
10. *The Sporting News*, September 17, 1990.
11. *Ibid.*
12. *Ibid.*, November 5, 1990.
13. Swaine, 34.
14. *The Sporting News*, September 17, 1990.
15. *Ibid.*
16. *Ibid.*, November 5, 1990.
17. Emily Witte, "A Few Witte Words," posted September 8, 2013.
18. *Montreal Gazette*, December 13, 1984.
19. *The Sporting News*, October 29, 1990.
20. *Ibid.*

Epilogue

1. Maury Allen, "National League," in *Street and Smith's Baseball* (New York: Conde Nast Publications, 1991), 77.
2. *Ibid.*
3. *Ibid.*
4. *The Sporting News*, October 9, 1992.
5. *Washington Post*, May 12, 1998.

Appendix F

1. Ted C. Oliver, *Kings of the Mound* (Los Angeles: privately published, 1947).
2. Faber, *Baseball Ratings*.

Bibliography

Achorn, Edward. *The Summer of Beer and Whiskey*. New York: Public Affairs, 2013.

Barzun, Jacques. *God's Country and Mine: A Declaration of Love Spiced with a Few Harsh Words*. New York: Little, Brown and Co., 1954.

Clark, Dick L., and Larry Lester, eds. *The Negro Leagues Book*. Cleveland: Society for American Baseball Research, 1994.

Cook, William A. *August "Garry" Herrmann: A Baseball Biography*. Jefferson, NC: McFarland, 2008.

Daugherty, Paul. *Fair Game*. Wilmington, OH: Orange Frazer Press, 1999.

Erardi, John, and Joel Luckhaupt. *Wire to Wire 1990 Cincinnati Reds*. Cincinnati: Clerisy, 2010.

Faber, Charles F. *Baseball Ratings: The All-Time Best Players at Each Position, 1876 to the Present*, 3rd ed. Jefferson, NC: McFarland, 2008.

Faber, Charles F., ed. *The 1934 St. Cardinals: The World Champion Gas House Gang*. Phoenix: Society for American Baseball Research, 2014.

Faber, Charles F., and Richard B. Faber. *Spitballers: The Last Legal Hurlers of the Wet One*. Jefferson, NC: McFarland, 2006.

Felber, Bill, ed. *Inventing Baseball: The 100 Greatest Games of the Nineteenth Century*. Phoenix: Society for American Baseball Research, 2013.

Heaphy, Leslie A. *The Negro Leagues, 1869–1960*. Jefferson, NC: McFarland, 2003.

James, Bill. *The Bill James Historical Baseball Abstract*. New York: Villard, 1988.

Jensen, Chris. *Baseball State by State*. Jefferson, NC: McFarland, 2012.

Kaiser, Ken, and David Fisher. *Planet of the Umps*. New York: St. Martin's Press, 2003.

Kurkjian, Tim. *Is This a Great Game or What?* New York: St. Martin's Press, 2007.

Lowry, Philip J. *Green Cathedrals*. New York: Walker & Co., 2006.

Meany, Tom. *Baseball's Greatest Teams*. New York: A. S. Barnes, 1949.

Nemec, David, et al. *The Baseball Chronicle*. Lincolnwood, IL: Publications International, 2008.

Palmer, Pete, and Gary Gillette, eds. *The Baseball Encyclopedia*. New York: Barnes & Noble, 2004.

Peterson, Robert. *Only the Ball Was White*. New York: Oxford University Press, 1970.

Posnanski, Joe. *The Machine*. New York: HarperCollins, 2009.

Rhodes, Greg, and John Erardi. *The First Boys of Summer*. Cincinnati: Road West, 1994.

Riley, James A. *The Biographical Encyclopedia of the Negro Baseball Leagues*. New York: Carroll & Graf, 2002.

Ritter, Lawrence S. *The Glory of Their Times: The Story of the Early Days of Baseball Told by the Men Who Played It*, new enlarged ed. New York: HarperCollins, 1992.

Salisbury, Luke. *The Anwer Is Baseball*. New York: Vintage Books, 1989.

Sandoval, Jim, and Bill Nowlin, eds. *Can He Play? A Look at Baseball Scouts and Their Profession.* Phoenix: Society for American Baseball Research, 2011.

Shatzkin, Mike, ed. *The Ballplayers.* New York: Arbor House, 1990.

Spatz, Lyle, ed. *The SABR Baseball List and Record Book.* New York: Scribner, 2007.

Stang, Mark, and Dick Miller, eds. *Baseball in the Buckeye State.* Cleveland: Society for American Baseball Research, 2004.

Swaine, Rick. *Baseball's Comeback Players.* Jefferson, NC: McFarland, 2014.

Thorn, John. *Baseball in the Garden of Eden: The Secret History of the Early Game.* New York: Simon & Shuster, 2011.

Thorn, John, et al., eds. *Total Baseball: The Ultimate Baseball Encyclopedia,* 8th ed. Wilmington, DE: 2004.

Wallace, Joseph. *World Series: An Opinionated Chronicle of 100 Years.* New York: Harry N. Abrams, 2003.

Werber, Bill, and C. Paul Rogers III. *Memories of a BallPlayer: Bill Werber and Baseball in the 1930s.* Cleveland: Society for American Baseball Research, 2001.

Newspapers

Associated Press
Boston Globe
Chicago Tribune
Cincinnati Enquirer
Cincinnati Post
Lexington Herald-Leader
Los Angeles Times
Milwaukee Sentinel
New York Daily News
New York Times
Philadelphia Inquirer
The Sporting News
Washington Post

Websites

www.artssci.uc.edu.
www.baseball-almanac.com.
www.baseball-reference.com.
www.baseball-statistics.com.
www.bleacherreport.com.
www.caribvoice.org.
www.cincinnati.com.
www.cincinnati.reds.mlb.com.
www.cincinnativiews.net.
www.crosley-field.com.
www.gocincy.com.
www.sabr.org
www.snakepit.com.
www.wikipedia.org.

Journals and Yearbooks

Athlon's Baseball '90
The 1992 Official Cincinnati Reds Yearbook Program.
Street and Smith's Baseball, 1991.

Court Cases

Baltimore Federal Baseball Club v. National League (259 US 200).
Flood v. Kuhn (407 US 258).

Index